Marshal Joffre

Marshal Joffre

The Triumphs, Failures and Controversies of France's Commander-in-Chief in the Great War

André Bourachot

Translated by Andrew Uffindell

Pen & Sword
MILITARY

First published in France by Bernard Giovanangeli Éditeur 2010
First published in Great Britain in 2014 by
PEN & SWORD MILITARY
An imprint of
Pen & Sword Books Ltd
47 Church Street
Barnsley
South Yorkshire
S70 2AS

ISBN 978-1-78346-165-3

The right of André Bourachot to be identified as the Author of this Work has been
asserted by him in accordance with the Copyright, Designs and Patents Act 1988.

A CIP catalogue record for this book is available from the British Library.

Typeset by Concept, Huddersfield, West Yorkshire, HD4 5JL.
Printed and bound in England by CPI Group (UK) Ltd, Croydon CR0 4YY.

Pen & Sword Books Ltd incorporates the imprints of Pen & Sword Archaeology,
Atlas, Aviation, Battleground, Discovery, Family History, History, Maritime,
Military, Naval, Politics, Railways, Select, Social History, Transport, True Crime,
and Claymore Press, Frontline Books, Leo Cooper, Praetorian Press,
Remember When, Seaforth Publishing and Wharncliffe.

For a complete list of Pen & Sword titles please contact
PEN & SWORD BOOKS LIMITED
47 Church Street, Barnsley, South Yorkshire, S70 2AS, England
E-mail: enquiries@pen-and-sword.co.uk
Website: www.pen-and-sword.co.uk

Contents

List of Plates

Joffre at his desk at GQG.

French soldiers at rest.

French troops in a primitive trench in the early stages of the war.

By the time of the Battle of Verdun in 1916, the French infantry had been equipped with helmets and had more sophisticated defensive systems.

The French army relied on the famous 75mm gun at the start of the war, but suffered from its shortage of modern heavy artillery following the onset of trench warfare.

A heavy artillery piece.

The Senate's Army Commission, 1916.

Lieutenant-Colonel Emile Driant.

Clemenceau with a group of British and French officers. Clemenceau was fluent in English.

General Joseph Galliéni.

General Maurice Sarrail, probably photographed in Salonika in late 1916.

General Charles Lanrezac.

Fort Douaumont, seen from the air on 19 May 1916.

Inside Fort Douaumont after its recapture by the French in October 1916.

Joffre on a visit to the Verdun sector during the battle.

Joffre decorates one of the heroes of the Battle of Verdun, General Maurice Balfourier, the commander of the 20th Corps.

Joffre as coalition commander. British, French, Belgian, Russian, Italian and Serbian representatives are all present at this Allied conference held at GQG, at Chantilly, in March 1916.

Joffre with the President of the Republic, Raymond Poincaré.

A train brings Joffre back from a visit to the Verdun sector in spring 1916. He is accompanied by two of his closest assistants: General Pellé and General de Castelnau.

List of Tables

List of Maps

Key to Maps

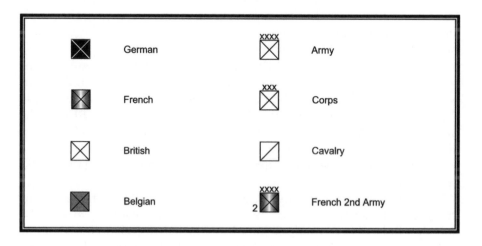

German		Army
French		Corps
British		Cavalry
Belgian		French 2nd Army

Preface to the English Edition

In a few months' time, France and its allies of the First World War will mark the centenary of the conflict's outbreak. In commemorating this event, the French will not overlook the people of either the United Kingdom or, more widely, the Commonwealth. Even though it is not the main purpose of this book, I am pleased that its appearance will serve to remind British readers, and Anglo-Saxon ones in general, of the extent to which the British and French armies fought alongside each other, shoulder-to-shoulder, until the final victory. The British army played a vital role in that victory. Without Sir John French's divisions, few in number though they may have been, France would have lost the Battle of the Marne. Europe would have been well and truly subjugated to Germany and history would have taken a different turn.

British participation in the defence of France was not a foregone conclusion. It took a big effort for British and French politicians to jettison resentments and rivalries that had continued without a break ever since the Hundred Years' War and the burning of Joan of Arc at the stake at Rouen in May 1431. By 1914, fewer than 100 years had elapsed since Napoleon's death on Saint Helena, and the Fashoda Incident was only sixteen years in the past. What history knows as the *Entente Cordiale* of 1904 was a mere ten years-old. Initially, the *Entente Cordiale* was just a settling of colonial antagonisms, and it did not commit Britain to intervening on the French side in the event of a Franco-German war, for it had never been a military alliance.

Nevertheless, the French and British staffs, working with the greatest discretion, made detailed studies and plans for British intervention. After the politicians gave it the green light, the intervention took the form of sending to the Continent what was called the British Expeditionary Force (BEF) under the command of Sir John French. On the British side, the future Field Marshal Sir Henry Hughes Wilson played a vital role in these staff conversations – to such an extent that at the start of the war the French often referred to the BEF as 'Army W'.

It goes without saying that Joffre's role will be frequently mentioned during this period of commemorations – and it will come in for some criticism. But nobody will be able to overlook him. Joffre had attentively followed all the pre-war negotiations between the French and British staffs, and he exerted the whole of the influence at his disposal to ensure that the British army was sent to the Continent. But the decisive moment that made possible the turn-around of the Marne was his meeting with Sir John French at the *Château* of

Vaux-le-Pénil near Melun on 5 September 1914. Joffre had come to check for himself that the British were willing to resume the offensive after a long and demoralizing retreat. He managed to find the right words. Turning to Sir John, and appealing to him in French, he closed by saying: '*Monsieur le maréchal*, the honour of England is at stake.'

'I will do all I possibly can,' said Sir John – a reply which Wilson, who was present at the meeting, translated into French as: '*Le maréchal a dit: oui.*' ('The Field Marshal says: yes.') The two commanders and their subordinates then sealed their agreement by following the fine British custom of having a cup of tea.

Readers will find in this book an account of what happened between July 1911 and the end of 1916: the period from Joffre's appointment as Chief of the General Staff (and as Commander-in-Chief in the event of war) up until his removal. Thus Joffre – he was made a marshal in due course – had three years to prepare France for hostilities. The French army that went to war at the start of August 1914 was Joffre's army. It was unfortunate that he had been given neither the time nor all the means he sought in order to turn it into the tool he believed was essential. Nevertheless, he was in charge of waging the war, and did so with the armies he had prepared, with equipment he was partly responsible for having produced, with the men he had trained, and with a doctrine he had developed.

It has not been my intention to sing Marshal Joffre's praises. He himself found flattery distasteful. Besides, I do not believe in great men. In most cases, they are produced by chance and circumstances. They all have their dark side, and all make errors to a greater or lesser extent, yet I find their mistakes just as instructive as their successes. All that matters is to ascertain whether they proved equal to the events for which they had been appointed and whether, to use one of today's expressions, they knew how 'to do the job'. Joffre unarguably knew how to do his job, and that is sufficient glory for him. For this, he deserves France's gratitude even today.

To end this preface, I have great pleasure in thanking Pen & Sword publishers, who readily took up the challenge of publishing a book by a French general. Thanks also to Rupert Harding, with whom I have worked with confidence to put the finishing touches to the text. I must also emphasize the very high quality of the translation by Andrew Uffindell and congratulate him on his work. His striving to understand the French text and his questioning have resulted in the English version being more accurate than the French, owing to the correction of errors and omissions. Finally, I must thank my friend, Doctor Bruno Carré, the most British of Frenchmen, who was a great help to me in finding a publisher, and without whom this book would not have seen the light of day.

General André Bourachot
December 2013

Preface to the French Edition

I have thought carefully about the risks involved in writing this book. Joffre is a divisive figure who is either adored or hated. Some see him as a bloodthirsty idiot, but others as a doting papa. These superficial extremes seem to be the only two answers that are ever given when questions are asked about this controversial personality.

Nor does the passage of time make everything fall naturally into place. Even though Joffre was the target of plenty of doubts and criticisms during the Great War itself, it seems as if France has only belatedly come to realize the true nature of the conflict. It is something of a paradox that people today find it more difficult than their predecessors to stomach the infinite scale of the human losses and the extent of the destruction. Frenchmen in the year 2000 are less understanding, reflective and tolerant than the Frenchmen of 1914–18. The isolated, individual protests of the past have now given way to collective indignation on the part of the national community as a whole.

Comments similar to those that crop up today would never have been written at the time of the war. It is of course true that people's sufferings, the constant presence of death, the loss of loved ones and protests against a most dismal fate found their way into words. People expressed these things where an active and vigilant censorship left them free to do so – nearly always in personal communications. Yet we must not overlook the opposite side to the coin. Alongside the long complaints in the diaries of the ordinary French soldiers or in letters written at the time, we also find expressions of courage, confidence, pride and patriotism.

Nowadays, we see nothing of that positive side of the war. The entire picture is filled with the human misery and with the compassion it understandably arouses. This is a pity, for ideology has shaped and interpreted the misery, always foisting the same explanation and slant on to the torment. The military and politicians alike – particularly the military – are accused of having deliberately sought and knowingly encouraged the massive bloodbaths of the four-year conflict. The key players of that era have all now passed away, which is fortunate for them since they are inevitably put on trial by the tender conscience of our era. The military – especially the generals – all receive the same pitiless sentence of posthumous infamy, now that it is too late to condemn them in their own lifetime.

When will there be a proper trial conducted before the bar of history? It is high time for one to be held in response to the tide of public opinion. Who will be bold enough to suggest that the situation might actually have been more complex? Who will ask modern-day Frenchmen to pause and try to understand why the military and the politicians acted as they did? Until 1914, none of these men had the slightest notion what a modern European war would be like. As for the generals, few of them had anticipated the nature of the coming conflict. We will go into the reasons for this in due course, but one of these generals, Joseph Jacques Césaire Joffre, bore a particularly heavy responsibility: that of commanding France's armies in battle and of holding the country's fate in his hands during the dark weeks of August and September 1914.

Joffre was born on 12 January 1852 at Rivesaltes in the Department of the Pyrénées-Orientales. He was the third of eleven children. His father, a comfortably-off cooper, subsequently changed profession to become a cultivator of vines and a wine-merchant. Joseph Joffre never forgot his Catalan origins: he often returned to the region and could speak its language. After primary education at the hands of the Brothers of the Christian Doctrine at Rivesaltes, he joined the secondary school of Perpignan at the age of 11. He proved himself a brilliant pupil by obtaining his *baccalauréat* qualification at just 16½, having already enjoyed several successes at the *concours général* competitive examinations. He then 'went up' to Paris, where he studied at the Charlemagne secondary school as preparation for the entrance exam to the *Ecole polytechnique* (the Polytechnic School). On 1 November 1869, he was admitted to the *Polytechnique* at his first attempt and was the youngest in his year's class.

On leaving the *Ecole polytechnique*, Joffre chose to become an engineer officer – his options were somewhat restricted by his ranking. His subsequent career can be divided into three phases. He began by learning his trade as a sapper at the Joint School of Artillery and Military Engineering at Fontaine-bleau and was then employed within his arm in both unit commands and engineering tasks. In particular, he helped construct the Séré de Rivières forts. The second phase of Joffre's career began in 1885, and took him to Formosa, Tonkin, the Sudan and also to Madagascar alongside Galliéni. In between these postings, he spent periods employed as a sapper in mainland France, for example within the specialist railway regiment, the 5th Engineers. Finally, during the third phase from 1906 onwards, he became an inter-arm commander, entrusted first with a division and then with an army corps.

Our account begins in 1911, at the moment when Joffre landed the top job, and finishes in 1916, the year of his disgrace. Thereafter, having been appointed a Marshal of France, he was removed from the centre of affairs. He carried out a successful mission to the United States, but after that he was no longer consulted by successive governments except out of politeness. He died at Paris on 3 January 1931, following the passing of two other great figures of the war, Foch and Clemenceau. He and his wife are buried at Louveciennes, in the garden of the house they had built for themselves in 1923.

Even though so much has been written about Joffre, he remains somewhat enigmatic. The rarity with which he spoke in public, the discretion of his private life, his natural reserve and his aversion to controversy have added to the air of mystery about him. His memoirs tend to be so sober in tone that they leave the reader wanting something more. (Although these memoirs were written by the officers of Joffre's personal staff, he himself read and re-read them carefully.) Yet what a journey it was for this young, unrefined man from the *Ecole polytechnique*, who failed to make a mark for himself at the Joint School of Artillery and Military Engineering at Fontainebleau and yet ended up as a Marshal of France. The evidence suggests that Joffre was a more complex man than he seems.

The aim of this little book is to help decipher Joffre through the key events of his military life between 1911, the year of his appointment as Chief of the General Staff, and 1916, the year of his departure. This is not a new biography – plenty of them exist already. Rather, it is an attempt to under- stand why Joffre took the actions he did while he was in power and to re- establish the truth about him – a truth that has often been much distorted.

Chapter 1

An Unconventional Choice

On 28 July 1911, the *Journal officiel de la République française* published a decree appointing a Chief of the General Staff. Practically nobody in France had heard of the appointee, except to a limited extent in the heart of the army. *Général de division* Joffre was young for the post, being 59 years of age. He was the replacement for General Michel, who had resigned from the Vice-Presidency of the Supreme War Council after finding himself completely isolated within the council over the question of how the reserve units should be used. Joffre immediately also became the Commander-in-Chief designate of the French armies, meaning that he would command in the event of war breaking out. Provided he retained the government's favour, he could antici-pate holding his post for five years until he reached the age-limit.

The sapper
The fact that the new appointee was a sapper came as a surprise. It was the first and last time that an engineer officer became the 'boss' of the French army. The twists and turns that accompanied his appointment are well known and we won't go into them any more than is necessary to explain the ensuing events. But we should start by noting one point: we can bet that Joffre would never have been appointed if a credible fortune-teller had managed to persuade the French government – and its Minister of War, Adolphe Messimy, a dyed-in-the-wool Radical-Socialist – that the war would break out three years later almost to the day. In those circumstances, Joffre's opera-tional military experience would have appeared very thin (as we shall see in due course) and it is not even certain that he himself would have accepted the post.[1]

Michel was perceived as a lukewarm Republican and it would have been impossible to replace him following his departure with a general who was labelled a reactionary. Joffre, on the other hand, fitted the bill. He was not only an affirmed Republican, but also a more-or-less lapsed Freemason and a rather unobtrusive figure with an irreproachable lifestyle. Ironically, he had a private life that was more in line with the Radical-Socialist ideal than did someone such as Jaurès (the Socialist leader).[2] Joffre's political discretion made him what would nowadays be called a consensus candidate.

Politics, indeed, played a major role in the future marshal's appointment. We have to remember that at the start of the twentieth century 'fear of the military formed the basis of Republican wisdom', in the words of a memorable saying attributed to Castelnau. Republicans could only hope that even if officers dedicated themselves to serving France rather than the Republic, they would at least obey the latter. These concerns did not prevent some men on the 'Left' from being infuriated by Joffre's appointment. They accused the government of having chosen him merely to smooth the same path for Castelnau, the man who became a sort of deputy to him.[3] For the odd thing was that Castelnau was a devout, militant Catholic and made no attempt to hide it.

One contemporary article examined what we might term the high command at the time of Joffre's appointment in 1911 and identified twenty-three Republican generals and eleven reactionary ones. According to the same article, by 1913 there were twenty-eight generals described as reactionary and only six as Republican.[4] The article's writer saw this as proof that Joffre's appointment was intended to conceal a vast and almost subversive venture controlled from afar by the Jesuits, the ultimate symbol and embodiment of clerical reactionaryism. The Jesuits have frequently been used as a pretext by regimes spanning the entire spectrum from republic to monarchy, and seem to have been an indispensable scapegoat.

The French army was Jacobin in tradition. Most of its officers had been freethinkers since the time of the Revolution and Empire and they were disgusted with the 'homilies' of some of the senior ranks. But during the last quarter of the nineteenth century, the Church supposedly managed to regain a hold on the officer corps by using a very simple means, namely the tuition provided at an excellent school to prepare candidates for the entrance exam to Saint-Cyr, where cadets trained to be officers. The school in question was the *Ecole Sainte-Geneviève*, which was located at Versailles in a street called the *rue des Postes* and was often called simply the *Ecole des Postes*. It was alleged that the headmaster, Father du Lac, carefully pruned the promotion lists with the complicity of some senior generals, removing the 'Republican' officers in order to advance the interests of the Church. The *Ecole des Postes*, followed inevitably by part of the army, would become the 'nest of Jesuits' that so preoccupied Clemenceau. This conspiracy theory seems a bit overdone to be true and yet it was adopted to various degrees by several men on the Left, including Clemenceau and Jaurès.

Thus the French army was deeply divided. The Dreyfus Affair was still in the recent past. General André's arrival at the Ministry of War had made it easier for officers to reach posts of responsibility if they were known to be of the correct political persuasion, for such information began to be secretly noted on their personal files.[5] All officers, regardless of how long they had served, kept a beady, wary eye on each other and tried to ascertain the hidden motives behind the appointment of a particular person and work out his allegiances. The officer corps had been further perturbed by the Two-Year Law, which had been prepared by André and passed in 1905 after he had left his post. Some officers had found it difficult to understand what André had been trying to achieve with this law, for they could see the French army's strength diminishing like snow melting in the sun, even as the German army grew ever stronger.

*   *   *

Joffre's appointment as Commander-in-Chief designate was a different type of heresy. Although he was responsible for conducting operations in the event of war, he was neither an infantryman nor a cavalryman, nor even a gunner. On leaving the *Ecole polytechique*, he had become a soldier after finding (in common with many other graduates of the *Ecole* at this time) that a civil career was not open to him. The only choice he could make was between the artillery and the engineers. Had he opted for the artillery, no one would have objected to his subsequent appointment, for some of his predecessors had also been gunners.

The school at Saint-Cyr trained only those officers who were destined for the infantry and cavalry, in either the mainland army or the colonial army. The situation is different nowadays, although the changes did not happen until as late as 1945. In Joffre's time, the officers of the so-called scientific arms – the engineers and artillery – did two years of specialist training at their own school at Fontainebleau after studying at the *Ecole polytechnique*.

Gaining admission to the *Ecole polytechnique* – which was commonly known as the X – was reckoned to be much more difficult than getting into Saint-Cyr. The Xs, as the pupils were known, tended to develop a superiority complex. The Saint-Cyr cadets claimed that many Xs became officers only because they were incapable of doing anything else, but such remarks were exaggerated.[6] The reality was that the *Ecole polytechnique* did provide a route into the major State-run corps – such as the Corps of Bridges and Highroads, or the Corps of Mines – but pupils who wanted to enter these corps rather than become a military officer needed to be graded in 'the boot' at the end of their second year. This meant that they had to be ranked among the top few, depending on the precise number of positions that were made available in the State-run corps that year. Joffre admitted that he had been unable to opt for one of the State-run corps since he had not been a 'booter', but the number of civil positions available to those who left the *Ecole polytechnique* that year, in the immediate aftermath of the 1870 war, was lower than it had been for the previous classes.

At the time of 1875, the Joint School of Artillery and Military Engineering at Fontainebleau taught sappers about permanent fortification and everything related to it. There were lessons in construction, in earthworks and also in drawing, the legacy of which can be seen in the archives in the form of some magnificent wash drawings that are not just architectural drawings but real works of art.[7] Fontainebleau transformed a man who had specialized almost wholly in pure mathematics into a public works engineer who could design practically any element of the infrastructure that was built at that time, such as roads, bridges, tunnels, public buildings, factories, weirs, railways and water-ways. Joffre left Fontainebleau with an unexceptional ranking (thirteenth out of twenty-six), but he always remained conscious that it had given him a solid training as an engineer.

Joffre's immediate future was that of any other young engineer officer. He supervised the construction and maintenance of forts in the area around Paris, in the Jura and even in the Pyrenees. He then went to the colonies, where his many tasks included the building of small forts, or *bicoques* as they were known. He served at Formosa, at Tonkin and, as a glorious culmination, at Madagascar under Galliéni's orders. He subsequently became Director of Engineers – this was the logical result of an ascent within his arm that had seen him exercise responsibilities within the Railways Regiment and serve as Secretary of the Commission of Inventions. His final post before his appoint-ment as potential Commander-in-Chief was Director designate of the Rear Zone. This made him a sort of logistics commander, in charge of all the supply services for the frontline armies.

The first part of Joffre's career, therefore, had been devoted to public works and he was frequently noted as being suitable for employment in 'very large-scale construction projects'. Not until Tonkin, after fifteen or so years of service, was he recorded as being 'a good engineer and equally good as a soldier'. When he was appointed Commander-in-Chief designate, he was received by the President of the Republic, Fallières, who told him: 'I am pleased to see an engineer officer at the head of the army. War, in my view, has become the art of an engineer.'[8] Joffre in relating this comment wrote: 'I have often thought of these words and they are profoundly true.' Fallières probably made the remark simply as something appropriate to say, but that did not stop Joffre from investing great importance in it. It does at least prove that the government knew full well what it was doing when it appointed an engineer.

On the other hand, Joffre did have the disadvantage of never having com-manded an infantry section, nor a company, battalion or regiment. His only experience outside that pertaining exclusively to an engineer officer had been at Tonkin and also in the Sudan during his march to Timbuktu – a march he made in conjunction with his superior (Colonel Bonnier, who died in the venture), but by a separate route.[9] This dramatic episode has been retold many times and it made Joffre's reputation. Yet it was more in the nature of a prudent exploration by a Livingstone than a warlike raid into enemy territory. It was overrated, as indeed were all the ventures that occurred at that time.

Even so, Timbuktu remains important because of what it reveals about Joffre's character. The engineer in him can be seen in the way he prepared and led the expedition. He was criticized for having dawdled and for having taken his time. If there is any truth to such criticisms, it was because Joffre was not a hothead liable to charge head down whenever he saw someone in an Arab cloak – and perhaps his prudence was something that Bonnier lacked. He did things logically, one after the other, and never took an uncalculated risk. Such a man, so calm and level-headed, could never have deliberately turned himself into a bloodthirsty firebrand twenty years later during the Great War, as one author would have us believe.[10]

Joffre knew nothing of infantry combat, for he lacked any personal experience of it. He had never given the order: 'Fix bayonets!' He had never led his troops to an assault. It is not even clear if he had ever fired a rifle shot anywhere other than on a firing range. Of course, a general who is Commander-in-Chief does not need the same skills as a newly-commissioned officer. Yet an officer grasps the realities of combat by being immersed in them at a young age. The first time he hears bullets whistling around him is a sort of initiation rite and it leaves its mark on him for life. By the time Joffre became Chief of the General Staff, he had long ceased to be in direct command of the soldiers within the units under his orders. If he had been 'baptized' at all, it could only have been at Tonkin or in the Sudan, and even that would have been relatively late in his career.[11]

He was hardly exceptional in this respect. How many infantry, cavalry or artillery soldiers had ever previously been under fire when war broke out in 1914? Few officers and NCOs had served in the colonies and, even if they had, it was in a totally different environment from that of Western Europe. Similarly, few officers had the gut awareness that bullets killed and were becoming increasingly efficient in killing more and more men. But the survivors of the 1870 war, such as Pau, Galliéni, Castelnau, Lanrezac and Michel, knew what war was like. They had been very young officers in 1870 and all – or almost all – of them had been in the infantry or cavalry. They had been initiated and this initiation was a real blessing that Joffre the sapper had undergone only to a minor extent, if at all.[12] In 1870, he had still been a pupil at the *Ecole polytechnique* and had been attached to the artillery to help defend Bastion 39 between the *Porte de Saint-Ouen* and the *Poterne de Montmartre*.[13] Yet neither did any of Joffre's peers have experience of major operational commands in a war of the sort waged in the Western world, so in this respect he had no cause for any envy.

* * *

Joffre's duties as Commander-in-Chief designate required much rational knowledge and intelligence and he constantly had to use his analytical skills to find the correct solution to a problem. He also had to draw on his stock of images, feelings and memories to fill any gaps that were left when pure reasoning was unable to provide the whole of the answer. Joffre certainly reasoned, but did he also have an intuition about people and, in particular, about situations?[14] He had a geometric mind and perhaps a shrewd one. But if shrewdness is absent, it can not be compensated for by a personality devoid of any imagination.

Joffre's experience of military tactics was practically non-existent, but what of his strategic knowledge? Surprisingly, he had never taken a course in what might be termed higher military training. (Those officers who had undertaken such training could not resist calling it the 'advanced sciences', with a hint of condescension towards those of their peers who had not enjoyed the same opportunity.)

Even if Joffre had wanted to do a course in the 'advanced sciences' (and that is by no means certain), he simply would not have had the time. He was never taught, therefore, at the Staff College, which had been founded in 1876. Someone like Galliéni managed to attend the Staff College's courses when he was almost ten years older than his fellow pupils. Joffre, in contrast, never knew the famous professors of this eminent establishment, such as Bonnal, Langlois and Négrier, who made a deep impression on their pupils. It is not obvious where else he might have found the opportunity to study the campaigns of the First Empire. Where else could he have compared the respective advantages of outflanking attacks (as in the Battle of Cannae, with which Schlieffen was so enamoured) and frontal attacks (as at Austerlitz, for which Foch had a soft spot)? Joffre's favourite reading did not include either Clausewitz, Guibert or Jomini. He probably knew nothing of Napoleon's campaigns. He is unlikely to have read Napoleon or Moltke and his memoirs contain no reference to any of the great captains. According to legend, Joffre was not in the habit of reading and when he did read – in his youth at least – he supposedly preferred mathematical books.[15] Yet in Emile Mayer's opinion, this legend was completely false. Mayer implied that Joffre did educate himself, but only if the knowledge he acquired was likely to prove useful, for he was uninterested in knowledge for its own sake. Mayer may have been right and his interpretation is in keeping with Joffre's pragmatic character.

Most likely, however, Joffre acquired his strategic education 'on the job', whilst commanding the 6th Infantry Division and the 2nd Corps.[16] He liked to surround himself with men younger than himself who were qualified staff officers – men such as Gamelin, who accompanied him to the General Staff and then in 1914 to the *Grand Quartier Général* (the General Headquarters or GQG). It was a sort of Socratic apprenticeship that removed the constraints of the hierarchy but without subverting it. This was the way in which Joffre learned how to carry out his new duties.

In his memoirs, Joffre stated that he insisted on obtaining Castelnau as the man who would be his chief-of-staff in the event of war as he was unable to obtain Foch to help him learn the techniques of staffwork. He probably also found certain personalities intriguing, including the man known as the 'hooligan', Lanrezac. A loudmouth and a connoisseur of coarse language,

Lanrezac was an officer who readily dissented, but he was also a brilliant, omniscient professor respected by his pupils, someone who was loquacious and able to express himself well – someone, in short, who had all the gifts that Joffre lacked. Joffre was an engineer and that's what he wanted to be. Yet he sensed there was something missing and occasionally confided this to friends. There is no doubt that he wanted someone at his side who would bolster his credibility and provide a sort of guarantee to allay any concerns that had been raised by his appointment.

Did Joffre inevitably become beholden to those around him, given that he was so different from them? Many commentators have suggested that he might have been the prisoner of his entourage, the obedient tool of some sort of secret and power-hungry cabal pursuing aims that had nothing Republican about them.

I'll leave aside the fact that nobody has ever clarified exactly what these aims might have been. The one thing that is clear about Joffre is his determination to be master in his own domain. That aspect of his personality has never been disputed. He had many enemies – his success made that inevitable – and probably few friends. But he could not have been a slave of the General Staff, for he never gave allegiance to anyone or anything. He was his own man. His mistakes were his and his success belonged to him alone.

It is difficult to believe Emile Mayer's claim that an officer said: 'There's no need to worry about [Joffre's] inadequacies. We're around. We know what must be done. He'll endorse our decisions and all will go well.'[17] This immediately raises doubts. Who was this officer? What rank did he hold and when did he make the remark? If he existed at all, he must have become very disappointed when he found out what it was really like to work with Joffre. Quite apart from the fact that it takes a good deal of cheek for a subordinate to speak in such terms, the notion of a commander so swallowed up by his staff that he becomes its hostage was no more realistic in 1911 than it is today. A staff is not a soviet. It does not function like a modern shareholder company where a handful of leaders can manipulate the hesitant and impose their views and decisions. General Staff officers are ambitious, self-confident, conscious of their worth and know that they have not got where they are by chance. They defend their opinions passionately in order to become firmly established with their boss. It is only natural that they should try and influence him. It is their job to be intelligent, to find solutions to the problems that occur and to propose them to the Commander-in-Chief. But it is too big a leap to suggest that they become Father Joseph figures to their general. ('Father Joseph' – no pun intended – was Cardinal Richelieu's influential confidant in the seventeenth century.) The officers soon learn, if they are not already aware, that the Tarpeian Rock – the execution site in Ancient Rome – lies just a short distance from the Capitol. Joffre alternately took men from, and threw them back into, the pool of officers who had graduated from the Staff College or from the Centre for Advanced Military Studies. He did so decisively and not always tactfully.

Everyone who served under Joffre, or saw how GQG worked, emphasized that he was his own man. Even Jean de Pierrefeu wrote: 'He was incontestably the master and few men did not quake in his presence. ... His strength and authority [were] indisputable.'[18] General Legrand-Girarde explained: 'Joffre kept tight control over his closest assistants, and tolerated no initiative in them.'[19] Some officers may well have tried to win him over to their views, but whether they actually managed to do so was another matter.

Joffre's awesome capacity for silence, and his reluctance – or even incapacity – to communicate, raised a barrier around him that was difficult to cross.[20] He never put on an act and never exaggerated. You had to take him as he was. Some almost considered him, if not an idiot then at least a somewhat sly and crafty simpleton who was fairly easy to manipulate. ('Foxy' and 'cunning', wrote Galliéni in his diaries.) The critics' insistence on attacking Joffre by attacking GQG clearly indicates that they thought of him – they wanted to think of him – as an irrelevance. Indeed, most of the time, they did not even mention him by name. It was simply one further way of denigrating him and regarding him as a figurehead.

'A perfectly good stationmaster'

We know not how Joffre's colleagues reacted to the news of his appointment, but we can easily guess. Comments and gossip were certainly rife in the officers' messes and within the staffs. No sapper had ever been appointed to the post before, and no other sapper would be afterwards, and the reason was that a permanent, unwritten rule existed forbidding it. In theory, general officers were interchangeable, because once they had been appointed they no longer belonged to their arm of origin. But what happened in practice was a different matter. It was 'understood' that the Commander-in-Chief had to be either an infantryman or a cavalryman, or possibly a gunner. Since Messimy, the Minister of War, was perfectly aware of this rule, it is all the more astonishing that he appointed Joffre. Here is how General Sérot Alméras Latour reacted to Joffre's appointment:

> I was greatly surprised, as were all my comrades in the army's General Staff. All of us had the impression that General Joffre was a colonial, a leader whose record in this respect was universally admitted to be distinguished. But he seemed reserved and did not find it easy to communicate verbally. He looked like a good bourgeois citizen who had occasionally put on a uniform. He was hardly regarded as a strategist and certainly not as the supreme commander.[21]

Nor did Joffre find it easy to maintain a correct seat in the saddle when horse-riding and this was a serious deficiency at that period.[22] His general appearance – his plainness – did not make him a man who attracted attention. In short, he did not even 'look' right for his post.[23] Looking right has always been important for a soldier and it was even more important back then than it is today. Reactions were therefore mixed.

More seriously, Joffre's competence was immediately thrown into doubt and remained so. Major Driant – the Deputy for the Meurthe-et-Moselle, a member of the Army Commission in the Chamber of Deputies and a man whom we shall come across again in due course – supposedly declared: 'Joffre! He'd make a perfectly good stationmaster.' It is clear that his past had been noted.

After the war, Sarrail published a series of four articles containing some thoughts about his relations with Joffre.[24] It was common knowledge that the two men loathed each other. In the following extract, for example, Sarrail managed to convey exactly what he thought of Joffre, without actually mentioning him by name:

> According to Napoleon, gunners are no good as army commanders, and he was in a position to know, since he came from that arm. He would have made a similar, and even more justified, remark, if ever there had been a question of resorting to a sapper during the period of the Revolution and Empire.

Sarrail was ostensibly writing in this section of his article about the *grignotage*, the attrition of 1915, but seems to have intended his comment to be applicable as early as 1911.

Liddell Hart, a British officer whose military experience was limited to brief periods on the Western Front during the Great War and whose inflated reputation bears no relation to the actual worth of his writings, wrote a book that assessed the generals of 1914.[25] He approved of very few of them. This is what he had to say about Joffre:

> His slow wits, combined with his inexperience of higher war studies, made him a modern Delphic oracle, the mere mouthpiece of a military priesthood among whom de Grandmaison was the leading intellectual influence and de Castelnau the acting high priest. ... His ignorance of European warfare had been officially recognized by the nomination of General de Castelnau as his assistant.

Liddell Hart's conclusion is usually quoted as well: 'Joffre was not a general, but a national nerve sedative.'

The allegation that Grandmaison could have possessed a 'leading influence' is definitely false, for he was a mere lieutenant-colonel and left the General Staff at the time Joffre became its chief (see Chapter 2). In any case, whom did Liddell Hart have in mind when he claimed that people had 'officially recognized' Joffre's ignorance? Any fool can blame 'them' – political authorities or shadowy figures manipulating events from the background. Any fool can accuse 'them' of machiavellianism and allege that their every move is calculated and that all their blunders are deliberate. 'Since we don't understand what's happening', the reasoning runs, 'let's pretend we know who's behind it.' Conspiracy theories are just a smokescreen and generally fail to hide the fact that the people who make such allegations have not bothered to think or do any research.

In 1913, General Bonnal, a former professor at the Staff College, wrote: 'There is no way that General Joffre, the Vice-President of the Supreme War Council, can have acquired in late middle age a knowledge and experience of matters of strategy and general tactics, given that he almost completely lacked them when he first became a general.'[26] Bonnal was retired and so he was able to say openly what many officers were thinking privately.

I will often mention General Percin in this book. He was General André's Principal private secretary at the Ministry of War, and was fully implicated in the controversy about the officers' personal files. On several occasions, he gave full vent to his doubts about Joffre's military qualifications, though the word 'doubts' is putting it mildly. After the war, for example, he wrote in a private letter:

> In my view, the incapable Joffre is more to be pitied than blamed. He was picked almost against his will. He was chosen not in spite of his incompetence, but precisely because of it, in order to ensure that General de Castelnau could rule supreme.[27] It was Messimy and General Pau who committed this crime.

Nothing less than a 'crime', be it noted. Percin made similar comments in his book about the high command: 'In all likelihood, they deliberately chose someone who knew nothing about what he had to do, so they would find it easier to make him do what they wanted.'[28] Once again the nameless 'they' are blamed. Percin's hatred for Joffre was largely politically-motivated and continued until he died.

Fabry, who served as the head of Joffre's personal staff after the Commander-in-Chief's fall from power, wrote that he was 'a controversial figure before the war and [was] reckoned by many of his peers to be unequal to the crushing task he had taken on …'.[29] Poincaré, the President of the Republic, related what Doumer told him on 1 September 1914: 'He had harsh words to say about … General Joffre. He claimed that the Commander-in-Chief was a first-rate engineer, but in no way a strategist or even a tactician.'[30] Yet Doumer had always been Joffre's enemy and would hardly have said anything else.

According to Messimy's memoirs, Joffre was fiercely criticized following the Battle of the Frontiers: 'after Charleroi, after Morhange, opinion within government circles and in the corridors of parliament was violently hostile to [Joffre]. He was openly accused of being useless and incompetent.'[31] When Messimy gave evidence to the Briey Commission in 1919, he said much the same thing, conveniently forgetting all the strengths he had seen in Joffre some years previously and forgetting also that he himself had appointed him.

General de Lardemelle, who was Franchet d'Esperey's former chief-of-staff, stated: 'This astonishing man had a serious chink in his armour. Neither his period at Tonkin as a captain, nor his raid on Timbuktu, ... nor his period as Director of the Rear Zone ... could prepare him, as Napoleon put it, to understand full-scale warfare.'[32] That's true enough – and yet no one, even in the rest of Europe, was any better prepared. Who was there with a better understanding of 'full-scale warfare' than Joffre?

General Alexandre was one of Joffre's officers and spent much of his career with him. He tells us: 'The candidates who dreamed of taking [Joffre's] place had no hesitation in intriguing against him – in military as much as in political circles – under the pretext that his military experience did not make him sufficiently qualified for his current post.'[33]

There were also press campaigns to remove Joffre or force him to resign. He survived only narrowly on at least two occasions, in 1912 and 1914.[34] As Alexandre pointed out, Joffre's military experience and background as a sapper clearly endangered his continued tenure of the positions of Chief of the General Staff and Commander-in-Chief designate. Yet the fact remains that no other Allied general showed sufficient mastery of the art of war to be equal to the realities of the conflict. A few of them gained some rare successes, but only as a result of surprise, luck or simply the exhaustion of the enemy. As a general, Joffre was neither better nor worse than his peers. As a coalition commander, he was actually rather better than them, especially considering that the coalition was still informal and that he had managed to create it only by sheer force of character.

* * *

It was during the war, several years after Joffre's appointment, that attacks on him were really unleashed both inside and outside the army. This wave of criticism was not long delayed, despite the wartime restrictions imposed on the release of information – restrictions that continued after Joffre's dismissal. The misleading allusions to his lack of military experience were now heard in conversations everywhere – not just in parliament, but also within the Parisian smart set, which still existed regardless of the war. At least censorship ensured that such criticism remained fairly muted in the press. In 1916, parliament began to hold closed sessions, but the supposed secrecy of the debates did not last long. Joffre came in for no end of stick during these sessions and the well-informed eagerly spread the gossip to everyone they knew.

The signing of the armistice removed any reason for restraint and produced a real fireworks display of disparagement. Throughout books, newspapers and journal articles, men such as Grouard, Le Gros, Palat, Percin, Regnault and Sarrail – to mention just the most prominent – ferociously tore Joffre and GQG to pieces. Initially at least, it was GQG that was attacked more often than the Commander-in-Chief. But the criticism was repeated and intensified by the so-called *limogés*, officers who had been dismissed during the war, and by their friends. They included Lanrezac, and others were even more extreme.

It is curious to find that most of these critics – military and civilian alike – were regarded as being politically on the Left, even though Joffre himself was Republican and a Freemason. Perhaps he had disappointed them. Everything suggests that a certain political class had confidently expected Joffre to be another André, only to find itself saddled with a second Castelnau. At any rate, it reacted in a way that seems suspiciously like annoyance and frustration.

The breach that emerged between Joffre and the fellow soldiers who criticized him can also be explained. These military critics were old generals or colonels – the pre-war set, as we might call them. They were all connected: they had scratched each other's back and done small favours for each other in order to advance the career of such-and-such a person whom Joffre had always passed over. Among the generals who tried to undermine him were two of his more plausible enemies and these two men united all those who had a grievance against him. They were Galliéni, who was credited with the victory of the Marne, and Lanrezac, who was regarded as having saved the French army and won the Battle of Guise. Those who campaigned to bring down Joffre succeeded in having Galliéni made a Marshal of France. Galliéni may have deserved the distinction, but not for what he did as a commander during the war.[35]

Joffre's relations with all his chief subordinates were rather abrasive at one time or another. But this was something completely different from the personal attacks such as those quoted earlier. Foch, Castelnau, de Langle de Cary, Dubail and others were all scathing about their commander, most frequently in their private correspondence. But it was inevitable that these men – all of whom were strong characters – should have become irritated during such a fraught period.

All the young, or youngish, officers were more guarded in what they said. They retained a great admiration for their former chief.[36] It might be thought that they were simply sensible enough to refrain from biting the hand that fed them, but there was more to it than that. Men who had been lieutenant-colonels and colonels in 1914, and had been brought forward by Joffre during the war, rarely disparaged their former chief even after they had become generals and had commanded divisions, then army corps and armies. Their gratitude stemmed from more than just self-interest. It was also the gratitude that came from having seen their Commander-in-Chief at work and having realized his qualities. This was the true nature of Joffre's relationship with his entourage. It was he who commanded them, instead of them controlling him.

This completely refutes what Emile Mayer claimed to have been told by the unnamed officer quoted earlier. The General Staff put its heart and soul into serving its chief. After the Marne, Joffre no longer had anything to prove, even to those who might have had doubts as a result of difficult moments earlier on. He had become the 'Boss'. It was two years before the members of parliament were able to rid themselves of him.

Let's turn again to Pierrefeu. However critical he may have been, Pierrefeu understood better than anyone the links that were swiftly forged between Joffre and his officers:

> [Joffre's] need for guidance ... made him prefer not officers of the same political hue as himself, but men who loved their profession and who believed in a simple, unquestioning way in the necessities of war ... men who as a result were his men entirely .... .

Joffre really did chose his officers from the pool of the Staff College and the Centre for Advanced Military Studies without consulting the yearbook of the Grand Orient to see if they were Freemasons, and without talking to the Church authorities or the Apostolic Nuncio. Having held the post of Inspector of Military Schools for almost four years, he was familiar with the best of the best, for most of the pupils had already gained admission to their schools by rigorous competitive examinations. Joffre also spotted men who were outstanding even though they had not qualified as staff officers. One of them was Weygand, an instructor at the Cavalry School of Saumur who later became Foch's chief-of-staff.

This also explains why GQG's liaison officers – men who were entirely loyal to their superiors – were sometimes rather extreme in their assessments of such-and-such a person. They did not necessarily want to undermine the person in question out of malice; more often than not they simply identified with the commander they served, to such an extent that they became completely absorbed in him. War, by its very nature, does not call for intelligent discernment or sophisticated thinking. There is no subtlety in a combat environment. Nobody has time any longer to find the perfect solution to a problem. A decision is often taken as soon as the problem has been assessed and it is rarely reconsidered afterwards.

After the war, it soon became the turn of civilian critics to take up the attacks made by hostile soldiers.[37] Naturally enough, they included Jean de Pierrefeu again. Initially at least, his books attacked the staff more readily than Joffre himself, but his criticism grew ever harsher and more caustic.

To crown it all, Galliéni's champions now tried to rob Joffre of something that had hitherto remained relatively unchallenged – the victory of the Marne. A man called Gheusi, who had known Galliéni for twenty-odd years, became a fervent defender of his idol. Gheusi had been the Director of the *Opéra-Comique* at the start of the war, and after being mobilized he had served on Galliéni's staff and helped steer him through the world of politics. Gheusi was far from being Galliéni's only champion, since the whole of the Left was more or less involved and a real campaign developed to try and shape public understanding of Galliéni's actions.

Another early pamphleteer worth mentioning is Victor Margueritte.[38] In 1919, he became one of the first – possibly the very first – to launch the campaign to belittle Joffre, while also settling some political accounts. The violence of his language was never exceeded: '[We] can not accept that an incompetent who nearly caused the complete ruin of his country should be acclaimed. In the past, less pathetic generals would have been sent straight to the guillotine for doing what he has done.'

Riding out the storms

Besides Joffre's competence, there was also the question of his character. But he came under less attack on this account, even if his determination was often portrayed as stubbornness. Let's go back a century to when Napoleon was in exile on the island of Saint Helena, dictating what might be called his memoirs. Las Cases, one of Napoleon's so-called 'four evangelists', noted down the following:[39]

> What was most desirable – what immediately made someone stand out – was that there should exist a balance between his intelligence or ability on the one hand and his physical character or courage on the other. This is what [Napoleon] called being square, with the base equalling the height.[40]

Las Cases continued: 'As for moral courage, [Napoleon] said that he had very rarely encountered two o'clock in the morning courage'. Las Cases also recorded a final remark:

> 'I know what I call the "draught" of every one of my generals', the Emperor said. 'Some', he explained with a gesture, 'displace water up to their waist and some up to their chin – but others do so right over their head, and believe me the number of these is very small indeed.'

Was Joffre one of this very small number? That is the key question and it can only ever be answered with hindsight since there is no way of assessing a man's 'draught' until it comes to the crunch. Only the actual test of war can determine his displacement. An assessment can be made only after the event and only about those men for whom the question is relevant. Rarely, in fact, is it relevant: as de Gaulle pointed out, it takes great clashes to produce great men and such clashes are mercifully few. The person who is assessing the general needs to be modest and reasonable, and yet the question of the critic or judge's own 'draught' has rarely been considered. Joffre lived in an age when people accepted no limits to what they could say. Our own era might appear excessive in terms of media coverage, yet it actually seems well regulated by comparison with the past, and standards of behaviour are calmer now than they once were.

It is not in the Sudan, at Madagascar or at Tonkin, or in the Directorate of Engineers that we must try to ascertain Joffre's 'draught'. Instead, we must do so during the black days of late August and early September 1914. The controlled, directed retreat of the French armies, the preparation for the Battle of the Marne and the rebound of the start of September were truly the indications of a general with exceptional 'draught', a man who was capable of surmounting events. We have to be wary when making sweeping statements, and yet even after careful consideration I can not think of any other general officer who could have absorbed so many disasters and found this 'two o'clock in the morning courage'.[41] Joffre was certainly aware of this absence of suitable generals to replace him and it explains his contempt for the attacks made on him. Why bother replying to men who are not on the same footing as the great and the good? And what would you tell them if you did reply? When Briand was urged by those around him at the end of 1915 or early 1916 to be rid of Joffre, it was this point about the lack of a viable alternative that he tried to get across to them. It was easy enough to say the Commander-in-Chief should be replaced, but the question was with whom?

Here is what Foch thought of Joffre – or 'Papa Joffre' as he called him, for he used the nickname that was common among many of the soldiers:

He is extraordinary. What marks him out is his very sound judgement. Yet he does nothing by himself. He has to be given recommendations, a plan has to be prepared for him. He knows how to motivate people to work. He himself considers and makes the decision. ... In his office, he never has anything in front of him, not a piece of paper, not a map. He does not do any writing.[42] ... At one time, he was called 'the buoy'. ... He always remains the same, riding out the tides and storms. He was a tower of strength. On 27 August 1914, the situation was rather worrying. Dangers on every side. Nobody knew what was happening! Yet he remained superbly impassive. His example prevailed. Around him, at his headquarters, despite the bad news, there was little agitation, let alone panic. Calm, order, coolness – the decisions were taken with coolness.[43]

Ultimately, few men have been so adored and loathed as Joffre was during and after the war. To the common man he was an idol, a grandfatherly figure, while to the Parisian intelligensia he was a foil, a 'big daddy'. It is difficult to understand the hatred directed at Joffre. What did he do to deserve so much criticism? What were people unable to forgive him for? Was it his scorn for political manoeuvring, his cold-shouldering of politicians and his refusal to become the hostage of any one party? It may have been. Was it his confidence and self-assurance, which often belied the reality of what was happening? That's perfectly possible. His reluctance to compromise? Certainly. The casualties of the first phase of the war? Yes, although that is not the core reason.

All these reasons contain an element of truth. Yet the answer is more than simply the sum of them all. You'll have to try and figure it out! Many soldiers clearly saw Joffre as a usurper, as they had never come to terms with being 'leap-frogged'. As for civilians, they often thought of him as a pretentious simpleton, especially if they were politicians – for Joffre had always held politicians at arm's length, with the exception of just a few trustworthy friends.

Chapter 2

The Offensive

It's impossible to open a book about the Great War and the men who waged it without coming across a mention of 'the offensive'. More often than not the author is condemning it, and the same old band of suspects are always blamed one after another: Grandmaison, the Staff College and the *Regulation on the handling of large units*. The Centre for Advanced Military Studies has a slightly lower profile, but its 'Young Turks' and those of the Staff College are accused of having propagated a doctrine that led directly to the bloodbaths of the war, especially during its opening phase.[1]

Even if these allegations about the offensive were true, it would still be necessary to assess just how much responsibility Joffre personally bore for the drafting of the regulations and for the development of the French army's doctrine. The importance of this chapter makes it somewhat longer than the others, yet I should explain that it is meant simply to fill in the background, since the issue of the offensive pervades the entire book.

Tangled meanings
What do we mean by 'offensive'? The answer is not as straightforward as you might think. Can someone take the offensive without even realizing that is what he is doing? Is the offensive a general attitude with no specific aim – or is it instead a course of action, a method of fighting the battle? At the start of the twentieth century, words lacked clarity and were vaguely defined – and this hasn't changed much since. People at the time might assume they were talking about the same thing when this was not in fact the case. Although we can definitely call it an offensive-minded era, it is difficult to work out the implications of this collective mindset.

To complicate the discussion even further, strategy and tactics tend to be confused. Military action can in fact occur on two levels: on the strategic level, where it aims to have an overall impact on the way a conflict develops, and on the tactical level, which is a lower level (often much lower). A strategic offensive is a concept, whereas a tactical offensive is no more than a means employed in a limited area and during a limited period of time. It is possible to conduct an offensive war, while remaining on the defensive in some zones. The strategic offensive does not mean attacking everywhere all the time.

All this resulted, both during and after the war, in a tangle of criticisms and accusations being directed at Joffre, and it is very difficult to make head or tail of it. What exactly is being held against him – a strategic offensive concept, or tactically-offensive means of action, or indeed offensive battles? He himself was ambiguous at times. He frequently spoke of 'strategic offensive' and, at his level, it could not be a matter of anything else. Yet, as we shall see in due course, many of his reactions during the Battle of the Frontiers suggest that he did not always distinguish between the tactical engagement of his troops on the actual ground – in other words, a battle pure and simple – and the strategic objectives he had set himself. The General Staff and GQG were hardly any clearer in their thinking between 1910 and 1914. The Staff College during the period 1880–1900 was not particularly sure whether it was teaching strategy or tactics, since it failed to clarify the terms it used. Not until the creation of the Centre for Advanced Military Studies, which was dedicated to teaching strategy, was a clearer distinction drawn.

Nevertheless, both the army and France more generally had an offensive frame of mind. That much is not in doubt. Joffre stated in his memoirs:

> During a session of the Supreme National Defence Council at the Elysée palace on 9 January 1912, even the peace-loving *Monsieur* Fallières expressed his pleasure at the abandonment of defensive plans that amounted in his view to an admission of inferiority. 'We are determined', he added, 'to march straight at the enemy without any hesitation. The offensive suits the temperament of our soldiers, and should guarantee us victory provided we commit all our active forces to the struggle without any exceptions.'[2]

What did the good *Monsieur* Fallières really mean by these words? He was, of course, expressing a shared mindset and possibly also his own personal attitude. Yet he would have been taken aback had it been pointed out to him that one of the logical consequences of the offensive was nothing less than the aim of capturing Berlin. The offensive is more than just an attitude. People might well talk about it – they might revel in the word – but they failed to realize its full implications, including the fact that it entailed a virtual obligation for their country to start the war. Of course they wanted the offensive, but they had not bothered to think through what they wanted the offensive to achieve.

Members of parliament were often more offensive-minded than soldiers. The most memorable moments came during the annual vote for the Ministry of War's budget. I could fill entire pages by quoting what was said, but here is just one example:

> We are convinced that once resort has been made to armed force, a great people impatient for action and for justice can think of only one way of winning and that is by taking the offensive. It is the only way, because it is prompted by the most manly determination and by the keenest and sharpest brains – the sort of brains that take the most direct approach. It is the only way, because it alone achieves great results.

These words were spoken in the Chamber of Deputies on 3 December 1912 by *Monsieur* Treignier, the Deputy for the Loir-et-Cher and *rapporteur* for the budget. Yet I shall repeat the same question as I asked about *Monsieur* Fallières – what did *Monsieur* Treignier really mean by the word 'offensive'? In my view, he meant nothing at all. In common with most of his fellow members of parliament, he was simply pandering to his constituents and hoping they would reelect him.

One advocate of the offensive who made a name for himself was Major Driant. He was the Deputy for the Meurthe-et-Moselle and was later killed as a lieutenant-colonel at Caures Wood at the start of the German attack on Verdun. He challenged the Chamber of Deputies 'to find a battle in this era that was waged defensively and yet was not lost'. His words have added bite, since it was Driant's denunciations of Verdun's inadequate defences that intensified the dispute between Galliéni and Joffre.

Ministers themselves gave a lead in speaking of the offensive. Messimy, the Minister of War, stated in an article published in the newspaper *Le Matin* on 1 August 1911:

> With these three men [Joffre, Dubail and Castelnau, whom Messimy had appointed several days earlier], men who are both capable and energetic, I will strive to develop the offensive doctrine in which our army is beginning to immerse itself ...

Since that was all Messimy said on the subject on this occasion, it is unclear whether he actually believed what he was saying, or was simply conforming to the atmosphere of the time. People have spoken of a mystique of the offensive and they seem to be near the mark. It would be fascinating to do a psychiatric assessment of French society as a whole back then, if only that were possible.

*   *   *

As Joffre was always repeating, you will not win if you remain on the defensive. He was right and his view was echoed by military circles at the time. The need to win is what justifies the offensive and this eternal truth can not be questioned today any more than in the past. But once you have opted for either attack or defence, at whatever level, you have to answer the question: 'What I am going to do?' Equally importantly, you have to work out 'why and how am I going to do it?' You have to be clear about your intent, your desired outcomes, your objectives and in particular your means. In short, you have to undertake a comprehensive analysis and continually repeat it, and you may well conclude that the offensive is impossible in practice. Yet such a discussion was never likely to be held in the 1910s – not in France at any rate, despite the undeniable progress that had been made in military thinking since the Second Empire. The Germans were more advanced, as can be seen in the development of the Schlieffen Plan.

If we were to trace the history of the offensive in France, we would have no trouble in showing that the army was always offensive-minded, despite having a succession of different political masters. In the aftermath of defeat in 1870, France was left stunned. Much of the population regarded revenge and the recovery of the lost provinces as the only great national cause worth pursuing, but France's governments were more wary and carefully avoided antagonizing the ever-vigilant Bismarck. Their cautious approach can be seen on several occasions when Germany basically provoked various incidents, for example in 1875. It was during this period that Gambetta remarked about the loss of Alsace-Lorraine in Juliette Adam's *Nouvelle revue*: 'Think of it always, but never mention it.' Even though the army remained offensive to its very core, the politicians thought only of self-defence against a Prussia that had been transformed into a German Empire. They seem to have been wise, for the German Empire soon began to leave France behind in every sphere, especially the economy and population growth. Imperial Germany was growing imperialistic.

France began building fortifications to protect itself. These were not the same as the previous set of fortifications dating from 1840. They were instead based on the concept of 'fortified systems', which sought to incorporate manœuvre into the way fortresses were defended. Between 1874 and about 1885, the Séré de Rivières system – it was named after the man who inspired it – tried to turn France into a vast no-go zone that was devised in such a way as to make it easier to repel any enemy who dared to penetrate the country's frontiers or land on its coasts. Among the admirers of Séré de Rivières was Eugène Ténot, who advised him on relations with parliament and the media. Ténot wrote a book, which included the following passage in its introduction:

> An immense undertaking, crucially important for the country's security, is being completed even as I write. France's mainland frontier from Dunkirk to Nice is being covered with a vast system of forts, fortresses and entrenched camps, which is transforming and reviving Vauban's work in a most impressive way. At the same time, Paris – the ultimate bulwark of the nation's independence – is being surrounded by a fortified girdle so bold and impressive in concept that the new fortifications make those of 1840 seem a bit parsimonious and unassertive in comparison.[3]

In seeking to fortify itself, France was effectively in the grip of paranoia. The country was trying to seal itself off by using every possible means of protection against every conceivable threat. Even if the new German Empire was the main enemy, a suspicion remained that Italy or Spain might harbour warlike intentions and Britain at this stage was still regarded as 'Perfidious Albion'.[4]

In contrast to this defensive attitude, which prevailed in the high command and amongst some politicians, the soldiers of the field army remained just as tactically offensive as they had been in 1870. Furthermore, a change occurred around 1890–1910, when the offensive was restored to official favour – apparently as a reaction against the prevailing mindset of the French commanders in 1870, which had resulted in the surrender of Metz and the rout at Sedan. The new emphasis on the offensive can be seen in what typically happened during the Grand Manœuvres of the 1890s, as revealed in an article by a Captain Nachin: 'As soon as [the enemy] was located, he found himself clobbered by an unvarying ritual culminating in an assault carried out in dense masses to the sound of martial trumpets.'[5]

The infatuation with permanent fortifications had a rather suffocating effect on military thinking. But the reaction that began to set in during the 1890s was regarded in some quarters as salutary. Technological advances – the invention of melinite and the development of more powerful artillery – undermined defensive concepts that were based solely on the durability of forts constructed with masonry, covered with a layer of earth of some thickness and bristling with cannon that lacked any overhead cover. The Séré de Rivières system was fiercely criticized at the start of the 1890s in a series of articles written by Captain Gilbert.[6] This young man from the *Ecole polytechnique* – where he had studied alongside Joffre – had graduated top of the very first class of the newly-created Staff College, but he was soon paralysed by an incurable illness. Gilbert wrote: 'The governing principle of using permanent fortifications to enhance an army's strength is completely wrong.' Many of those who have poured scorn on the offensive see Captain Gilbert as the man who was really responsible for reviving the offensive spirit and they may well be right.

General Langlois, a distinguished gunner, who taught at the Staff College before becoming its commandant, wrote in 1905:

> After the battering France had received in the 1870–1 war, its immediate reaction was to protect itself by raising a real Great Wall of China on its threatened frontier. It was a psychological reaction – akin to a dog hiding behind a piece of furniture after it has received a beating, in the belief that it will be safe there.[7]

I admire the forcefulness of that image! General Langlois added: 'You have to seek battle and desire it with everything you have.' He was obviously an advocate of the pure offensive, but as is so often the case it is difficult to tell which offensive he had in mind.

General Cardot is credited with the well-known saying: 'A bullet is stupid, but a bayonet is wise.' (It actually originated with a Russian, Dragomirov.) Cardot had a reputation for making such comments and was one of the men who eulogized the idea of sacrifice. He declared:

> Losses? They're basically the price you pay for every step you take forward, for you advance only by men's blows. Winning is a matter of

advancing and everything depends on the price you are willing to pay for it. The brave men whose bodies lie along the road are what open the way for the others.

Another maxim attributed to Cardot was often quoted as an example to be followed: 'The only purpose of manœuvre is combat. Combat means attack – all-out, decisive, unrelenting attack, carried out in mass and without having any second-thoughts.'

The same theme was developed by Foch, who in common with Langlois became a commandant of the Staff College after teaching there. This brief extract is taken from the preface of one of Foch's books:

Commanding troops in war is increasingly a matter of making a set of preparations with the aim of fighting a battle – and of taking the offensive in that battle. The decisive attack is a superior concept that should occupy us fully in both mind and character and keep us equal to the difficulties that lie ahead, above the doubts that are going to assail us.[8]

In his previous book, Foch systematically praised the merits of the offensive: 'We have to take these decisions ourselves before they are imposed on us. We must seek out these responsibilities. We must retain the initiative everywhere. We must unleash the offensive at every point.'[9] Foch added:

Only one thing counts in modern warfare and that is the tactical outcome, the battle. All your forces are required for this and it is the role of strategy to bring them to the battlefield ... in order to produce the impact.

In neither France nor Germany did people expect the war to last long. By thinking in terms of a short war, they hoped it would become a self-fulfilling prophecy.

After the creation of the Staff College in the wake of the 1870 war, General Bonnal was instrumental in ensuring that Napoleon's campaigns were studied once more. The campaign of 1806 was a favourite, as it resulted in the defeat of Prussia and the French troops marching into Berlin. This was a purely academic revenge over the Prussians, but it was revenge nonetheless and had the advantage of showing that France had been powerful in the past and that there was no reason why it should not become powerful again if only it made the right choice, namely opting for the offensive. We might note in passing that the campaign reckoned to be Napoleon's masterpiece – the campaign of France in 1814 – received little attention because it was purely defensive.

We can now understand why people were so keen on the offensive and yet the word remains surrounded by vagueness. Was the purpose of the offensive to reach Berlin, or to defeat the German army on France's redrawn eastern frontier? In short, we have come back to the eternal question of what the offensive was meant to achieve. Few soldiers had anything to say about this question. Defeating the German army was an obvious aim, but it was unclear what was meant to happen after the battle – assuming of course it was a victory – and I shall return to this issue when discussing Plan XVII. However surprising it may seem, men simply wanted a battle and gave no consideration to how the war would develop after the initial encounter. A defeat for the German army would be enough to lay to rest the memory of 1870 and the loss of the eastern provinces. As far as I know, the military press, flourishing though it was at the time, never described how an offensive towards Berlin might unfold.

Once again the French army gave full expression to what it was, and had never ceased to be, at heart. It was offensive and had a burning desire to fight. The grand manœuvres always ended with a cavalry or infantry charge, as a little display of courage that delighted the politicians, and the same was true for the annual review held on 14 July. This mindset is revealed by the newspaper columnists who closely followed the grand manœuvres.[10] Their articles made the front pages for several days and were always pompous and jingoistic in tone. The journalists took delight in reporting the bayonet charges that invariably concluded the principal moves. The only point that seemed important was that 'the troops were cheerful and appeared full of spirit', for this was repeated several times.

Moral strength

We must also address the emphasis on 'moral strength', for this is something inextricably tied up in the desire for the offensive. I have deliberately put the phrase in quotation marks to underline how the association of the words 'moral' and 'strength' created a concept that gained a life of its own. It became the icing on the cake, the be-all and end-all of military thought. Yet it did not, in fact, have an exclusively military origin. A leading psychologist of the era, Gustave Le Bon, was always talking about the importance of moral strength in the life of societies.

All the military writers seem to have regarded 'moral strength' as the beginning and the end of everything. General Percin, a prolific author with Left-wing views, wrote a successful book published in 1914. The title of the very first chapter was: 'Aim of the fight: the fight is a struggle of moral strength.'[11]

The following passage is taken from another article, written by an anonymous author who was a *général de division* and probably serving on the General Staff:

> What is the point of vast numbers of soldiers and sophisticated cannon, what are the most skilful strategic conceptions or the best devised tactical combinations going to achieve, if the prime instrument of combat – the

human being – gives way in the face of death? Victory will be won more than ever before by moral strength.[12]

Note that the need for moral strength was always linked to offensive action and never to defensive action, and yet it was actually in defence that moral strength would find its fulfilment.

I could quote an infinite number of other examples, not least from the daily newspapers. In due course, the expression 'moral strength' even found its way into the regulations and imparted an almost ideological significance to these texts, which ought to have been purely technical. Indeed, it is impossible to ignore the fact that moral strength was also the expression of an ideology, a mixed secular and religious ideology that was not restricted to the upper classes of the time. It could also be found – in a slightly different and coarser form – in almost all of France's social structures, including those of the Left and Far Left.[13]

Society created rules of behaviour and a moral code that practically everyone accepted, largely as a result of school education. The almost universal acceptance of these rules and this code was unaffected by social friction, the rise of trade unionism and the quarrels over religion. When war was declared, the political class responded to Poincaré's appeals by laying aside its internal enmities, and hence the so-called *Union sacrée* ('Sacred Union') sprang into existence. This unanimity was also an expression of moral strength, even if it broke down in due course – indeed, it was a bit artificial from the start. When Frenchmen today wonder how their forefathers managed to 'hold on' during this appalling test 100 years earlier, they should ponder the importance of 'moral strength', even if they find the concept hard to grasp and a bit amusing.

Cran was another personal quality valued in that era – yet what exactly did it mean? The word is hardly ever used in France nowadays and it has no exact English translation, though 'guts' is the nearest equivalent. Having *cran* meant showing you were equal to events. It meant being neither afraid nor discouraged. It meant pursuing your convictions to the very end. It meant being true to your origins and your family, to what you believed you were and what you wanted to be. It meant accepting your fate. It meant having it within you to make a noble gesture. It meant one of Hemingway's ideals – showing that you were a man.

In 1914, some officers fresh from their training school at Saint-Cyr thought that they would be showing *cran* if they charged at the head of their men wearing the shakos of their dress-uniform (with red and white plumes of Casoar) and white gloves. *Cran* was the perfect partner for what amounted to a virtual mystique of the offensive, for the two fed off one another. Attacks were often badly organized and badly led, and they cost many lives, including those of the officers who had knowingly launched them with the sole purpose of showing that they were not 'chickening out'.

The unfortunate result of all this was that everyone monitored his own conduct and tried to elevate himself to match the image he wanted to project. Men felt obliged to prove themselves again and again, and in doing so they might strive to outdo each other in the way they behaved. It can be difficult to understand this today. When we read the political and military speeches of the time, we often find them worded in such extreme terms that we wonder whether the men who gave these speeches were actually putting on an act. We wonder whether they had a hole deep down inside that prevented them from being fully human, and whether they were hiding this hole behind their volubility and vainglory and behind their determination to press on regardless. It seems suspiciously as if they were concealing their true personalities behind a sort of screen – and yet if we scratch a little, we find that the extreme language hid something else as well, namely a genuine commitment and a strong set of values. It was often *cran* and moral strength that made it possible for men to hold on when everything else had gone.

The most obvious place for *cran* was in bayonet attacks, with flags and standards to the fore, bugles blowing and the officers, sometimes even the generals, leading their men in one wild dash. When *cran* made an appearance, it added something that went beyond mere obedience of a regulation or orders – it added the expression of an ideal and of beliefs. It was idiotic and yet sublime at the same time – admirable and yet ludicrous. The philosopher Pascal would have said that it was a question of different realms.[14] The realm of the heart is not the realm of the mind. The realm of the heart understands and admires *cran*, but that of the mind rejects and condemns it. In 1914, it was the realm of the mind that should have prevailed.

Self-sacrifice was likewise an expression of *cran* and moral strength. We often find the word sacrifice mentioned, but men do not always act out of religious motives when they lay down their lives. During the Great War, some men did so for secular reasons and their sacrifice was equally worthy of respect – perhaps more so – because it was made without any hope of an afterlife. Their actions should not be dismissed or derided. The so-called 'skull-stuffing', or propaganda, that allegedly spread this spirit of self-sacrifice was in fact seen only later on. At the outbreak of the war, the vast majority of Frenchmen had yet to grow sceptical. Hypocrisy was the preserve of no more than a few thousands of people – journalists, influential members of parliament, industrial and financial tycoons, academics and prosperous members of the middle-classes. Soldiers with few exceptions did not belong to these exclusive circles. At least at the start of the war, the military world was more in tune with the nation, which did not question or argue. The *Union sacrée* was a reality in the lower levels of society, even if at the top it soon became a mere sham and smokescreen. Almost all of France's citizens – whether they wore uniform or civilian clothes – did what they termed their duty. After the war, this created new solidarities and the well-known veteran spirit, which also conveyed a sort of nostalgia for the period when life had been much more difficult but also, in some respects, much simpler.

Tools for reform

What was Joffre's own attitude to the offensive? I am unaware of him having written anything that glorified it, and in 1913 he gave a lecture at the *Ecole polytechnique* in which he had strikingly little to say about doctrine and instead concentrated on the material conditions of the coming war. He was definitely offensive-minded by the time he took charge in July 1911, but he had not always been so. It is notable that he had been recorded as having a 'sluggish and very soft constitution' while he was studying at the Joint School of Artillery and Military Engineering at Fontainebleau. In contrast, Archinard (the future general) covered him with compliments in the Sudan in 1889 and praised his dynamism. In short, Joffre gradually developed his officer-qualities, but it was only when he took command of a division in 1906 and then of an army corps in 1908 that he became more of a warrior than an engineer. Emile Mayer saw this for himself when he met Joffre on the top deck of a bus in 1911: Joffre launched into a furious outburst against General Michel, accusing him of 'spouting false notions about war and the use of the reserves'.[15] Mayer was rather taken aback, as he had never seen Joffre in this light before.

Three years passed between Joffre's appointment as Chief of the General Staff and the outbreak of the war. During that time, he could either intensify or turn aside the offensive tendencies and desire for battle that were evident in both military and civilian society. So what happened during this period – and what influence did he have? As he himself recognized, he was endowed with powers that none of his predecessors had known. 'This reorganization was a big leap forward', he wrote, thinking in the logical way of an engineer. 'It placed a concentration of power in my hands that could be used to coordinate the military efforts effectively.'[16]

Joffre had three tools at his disposal for bringing about institutional change. They were the Staff College, the Centre for Advanced Military Studies and the publication of regulations and instructions, which were the only documents that were likely (if given enough time) to percolate down to fairly junior-ranking subordinates and win them over to their chief's way of thinking. In addition, he was able to instruct the staffs and check the state of their training by means of the annual grand manœuvres and so-called map exercises. Officially, Joffre was unable to appoint officers, especially generals, since the power to do so lay with the Minister of War. But in reality, he enjoyed sufficient influence with successive Ministers to have something more than simply a right of scrutiny. This can be seen in the remark he made in his memoirs that he had an extensive programme of replacing old and worn-out generals. It was hardly the first example in history of worn-out officers being culled, but unfortunately in this case the cull had to be continued during the early stages of the war since it proved impossible to complete in peacetime.

* * *

Before we go into the details of what Joffre did, we must say something about Colonel Loyzeau de Grandmaison. For years after the war, Grandmaison was accused of having caused the catastrophe and he became the perfect scapegoat. Yet the puzzling question is how a mere lieutenant-colonel managed to provoke so much controversy and acquire such importance that Joffre himself – the Commander-in-Chief of the French armies – felt obliged to mention him and his lectures in his memoirs twenty years later.

In February 1911, Lieutenant-Colonel de Grandmaison was head of the Operations Department of the army's General Staff, and was teaching and lecturing at the Centre for Advanced Military Studies.[17] He was an outstanding officer, undeniably charismatic, and had a flair for written and verbal communication (especially the latter).[18] General Debeney hit the nail on the head when he remarked:

> It's impossible to think of a more persuasive man than Grandmaison. Of keen intelligence, fiery in temperament and generous in character, he had a considerable power to inspire ..., but he was carried away by his imagination. ... He had subordinated his judgement to his temperament.[19]

Grandmaison gave two lectures entitled *The critical nature of the fronts and the concept of security* and *The mode of engagement for large units*.[20] They were given to the officers of the General Staff and of the Centre for Advanced Military Studies – but to them alone, and they amounted to only around fifty-odd people. Grandmaison did not deal at all with tactics at the level of small units, namely the section, company, battalion, regiment and even brigade. What he had to say applied solely at the level of the army and army group, and was intended to describe the engagement of forces only after they had been assembled in those formations. In other words, we are talking about strategy. Lieutenant-Colonel de Grandmaison was therefore attempting to define the correct method of engagement for units that he might never command, at a time when he personally had never led so much as a regiment. (We must remember, of course, that the whole point of the Centre for Advanced Military Studies was to teach men to think about the long-term.)

Grandmaison's lectures can be summed up by four points. First, the very speed of an attack provided whatever security was required for the flanks. Secondly, the progress made by attacking units made liaison between them pointless. Thirdly, the offensive had to be all-out and undertaken along the whole front simultaneously. Fourthly, a fighting retreat was impossible. Grandmaison also became bogged down in endless reasoning about the role and function of the advanced-guard, which were key discussion points within the military intelligensia at the start of the twentieth century but have now ceased to have any interest and are poorly understood. Grandmaison set out a whole series of recommendations, along such lines as: '. . . fostering anything associated in the slightest way with the offensive spirit – and doing so with a passionate and extravagant approach that goes to the very heart of training.' He concluded with the words: 'Let's go to extremes, for it is possible even that may not be enough'. This oratorical flourish was a deliberate figure of speech and should not be taken too seriously. Yet it naturally stuck in people's minds and the remark has resulted in Grandmaison being heavily criticized by modern-day commentators.

In the 1910s, an entire school of young officers tried to convince itself of the validity of this new way of thinking, in which the dynamism of the attack took priority over flank protection, on the basis that the very act of attacking would provide whatever protection was needed. This might seem contrary to commonsense, and even if you lack any military experience you might well question whether such an argument always held true regardless of the circumstances.

In order to understand Grandmaison's thinking, we need to leap thirty years forwards in time and consider what Guderian and Rommel did in 1940. Their rapid success was the first occasion on which an assailant unconcerned with ensuring the security of his advance managed to rout an enemy (in this case, the French army) by dislocating him with a series of uninterrupted attacks. There is no example in modern military history of so swift a victorious campaign. It was pure Grandmaison and proves that his arguments had some justification. Endlessly attacking again and again, giving your opponent not a minute's respite – 'pummelling' as it was termed in 1914 – was the right sort of approach. The problem was simply that the means available in Grandmaison's time were inadequate.

Grandmaison had previously written a small book about infantry combat.[21] He had been a major at the time and the book is not as well known as his other works, which is unfortunate since it is actually far more interesting. In this book, he really did address infantry fighting even at the lowest tactical levels, down to the squad of about fifteen men. But far from advocating a blind bayonet assault as the only form of attack, he placed much emphasis on an astute approach exploiting information gleaned by advanced-guards. For the combat itself he wrote: 'Experience confirms the dictates of commonsense by proving that envelopment [turning the enemy's flank] is by far the most common and advantageous form of the offensive.'[22] Most important of all is his statement that in an offensive action 'we risk going astray if we focus too narrowly on the infantry's fighting methods and fail to take account of the artillery'.[23]

Grandmaison certainly made his mark on the era, but it would be inaccurate to claim that he bore a heavy responsibility for the bloodbaths of 1914, even though this is what many authors have written. The simple fact is that he left the army's General Staff in 1911, far too early to have a hand in the development of Plan XVII. On leaving the Operations Department, he was rewarded by Messimy (who at least sympathized with his way of thinking) with the rank of colonel and command of a regiment.[24] Grandmaison enjoyed a meteoric rise after his famous lectures: having been made colonel on 14 August 1911, he rose to become *général de brigade* on 27 August 1914, followed by temporary *général de division* on 22 January 1915. This was not simply due to the war, for without a doubt he was an exceptional leader and his men would have followed him to the end of the world. In 1914, he led the 153rd Infantry Regiment, part of the 20th Corps under Foch, who referred to him in glowing terms. He was wounded three times within twenty-four hours at Morhange on 19 and 20 August, and ended up being mortally wounded on 19 February 1915 whilst commanding the 5th Group of Reserve Divisions.

Grandmaison was framed as the man responsible for the disasters and he made a perfect scapegoat since he was no longer around to defend himself. Yet it was hardly his fault that his message fell on fertile ground (that, indeed, was why it proved so successful). The problem was that his audience took what he said about the army corps and deliberately misapplied it to company level. The fact that none of the French armies in 1914 was led according to Grandmaison's ideas underlines the intoxicating nature of his two lectures. What he advocated for armies and army corps was put into effect at the level of smaller units – but this happened only because people wilfully overlooked the distinction between the two levels and ignored the reality of the situation. Everyone forgot Grandmaison's actual words and remembered just the background music of the offensive. He became the convenient symbol of pre-war mistakes.

Surely, a naïve person might wonder, at least some French officers were more level-headed? Since the principle of authority was so strong in the army, why was the man in charge unable to impose his will – assuming, of course, that he did not share the commonly-held views? This question has already been answered by Lanrezac, who commanded the 5th Army in 1914.[25] He noted in his book that people were bound to ask him: 'Why did you, as an army commander, not do what was necessary to impose more moderate tactics on your officers – tactics more appropriate for the means at your disposal?' His answer to this potential question was: 'Whatever I might have done on this matter would have been in vain, given that such a violent tide of opinion was sweeping our fellows along. In any case, once our troops are engaged with the enemy it is too late to try and instruct them.'[26]

We have already encountered General de Lardemelle, the chief-of-staff of Franchet d'Esperey's 1st Corps, which belonged to the 5th Army. He sought to defend Lanrezac in a couple of articles, which discussed at length how Grandmaison's rash statements and the excesses of the offensive spirit harmed the functioning of the staff of the 5th Army and its army corps.[27] Yet these arguments are only half-convincing. Lanrezac was an intelligent man and simply needed to have given strict orders and made some examples – this would have been enough to ensure his generals obeyed him and his infantry-men dug defensive positions.

Another man who was lukewarm about the offensive was Pétain. He was head of the infantry course at the Staff College and strangely enough got along well with Foch, at least at this time, who was the Commandant of the College. Cold and somewhat aloof, Pétain was nicknamed *Précis-le-Sec*, a reference to his dry and succinct manner of speech.[28] Sarcasm came readily to him and he ridiculed advocates of the all-out offensive rather than arguing with them. This may well have been the right approach – as well as being persuasive, it was less likely to provoke rebukes – though his lack of enthu-siasm for the prevailing doctrine may have contributed to his slow promotion. He also took the more subtle step of shifting the emphasis in his teaching by placing his own interpretation on the offensive: his maxim was 'firepower kills'. While retaining the concept of the offensive, he imposed so many restrictions as to deprive it of substance. But Pétain remained exceptional right up until the end of the war and beyond.

Regulations
Before examining the contents of the regulations that were in force at the time, we should note something that almost every historian has overlooked – and it has led to inaccuracies in what they have written. In 1914, there were two ways of waging war – ways that had emerged in the course of several centuries. The first was field warfare and the second was siege warfare (which also included the defence of fortresses since defending and besieging for-tresses were two sides of the same coin, just as in Vauban's time).

By 1913, there were regulations on siege warfare, namely the *Instructions on siege warfare* and *Instructions on fortress duties*, both of them issued in 1909. This type of war was conducted with specialized equipment and troops – sappers and artillerymen – who were grouped into siege parks. Fortresses that might be defended or besieged were protected almost entirely by permanent fortifications, with temporary fortifications being few and far between.[29]

Methods of attacking or defending a fortress took account of these specific circumstances. Heavy artillery was always used and naturally enough was called siege or fortress artillery. You would never besiege a fortress with just 75mm cannon. Conversely, you had no need of heavy artillery on campaign, since there were no permanent fortifications. The problem was that tempo-rary fortifications, such as trenches, barbed-wire and machine-gun posts, did not fall neatly into either of the two categories of warfare and instead belonged to warfare as a whole. Temporary fortifications straddled the two concepts of field and siege warfare, and no one – no one in France at any rate – claimed ownership of them or drew up regulations to govern their use. To make matters worse, just as there were two ways of waging war, there also existed two armies until 1915 – the field army and the army of the fortresses. Unlike the field army, which was under the Commander-in-Chief, the army of the fortresses was controlled by the Minister of War.

Joffre has been criticized on account of two regulations – yet we have to remember that both of them applied just to the field army. One was the *Regulation on the handling of large units* of October 1913. (A provisional version, not much different from the final text, appeared in December 1912 as an instruction approved by Millerand.)[30] The second was the *Field service regulation*, which was directed at much smaller, subordinate units. (We'll leave aside the *Regulation of infantry manœuvres*, which was issued at the end of April 1914, for its overall tone was much the same and it appeared too late to have the slightest effect one way or the other.)

The commission responsible for drafting the *Regulation on the handling of large units* consisted of eight members. Only two of them were generals – the others included two lieutenant-colonels and one who was merely a major. They were clearly chosen because of their alleged competence rather than their seniority. The same commission also drafted the *Field service regulation*, which applied to divisions and smaller units. This over-arching approach was exceptional and indicates a desire to standardize doctrine – and hence action – throughout the chain of command, from the very smallest to the very largest units.

The commission was presided over by General Pau, who had nearly been appointed to Joffre's post – indeed it was said he might well have been appointed if he had been more flexible in character and readier to bend with the wind. Other members included General Hély d'Oissel, who became Lanrezac's chief-of-staff a few years later, and Colonel Anthoine, who enjoyed a high-flying career, first with Joffre and subsequently as an army commander. Colonel Berthelot became an assistant chief-of-staff at GQG in 1914 and was accused of incompetence and all sorts of disgraceful actions, which I shall address in due course. Lieutenant-Colonel Brécard subsequently served as liaison officer with the Belgian army at the start of the war. Lieutenant-Colonel Hallouin was the Secretary of the Supreme War Council while the Three-Year Law was under discussion. He became the head of the Operations Department of the General Staff and in 1915 commanded an army corps. Major Brossé was the commission's secretary and did not hesitate after the war to criticize what he himself had minuted during the pre-war years – I shall say more about this, too, in due course.

Joffre without doubt had confidence in all the commission's members. In his memoirs, he elaborated at some length on the tasks entrusted to them and he clearly viewed their work as an important part of the reform of the French army.[31] Yet all these officers – not least Hély d'Oissel – later 'forgot' their role in drawing up the regulations, or at the very least kept quiet about it. In some cases, this was because they now felt a need to tone down the concept of the offensive. When a Deputy called Engerand made an official request in 1919 for the names of the commission's members, the Minister of War refused to comply.

Were these regulations really necessary? The French fondness for doctrine was a recent development, the result of following the example set by the Germans, and it replaced the pragmatic, improvised approach favoured by Napoleon that had prevailed during the wars of the Revolution and Empire. It was at this stage that regulations governing the handling of large units were drawn up for the first time in the French army's history. At the end of the nineteenth century, France's generals rediscovered Napoleon's strategic and tactical mastery – but since not all French soldiers were Napoleons, a regulation had to be written for them. This step was perfectly justified, if it was used as a means of standardizing the operating methods of the staffs so as to make them interchangeable. As Captain Z——— explained, 'the regulations provide a guard rail for mediocre men and are the only way to standardize an army's tactical concepts and the work it does'.[32] In 1921, Captain de Gaulle (the future general) wrote in an article:

> The mentality of the French army seems to recoil from recognizing the essentially empirical character that warfare ought to acquire. It is always striving to construct a doctrine that will automatically enable it at least to get a handle on the action and grasp its outline, without considering the circumstances on which it should be based.[33]

The question that has to be asked about the army's regulations is whether they were something original, or if they simply conceptualized and codified operating methods that in many cases were neither well-reasoned nor reasonable.

What is striking in France is that ever since the founding of the *Ecole polytechnique*, it has always been graduates of that school who have tried to put warfare on a theoretical basis. This can be seen with the creation of the Entrenched Camp of Paris in 1840, with Séré de Rivières' fortified systems of 1875, with Foch's championing of the offensive, and much closer to our own times with Colonel Argoud's theories of revolutionary warfare and with the deterrent established largely by General Ailleret. Nor should we forget the gunners and sappers – all of them graduates of the *Ecole polytechnique* – who decided, more or less autocratically, that heavy artillery was unnecessary or that permanent fortifications were essential for the nation's security.

We must also ask ourselves another question. Nobody thinks of raising it nowadays and yet the answer is not at all clear. Was the *Regulation on the handling of large units* actually read by those for whom it was intended, namely the generals commanding the armies and army corps? All of them were aged between 62 and 65 and reckoned that they already knew practically everything they needed to know. They were certainly sceptical about something many of them must have regarded as just another fad. The retired General Cherfils had a reputation for the incisive way in which he expressed himself and he often voiced his opinions in the newspapers *L'Echo de Paris* and *Le Gaulois*. Here is his comment about the *Regulation on the handling of large units*:

> This seems to be just a theoretical little book intended exclusively for high-level officers commanding an army. If these army commanders really need to learn what to do from a catechism on the art of command, it would have been better not to have appointed them and to have filled the posts with other officers who do have the necessary knowledge.[34]

I bet that Cherfils was simply putting into words what his peers were thinking. No commander of an army or army corps is likely to have read any more than the first chapter of the *Regulation on the handling of large units*. These generals were intent on waging war in the way they had learned, but unfortunately a long time had passed since they had begun their careers. All too many generals of 1914 had no personal experience of war except as a second-lieutenant back in 1870. A number of generals dismissed during the Great War unanimously condemned the regulation – but they waited until after the war to do so and the paradox is that most of them had not even read it. They simply saw an opportunity to try and hide the stain on their reputation and justify themselves by joining the howling wolf-pack.

On the other hand, the regulation was evidently discussed at the Staff College and at the Centre for Advanced Military Studies. Yet it was not a case of the officers all having to jump into line and conform with a sudden, drastic change, for the regulation simply formalized what had already been taught and practised for several years. The only novelty was the way in which the recommendations were presented in language that seems insufferable today, although it was not so at the time.

Hence the belated publication of the *Regulation on the handling of large units*, just months before the war, had little effect on the staffs. They had already been amply immersed in the ideas contained in the regulation – its first chapter simply repeated what they knew by heart – and they all believed they knew its key point, the offensive. But the army corps commanders and other generals simply leafed through the regulation hurriedly, if they actually opened it at all, even though they should have regarded it as their bedside reading.

*   *   *

Now let's examine the regulation itself, starting with the report that presented it to the Minister of War. The report was long, taking up as many as twenty-six of the 101 pages of the regulation, and it contained some phrases that were later picked up on by many critics. For instance: 'The conduct of war is governed by the need to give the operations a vigorous offensive impulse'. Above all, there was this sentence: 'The lessons of the past have borne fruit: the French army has returned to its traditions and now recognizes no rule in the conduct of operations other than the offensive.' (Incidentally, the provisional version of the regulation, published as an instruction in 1912, had been signed by Millerand, but the regulation itself was simply presented to the Minister of War.)

Article 3 of the regulation's first chapter was a reminder that the war would have to be short and recommended 'seeking a decision with the shortest possible delay'. We must never forget that the glorification of the offensive was in part a direct consequence of the widespread belief that the war had to be short. This seemed straightforward enough, for the syllogism (a type of logical argument) ran as follows: (1) the war had to be short, (2) only the offensive could ensure victory, (3) it was therefore necessary to take the offensive to ensure victory and shorten the duration of the war.

Article 5 of the same chapter followed on logically and summed up all the rest of the regulation:

> In order to win, it is necessary to break through the enemy's battle dispositions by force. A breakthrough requires attacks driven right up to the hilt without any hesitation and it can be achieved only at the cost of heavy casualties. Any other approach must be rejected as contrary to the very nature of war: a manœuvre can prepare the way to victory, but can not guarantee it – regardless of however skilfully it has been planned.

The regulation emphasized moral strength, as was only to be expected. Article 8 explained:

> Battles are above all moral struggles. Defeat becomes inevitable once there is no longer hope of victory. Success therefore goes not to the side that has suffered fewer losses, but to the one with greater determination and tougher morale.

The pomposity is obvious and the whole of the first chapter was written in similar style, being a mixture of a moral message, exhortations and philosophical points. Such language had no place in a regulation and was perhaps a way of elevating the argument above a purely technical level in a final attempt at persuasion. It was akin to a gloomy exhortation and reminds me of the Francoist war-cry in Spain in 1936: 'Long live death!'

The remainder of the regulation was less strident, and many of its provisions were more sensible than might be assumed from the earlier sections. The overall tone was very technical. The possibility of a retreat was foreseen and set out methodically. So was the organization of defensive fronts (Article 123), although this was always to be done with a view to bouncing back and counter-attacking. The emphasis placed on the offensive was offset by a series of recommendations, such as Article 117 about relying on artillery in order to spare the infantry. In fact, these recommendations virtually contradicted the repeated insistence on attacking. The regulation may not have explicitly recommended waging war in an intelligent way, but neither did it make it impossible to do so. In other words, it was possible at the tactical level to use procedures and combat methods that were appropriate for the situation and the mission. The regulation did not cause the bloodbath of the start of the war, nor could it have done so. All it did was assert a doctrine and it was merely the result of a process of thinking that had already been done elsewhere and in other ways.

*   *   *

We now turn to the *Field service regulation*, which was brought into force by the decree of 2 December 1913. It applied only to divisions and smaller units, and focused on combat at the divisional level. On the whole, it was a good regulation and it added to the credibility of the *Regulation on the handling of large units* since both had been written by the same team. It praised the offensive, but did so in a more balanced way. Above all, it stated that the offensive was the default means of action – all other procedures were accepted and recommended in certain circumstances, but only for temporary periods. Admittedly, it was exaggerated, but apart from some flights of rhetoric, which were equally out of place in this regulation, it described combat procedures that have stood the test of time. This will become clear if I quote some extracts about the role of the infantry and artillery, which I have taken from the second chapter. The first extract concerns the infantry:

> The combination of fire and movement is the infantry's means of action. *The power of modern weapons makes it impossible to make any attack in dense formation over open country in daylight.*[35] Offensive drive can be maintained only by using flexible formations whose vulnerability is as limited as possible.

As for the artillery:

> Artillery supports the infantry by destroying anything that might check its progress. Close, constant cooperation between the infantry and artillery is absolutely imperative, therefore, in action. Every attack entails the infantry and artillery's close cooperation.

Nowadays, many people seize on the statement: 'Artillery no longer prepares attacks; it supports them'. By criticizing this remark, they seek to emphasize the regulation's share of responsibility for the bloodbath that followed.[36] Yet such criticisms are actually a complete distortion of the truth, not least because artillery 'support' also entails 'preparation'. The regulation made this clear by stating: 'Artillery fire is the first obstacle the infantry encounters' –

the implication being that this artillery fire had to be silenced. The correctness of this view was demonstrated to an almost ridiculous degree by the disastrous initial clashes of the war, which were often caused by each arm trying to wage its own, separate war. Nor should we need reminding that this regulation dealt just with field service, whereas it was in siege warfare that attacks required artillery preparation.

The regulation also addressed the defensive. The whole of the fourth chapter of Section V was dedicated to this subject and the methods of action it advocated can not be faulted, such as establishing centres of resistance composed of strongpoints. Contrary to what has sometimes been claimed, the French army was not ignorant – or to be more precise, it had no excuse to be ignorant – of what a trench or a shelter was. For as Joffre pointed out, this was the first time that a regulation contained a section dealing specifically with fieldworks.[37] These pages might well have caused more than one infantryman to gag, out of a reluctance to turn himself into a navvy. For they contained the unambiguous statement that positions were to be prepared for defence by the same troops who were occupying the ground – in other words the infantrymen.

Yet another regulation existed, called *Instructions on fieldworks for the use of infantry units*. It was issued in October 1906 and updated in 1912. (Regulations were plentiful in this era.) It contained a good description of how to create trenches and lay out the ground. Yet it is a safe bet that no unit in peacetime ever dug so much as 1 metre of real trench on a field of manœuvre, particularly as it would have been necessary to fill in the trench afterwards and also because in many cases the field of manœuvre did not even exist.

It would be wrong to claim that the *Field service regulation* of 1913 aggravated the situation. We should instead regret that it came too late to change the prevailing mindset or to be put into practice as part of the infantrymen's training. In any case, training camps would have been necessary for any attempt to impart hands-on experience of combined-arms fighting at the basic level of the division. As far as most regiments were concerned, training camps were practically non-existent.

It is doubtful whether this regulation was read any more than the previous one. After the war, Colonel Brossé described what he called the general trends of pre-war thinking:

1. The defensive will inevitably end in defeat. It is to be totally rejected.
2. Morale is by far the most important factor in war. Infantry will overcome any difficulties, provided it is brave and has vigorous leaders.
3. An all-out attack is suitable whatever the circumstances. The casualties are always worth it. For anyone in charge of the fighting, the basic rule consists of just three words: 'Let's pile in.'

4. The attacker's morale is far higher than the defender's. A soldier who is advancing believes in success. But a soldier on the defensive has to endure all the doubts caused by the strain of waiting.
5. Moral ascendancy is acquired by whichever side seizes the initiative of the operations. His opponent is obliged to take steps to protect himself: his willpower is thereby paralysed, he abandons his offensive plans and gives in to passivity, which leads to defeat.
6. Any counter-offensive manœuvre is doomed to failure, regardless of whether it is launched immediately or after being methodically prepared.
7. If an operation is intended to have a decisive outcome, attack everywhere.[38]

It's a pity that Brossé made no mention of the fact he had been secretary of the commission that produced the *Field service regulation* – he did not even refer to the regulation he had helped to create. This says much about the mentality of the officer corps, which was clearly uninterested in what the General Staff was trying to impose on it. In the eyes of Colonel Brossé, who was simply describing what must have been a general outlook, the regulation that was in force – the one that had been issued and was to be put into effect – could be summed up by just the seven points quoted above, and all the rest could be ignored. It was a regrettable attitude, since many lives would have been saved if only the Battle of the Frontiers had been fought in the spirit of the regulation.

To conclude this section, I will quote from a US army regulation of 1986, called *Field Manual 100-5*:

> The offensive is the decisive form of war – the commander's ultimate means of imposing his will upon the enemy. While strategic, operational, or tactical considerations may require defending, defeat of an enemy force at any level will sooner or later require shifting to the offensive.

These sentences could have been taken word for word from the two French regulations seventy-three years earlier. *FM 100-5* formed the basis of the US doctrine for infantry combat in Iraq in both 1991 and 2003.

Staff training
I shall now say something about the work of the Staff College and the Centre for Advanced Military Studies. Joffre obtained control of both these institutions as a result of his appointment. The Staff College had been created in 1875–6, on the lines of the German *Kriegsakademie*, while the Centre for Advanced Military Studies was established at the end of 1910. The trainees of the Centre for Advanced Military Studies were called the 'apprentice-marshals' (this remains the case today), since they were mostly selected on the

strength of their record after leaving the Staff College and had a glittering future ahead of them in the senior ranks. The 'military studies' in the Centre's name consisted of studying strategy, large-unit tactics and also what would now be called logistics.

We are told that between 1910 and 1914, three classes of officers were supposedly trained in the cult of the offensive at the Staff College and the Centre for Advanced Military Studies. Yet the instructions that Joffre gave the Centre for the year 1912 stated:

> The focus of the teaching is to be restricted to the handling of large units (division, army corps, army), *excluding matters of minor tactics*.[39] In order to maintain the practical slant of the teaching, no lectures are to be given of an academic nature about either strategic or tactical matters.[40]

In short, authoritative lectures on the lines of those given by Grandmaison were to be replaced by training, training and yet more training. Joffre's instructions then made a number of specific points. The instructions are too long to be quoted in full, but they concentrated on staff techniques and *not once* did they address the offensive.

Officers who graduated from the Staff College were *brevetés* – qualified staff officers – and they took up posts on the staffs of large units such as army, army corps and division. The staffs of these units were organized into departments, but only the Third Department (Operations), which was a sort of inner sanctum, made it possible for *brevetés* to get to grips with matters of strategy and more frequently of tactics. The *brevetés* of the Operations Department were widely detested: by comrades who had failed the competitive examination for entering the Staff College; by reservist officers; by politicians who disparaged them for manipulating their superiors; and by the soldiers who – sometimes rightly, but by no means always so – accused them of holding their lives in scant regard by hurling them into offensives without properly understanding what these offensives were meant to achieve.

But the other departments – First (Personnel, Manpower), Second (Intelligence) and Fourth (Logistics) – were likewise led and manned by *brevetés*. All these officers had learned their trade at the Staff College, which codified and taught the procedures for these duties – duties which may have been less glamorous than those of the Third Department but were just as vital. Joffre paid tribute to them in the speech he gave on 19 December 1918 when he was admitted into the *Académie française* (the prestigious body that regulates the French language): 'During the first weeks of the war, we would never have managed to do what we did if the army staffs had not remained like rocks in the storm, spreading clarity and coolness around them.'

During the period up to 1918, the senior commands were gradually filled by men drawn from the body of officers who were *brevetés* or products of the Centre for Advanced Military Studies. An army's most precious resource lies in having a pool from which it can pick officers of ability and character. Joffre selected the best of them with the valuable help of assistants such as Major Bel (even if Bel was disparaged by the many men he found wanting). Joffre had the knack of finding commanders for large units, and his successors were content to leave almost all his choices in place. At the 1925 commemorations to mark the fiftieth anniversary of the creation of the Staff College, tribute was paid to those *brevetés* who had died for France – they amounted to no fewer than 21 generals, 108 colonels or lieutenant-colonels and 115 majors. The 'Young Turks' had paid as high a price as their elders, if not higher.

* * *

It remains to be seen what Joffre tried to do in terms of training his officers. In his memoirs, he wrote at length about both map exercises and TEWTs (Tactical Exercises Without Troops), the latter being conducted in the field. The purpose of these exercises was to train the staffs to study and resolve situations that were likely to occur in real life. Joffre reported that during the first six months of 1914 alone, as many as seventy study sessions were held during army map exercises.[41]

The staffs of the large units were clearly kept busy, for in addition to these exercises they took part in the French army's traditional grand manœuvres, the last of which was held in South-Western France in the autumn of 1913. Joffre could not fail to be pleased with the excellent strategic sense shown by those taking part in the manœuvres (Galliéni and Marion in autumn 1912, Chomer and Pau in 1913), but he also deplored the many tactical mistakes that were made on the ground.

General Palat, who was no admirer of Joffre, wrote in an article: 'It can not be denied that the 1913 Manœuvres make disciplinary action necessary in order to avoid bloodbaths.'[42] Disciplinary action is indeed what happened, with Generals Faurié, Plagnol, Besset and Alba being removed from their posts. Faurié, the commander of the 16th Corps, was regarded as a Republican general. He believed that he was being removed for political reasons and mobilized the press and parliament to try and retain his post. Even Clemenceau supported him, but in vain. Palat was making public criticisms in his article about the manœuvres and probably felt obliged to tone down his remarks. Even so, he claimed that the divisional generals failed to command and simply left their units to their own devices on the ground:

> Infantry could be seen launching premature assaults and advancing without worrying about the effect of incoming fire, without exploiting cover and hidden paths and without ensuring liaison with either neighbouring units or the echelons further back ...

This is exactly what happened later, during the Battle of the Frontiers in August and September 1914. Palat's account is significant, for it shows that as early as 1911 Joffre was fully aware of the inadequacies of some of his senior subordinates. Otherwise, he would not have dismissed them before the war.

The grand manœuvres were observed by foreign military attachés from various European countries. Just as the French attaché attended the German manœuvres, his German opposite number attended the French ones. The report by the German attaché on the 1912 Manœuvres makes interesting reading:

> Infantry: ... individual marksmanship and combat training were not up to scratch. Often, no account was taken of the effectiveness of hostile fire .... Nor, in many cases, did the infantry await the result of a serious preparation fire; they instead simply dashed to the assault in a dense line and from too far away.[43]

His verdict on the artillery was: 'The liaison with the infantry was clearly inadequate.' As for the cavalry: 'Cohesion, calmness and order were conspicuously absent during the movements of the units.' In this respect, too, the warning signs for what happened in 1914 can be seen in 1912.

Joffre stated in his memoirs that he had intended to provide a training camp for each army corps. By 1914, this work had barely begun and only the large camps existed, such as the already antiquated one at Châlons and the camp of Mailly. Completing the task would have taken several years owing to numerous problems, especially financial ones. Rural inhabitants did what they have always done, and artificially 'improved' their lands so they could sell them to the State for an inflated price.[44] Acquiring land by either expropriation or agreement proved tricky. Yet it was a sound idea to create training camps and no other way existed of 'drilling' regiments so as to teach them combined-arms manœuvres. If no training camp was available, the *Field service regulation* remained just empty rhetoric.

*   *   *

Before concluding, I shall take an overview of the rest of Europe. France was not alone in its offensive-mindedness: it was not an island surrounded by a sea of defensiveness. All European countries were aggressively-minded – especially the Germans, ever since Clausewitz had written:

> The defensive is just the deliberate postponement of the decisive act – the offensive act – and if this act is not forthcoming, a real sacrilege is being committed.

Since French soldiers practically worshipped Clausewitz, such words would hardly have made them more restrained. Yet in Germany, by contrast, Clausewitz's assertion was immediately tempered at the tactical level by a much greater awareness of realities. In 1909, for example, just a few years before the war, an article by von Schlieffen was published in the *Deutsche*

Revue. It was republished in France under the title 'German views, modern warfare' and contained this passage:

> It would now be unimaginable to deploy in two lines, as in the eighteenth century, with one line facing the other, and deliver volleys at the enemy at relatively close ranges. Just a few minutes of rapid fire would be enough to wipe out both armies.[45]

(This was not all that different in spirit from what was said in the French regulations of 1913.) In short, the Germans favoured the strategic offensive, but they were prudent in tactical terms. On campaign, they always strove – until the fronts became static – to make flank attacks, which cost far fewer lives.

The British, who had been taught a lesson by the South African war at the turn of the century, were also offensive-minded, as were the Russians, but both of them took the same point of view as the Germans. In fact, all the belligerents, including those in Asia, wanted to be offensive. Not a single exception to this existed, but the actual fighting methods could vary markedly between countries. The French approach was unarguably the most extreme – the one that demonstrated the greatest scorn for the enemy and the greatest ignorance of what a modern battle would be like.[46] It was in France, therefore, that losses were proportionately heaviest: 18.2 per cent of Frenchmen liable for military service were killed, compared with 11.3 per cent of Germans and just 8.8 per cent of Britons.

Joffre was undoubtedly an offensive-minded sapper, but with his head and not his heart. He never allowed his heart to rule his head except during those brief moments when a mighty, ferocious rage suddenly relieved the pressure that he, like any other human being, felt during times of tension. Ultimately, it was not at all in his nature to let himself be carried away by passionate enthusiasm, and he never changed in this respect.

Yet it is intriguing to read Joffre's memoirs, for they give the impression that he was taking a detached view of what he had authorized and approved, as if it was nothing to do with him. His memoirs, written in about 1930, clearly contradict the wording of the 1913 regulations. For example, he stated:

> [The officers] regarded the offensive as a sort of dogma and readily believed in it because of both tradition and temperament, but they had still not grasped all its requirements. In particular, too many of them tended to fail to take enough account of the conditions of modern warfare, in which it was no longer possible to attack in the same way as in the age of muzzle-loading muskets and cannon.[47]

The officers did indeed regard the offensive as a sort of dogma. But it was untrue that they could not be made to 'grasp all its requirements'. Suitable forms of action needed to be imposed on them and this was precisely what the regulations could have done, given enough time and much perseverance. Yet Joffre did not go down that route. Instead, he let his excellent intentions become smothered in words that caused the engine of the French army to race ahead instead of slowing down. Expressing regret for 'the over-doing of the offensive doctrine' was a positive step.[48] Deciding to 'lay down the reasonable foundations of an offensive doctrine' was even better.[49] But this intention should have been incorporated into the regulations and I can find nothing in them requiring that the men in charge of fighting a battle – the generals and colonels commanding the large and medium-sized units – should be 'reasonable'.

Not the slightest dampener existed, therefore, particularly in the text of the *Regulation on the handling of large units*. On the contrary, everything points to a deliberate effort being made to hide anything that might have weakened the offensive, out of a concern to avoid misunderstandings. This is what resulted in the discussion about the offensive being overstated. Fear of not going far enough caused the regulations to go too far. They fell on fertile ground and inevitably inflamed hot-heads who were already worked-up. It was partic-ularly dangerous to give the backing of a regulation to a mentality that was too widespread as it was. Ultimately, time was too short for what Joffre did to make a difference. Yet this fact alone does not completely excuse him for the excesses he encouraged – for he did encourage them, at least by failing to correct them, regardless of whether or not that failure was intentional. Nor did he fully grasp the potential consequences of those excesses.

The regulations were undoubtedly submitted for Joffre's approval before they were issued. Why, then, did he not try to tone them down? After all, at the end of August 1914 he issued numerous orders to correct conduct that was almost identical to what had been seen in the pre-war manœuvres. The answer may well be that it was an early sign of Joffre's lack of personal experience of infantry combat, as noted in Chapter 1. At the start of the war, the engineer in him – the intensely practical and realistic side to his character – made him try to correct what the general in him had thought he could justifiably tolerate. Joffre was offensive-minded out of reasoned conviction, whereas many others believed in the offensive simply by gut-instinct and never changed. They paid a high price for it – and even worse, they made their men pay for it.

Joffre certainly regarded the offensive as necessary for victory – yet unfor-tunately most of his colleagues saw it as not simply necessary but also sufficient on its own. Joffre failed to make the general in him give way to the engineer. Perhaps he did not want to. Or perhaps he lacked the ability to do so, or simply did not know how to go about it. Whatever the true reason, it was a real pity.

Chapter 3

Plans

The problem of Belgium

The treaty signed in London between Belgium and the Netherlands on 19 April 1839 stipulated in Article 7: 'Belgium ... shall form an independent and perpetually neutral State. It shall be bound to observe this same neutrality towards all other States.' The treaty was guaranteed on that same day by Austria, France, Great Britain, Prussia and Russia. On 11 May 1867, the same co-contracting parties, with the addition of Italy, signed a treaty that stated in Article 2: 'The Grand Duchy of Luxembourg ... shall henceforth form a perpetually neutral State.' Belgium and Luxembourg were therefore neutral, but it is often forgotten that their neutrality worked both ways. Neither of them was permitted to favour particular countries, and certainly not openly.

Both sides respected this neutrality during the 1870 war. But France found itself isolated in that war, lacking both allies and support. This was partly because Napoleon III's ambassador, Benedetti, had left a highly embarrassing document with Bismarck during an informal conversation at Berlin a few years earlier. When Bismarck deliberately had the document published in 1870, the Belgians learned that France had wanted to annex their country and had sought German diplomatic support in order to do so. The result was an outcry in Europe, among the neutral powers, and above all at London, which remained fiercely attached to Belgian neutrality.

The Belgians remembered this incident, and it increased the wariness of their relations with France. A strong pro-German party emerged in Belgium in the first years of the twentieth century, and the Kingdom tried to observe a strict neutrality, refusing any staff conversations however general in scope. The Belgians fortified Namur, Liège and Antwerp to ensure their country's neutrality was respected. Lieutenant-General Brialmont, a fortifications engineer whose fame equalled that of Séré de Rivières, surrounded these cities with entrenched camps, in much the same way as the French did at Verdun or Toul.

Belgium was a superb theatre for fighting a war, since the terrain between the Meuse and the North Sea had an excellent road net, many railways and practically no obstacles. It was an ideal invasion route between France and Germany and had been used as such for centuries, in both directions. The great plains of Northern France led directly to Paris along the Oise valley. This was one of the gaps that offered an easy passage between France and

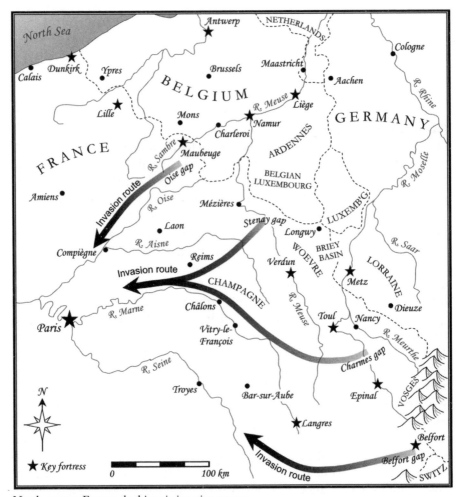

North-eastern France: the historic invasion routes.

Germany – others were the Stenay gap in the Ardennes and the Charmes gap south of Nancy, but these were far narrower.

France seemed for a long time to regard Belgian neutrality as sufficient protection against any German impulse to invade. Yet many people were unconvinced. Ténot, for example, wrote:

> Belgian neutrality is based on diplomatic agreements, whose sanction depends on the convenience and interests of the powers that have guaranteed it and on their ability to take action. Events might occur that would turn this neutrality into a disappointing figment of the imagination.[1]

During the period before 1870, the Franco-Belgian frontier had resurfaced from time to time as a cause for concern owing to the whims of international politics. But after that date, it became a permament source of anxiety and continued to preoccupy French soldiers and politicians not only until the Great War but long afterwards, up until 1940. This is clear from the archives preserved at the *Service historique de la défense* (the Historical Branch of the French armed forces).[2]

The frontier between France and Germany, as amended by the 1870 war, was 250km long from Switzerland to Longwy. France shared another 300km of frontier with Belgium and Luxembourg. That meant it had to watch almost 600km of frontier – a vast distance at a time when a division was reckoned to be able to hold only about 4km of front. A distance of 600km would require 150 divisions, or 2,250,000 men. Even if sufficient manpower had been available to put these numbers in the line, there would have been no depth to the defence and none of the troops would have been left in reserve. In any case, the manpower simply wasn't available. It was impossible for France to guard its frontiers with what was known as a 'cordon' of troops, stretching from Basle to Dunkirk.

If France adopted a defensive attitude and intended merely to react to attacks, it had to work out its priorities. In view of its limited manpower, it had to leave gaps somewhere along the line, but the problem lay in knowing where these gaps would pose the least possible risk. Such decisions could be based on information obtained by the intelligence services, but it was not always reliable or easy to obtain. Another option was to transform the terrain by engineering, and in doing so perhaps create some dead-ends into which an enemy advance could be expected to flow. Alternatively, a combination of these approaches could be adopted. Forming alliances might relieve the pressure on the French army by using another threat to divert some of the German troops. The French had to put together a plan that took account of these various options and constraints. If, for example, they took Belgian neutrality for granted, they would free up in theory almost ninety of their divisions.

Ideally, the French needed advance knowledge of the German army's composition, and more importantly of its axes of attack (lines of operations as they were called at the time). That was a matter for the intelligence services. Even if the French intelligence services appear to have been less active than their German counterparts owing to the reorganization that was necessary in the wake of the Dreyfus Affair, they existed nonetheless. The information they provided always had to be treated warily, and the risk of manipulation was high. Throughout history, governments have found it difficult to trust the information supplied by their intelligence services.

What about transforming the terrain by engineering? After the German annexation of Alsace-Lorraine, Séré de Rivières set out to give France another frontier – a military frontier a bit to the west of the formal, customs frontier. He created a couple of what he called defensive curtains, by which he meant lines of forts. One of these curtains was built between Verdun and Toul, and the other between Toul and Epinal. Each of these three towns was organized as an entrenched camp that acted as a 'pier-head'. The defensive curtains formed barriers between the pier-heads, but gaps (those of Charmes and Stenay) were deliberately left open so as to direct the enemy's advance into funnels that would leave him exposed to counter-attacks. Behind the defensive curtains, Séré de Rivières created second-line defences, which extended as far back as Paris since the thinking of the time held that the capital had to be the operational objective of the German armies. Shortage of funds meant that the northern invasion route was 'blocked' by just three entrenched camps at Dunkirk, Lille and Maubeuge, all three of which were intended to compartmentalize the terrain. Unfortunately, these entrenched camps were separated by some 70km of open space. Furthermore, on 2 May 1907 the Supreme War Council declared its intention to decommission the fortress of Lille: 'The only remaining fortifications now lack any justification for their continued existence ... This fortress is bypassed on all sides by numerous railways, ... the perimeter wall of Lille has been submerged by the suburbs and is impossible to defend.'[3]

Yet the problem could potentially be solved in an easier way, if the French army opted for an offensive posture. It would thereby secure the operational initiative and ensure that the enemy's own posture was largely shaped by the attacks made on him. This, indeed, was one of the advantages of the 'offensive' – advantages that Grandmaison dwelt on at such length.

War aims

How was a war between France and Germany expected to unfold? Before actual operations could begin, the armies of both sides had to go through some intermediate stages. Three phases had to be carried out regardless of the circumstances. Phase I entailed putting in place a covering force composed exclusively of active troops – in other words men belonging to those conscript classes that were already serving with the colours at the time of mobilization. The role of the covering force was to ensure that the next two phases could be carried out undisturbed, if necessary by thwarting a surprise enemy attack. Phase II was the mobilization of men recalled to military service. They came from all over France to rejoin their regiments, for the regiments had the double role of being both mobilization centres and combat units. Phase III was the concentration. It involved the various units being grouped into brigades, divisions and army corps, and taking up the concentration areas that had been assigned to them.

In French military terminology, these three phases jointly constituted a 'plan'. All the French plans had taken this form, ever since conscription had provided the necessary numbers of men. I must emphasize that these were not operational plans, even if there were particular reasons for the way the concentration was to be carried out. Instead, they were deployment plans. The most recent of them – Plan XVII – was structured in the same way as its predecessors. No trace of any operational plan for the period 1871–1914 can be found in the French military archives.

It is unclear exactly what role the political authorities played in determining the plans of concentration (or any possible operational plans). The Third Republic had never had to face a major foreign policy crisis within Europe of the same magnitude as the one that was about to break. It had constitutional documents to serve as a guide, but had no practical experience of using them for such an eventuality. The Constitutional Laws of 1875 stipulated that the President of the Republic 'had the army at his disposal' and that he made appointments 'to all civil and military posts'. The *Regulation on the handling of large units* specified in Article 1 of its first chapter: 'The government alone has authority to set the political objectives, ... it distributes the forces ... and places them at the full disposal of the generals'.

This was all very well in theory, but in practical terms what were the war aims and what control did the government have over the armies in the field? The *Regulation on the handling of large units* also stated: 'The conduct of military operations is the domain in which these generals exercise their authority with complete independence and on their own responsibility, in pursuit of the political aim of the war.' In other words, if I'm reading it correctly, the generals in command had complete freedom of action once the political aim of the war had been set. But even if we work on the assumption that this was the case after the declaration of war, the situation before that point remains unclear. Was a soldier free to plan the forthcoming war as he thought best? At the time that Plan XVII was developed, there had been no formal statement of political war aims – no document existed setting them out. Regaining Alsace-Lorraine was in everyone's mind, but otherwise the only obligations the French government accepted were of a diplomatic nature. It had to respect its treaty obligations, which meant it might have to wage war on behalf of the Tsar of All the Russias or for His Gracious Britannic Majesty.

These questions seem of fundamental importance today, and yet the political authorities of the time had no answers to them. They had never considered these questions, or rather they had not provided themselves with the tools that would have made it possible to consider them properly. In April 1906, they created the Supreme National Defence Council, which brought together the Ministers of War, Foreign Affairs, the Navy, Finance and the Colonies. The Council was modified in 1911 following Joffre's appointment and the changes in the army's general organization. It was a step in the right direction and the Council did have the potential to develop what was termed a war plan. But ultimately it was just an assembly of ministers and lacked a permanent secretariat. Even on the rare occasions when it actually met, it merely exchanged information and analytical reports, without synthesizing them into government directives.

The first session of the council was held in 1911. It was presided over by Caillaux (the President of the Council of Ministers), along with Fallières (the President of the Republic). Caillaux stated by way of introduction:

> In peacetime, the [Supreme National Defence] Council should under-take methodical reviews in order to ascertain the various possibilities of conflict. ... In wartime, ... it will be the council's task to facilitate the government's decisions in matters pertaining to the general conduct of the war.[4]

But Messimy immediately muddied the waters by adding: 'The council's remit will be to study any question that the commanders of the armed forces are unable to settle'.[5] This was far more restrictive, as it was so vague. Caillaux's approach sounds strikingly modern to us, and if his eminently sensible proposal had been implemented the military would never have been able to exert such a grip on power as it did at the start of the war. But to all intents and purposes, it was Messimy's point of view that prevailed, and it did so without a discussion – or at least without any discussion being recorded in the minutes of the meeting. The incident makes clear the danger in having a soldier as Minister of War (or in Messimy's case, someone who was a sort of soldier).

The result was that the soldiers had a free rein, for obviously they were able to 'settle' almost every question themselves. Joffre, who was present at this meeting by virtue of his new duties, clearly saw nothing wrong. It must have strengthened his view that he had the authority to decide how to wage the war once it was declared. He never wavered in believing that he was free to conduct the war as he saw fit, and this was basically what led to his dismissal in 1916.

Thus, the government never really came to a decision about the political objectives of a possible war. This was despite the fact that in October 1911 the General Staff's Operations Department had produced a six-page note that carefully spelled out why this war plan needed to be drawn up and what intelligence was required to enable it to be done.[6] (It is questionable whether it should really have been up to the General Staff to spell this out.)

Despite its limitations, the Supreme National Defence Council did discuss some matters during its meetings, notably Belgian neutrality. Joffre recorded a session on 9 January 1912 at which he set out the general conditions under which Plan XVII was to be developed, and he readily obtained approval of them.[7] But when the council intervened like this, it did so on a case-by-case basis as a result of matters that came under discussion.

The political authorities failed to fulfil their responsibilities. They should have stated their intentions and imposed them on the military. Not only did they fail to do so, they apparently did not even consider doing so. To give just one example, they let military conventions be signed with the Russians that explicitly committed each of the two allies to take the offensive should the other come under German attack. These military conventions are an early sign that successive French governments were well aware of the General Staff's desire for the strategic offensive. The political authorities should not have allowed these conventions to be signed unless the terms were what they genuinely wanted – and it is also worth noting that the conventions had not been debated in parliament.

Only when the crisis came in 1914 did the political authorities belatedly stir into life. Messimy dwelt at length in his memoirs on how difficult he found it, just before Joffre departed to join GQG, to obtain some clarifications about 'the whole of his strategic plan'. Joffre came with Berthelot, bringing no more than a lousy map on a scale of 1:320,000. He explained his plan for a general offensive, which involved cutting off the German right wing on the middle reaches of the Meuse, and Messimy shared the information with his ministerial colleagues the following day. Messimy added in his memoirs: 'We had left the general conduct of the war entirely in the hands of the professionals, and perhaps we should not have done so to quite such an extent.' He clearly forgot that he had said something quite different back in 1911.

Plan XVII

Now that I have described the constraints that Joffre faced from the moment he took up his appointment, I shall examine how Plan XVII was developed. It was a major undertaking. The archives held at the *Service historique de la défense* at Vincennes under the heading 'Plan XVII' fill as many as fourteen boxes. Even that is only a partial indication of the sheer volume of relevant material, for many more documents have a bearing on different subjects and can therefore be found scattered throughout other sets of papers.

Joffre's initial task was to update the existing plan, known as Plan XVI, and he produced two successive variations of it. For the purposes of this discussion, I'll leave aside the earliest plans and confine myself to Plans XV and XVI and their variations, which means going back as far as 1908. During that period, the centre of gravity of the French concentration was shifted very noticeably towards the Belgian frontier. The northernmost units now lay between Longwy and the northern side of Mézières, in other words roughly along the first section of the Franco-Belgian frontier. But the obvious implication of extending the dispositions northwards in this way was that it reduced their depth, since the overall numbers of troops remained almost the same. Nor were any forces allocated to watch the Belgian frontier between the North Sea and the Ardennes, and so a vast corridor, 300km wide, appears to have been left open to invasion.

This exposed corridor stretching all the way to Dunkirk could be found in every one of the earlier plans. (The only exception was General Michel's plan of 1911, which had never come to fruition.) For various reasons, the staffs had always discounted the likelihood of the Germans mounting an invasion through the centre of Belgium. Obviously, it was thought that the German armies might clip the corner of Belgian territory – basically the area known as Belgian Luxembourg – so they could use its communication routes.[8] But few analysts thought it possible that the Germans would extend north of the line formed by the Sambre and Meuse rivers.

A host of reasons seemed to support this conclusion, including the existence of the fortifications of Namur and Liège on the Sambre-Meuse line, the presence of the Belgian army defending its country, and the risk that a full-scale German invasion of Belgium would cause Britain to intervene in the war. Nor did the Germans appear to have enough troops to defend the Franco-German frontier while simultaneously attacking in Belgium. All these observations, and the inferences that were drawn from them, pointed in the same direction. The French General Staff was therefore strengthened in its belief that the two sides would fight it out along the Franco-German frontier of 1871 between Belgium and Switzerland. The fighting might well extend a long way to the south or north, but it was not expected to reach as far as the North Sea.

In 1904, the German plan for the invasion of France was apparently sold to the French intelligence services by a mysterious 'avenger'. The axis of the advance seemed to pass along the valley of the Meuse and Sambre, in the direction of Liège, Namur and Maubeuge. But no precise information was given about the scope of the movement. A Captain Sorb wrote in August 1907: 'The Germans are certainly not going to expose themselves, at the start of a campaign, to considerable delays and premature losses by going up against the defences of the Meuse and then those of Antwerp.'[9]

Opinion was pretty evenly divided as to whether or not the Germans would attack through Belgium. Even people who did anticipate such an attack tended to be unsure just how widely the German armies would extend as they moved through the country. Inevitably, all this was forgotten after the war, except for the names of the few clear-sighted men who did foresee accurately what would happen.

Nevertheless, during the years leading up to the outbreak of the war, many documents did appear indicating that the Germans would attack through Belgium. The information coming from Belgium itself was fairly worrying, since it was possible the Belgians might simply let the Germans march in without any opposition. The Belgian population was divided and wary, and some intelligent men – especially in Flanders – sensed that war was coming and suggested that the country should be ready to join the victorious side when it did break out. Belgian Catholics tended to be pro-German and dis-approved of the fact that France had turned itself into a secular state. Indeed, *Monsieur* Combes (a former President of the Council of Ministers) was con-sidered in Belgium to be the devil incarnate because of his role in the passing of the secularization laws. German trade was thriving and made much use of the port of Antwerp for its exports, while German businesses extended their reach throughout the country.

The Germans wrote much on the question of Belgium. One author, General von Bernhardi, who was apparently an adviser to the *Großer Generalstab*, published a book in 1912, entitled *On war of the present day*.[10] It contained numerous allusions to what the Germans might do, including the following example:

> In the event of a war against France, we can imagine the Germans taking the offensive in such a way that on their northern wing an array of armies would advance across Holland and Belgium, marching along the coast on the far right, whilst those German forces that were in the south would evade the enemy's blow.

In 1900, a Belgian called Colonel Ducarne reckoned that no German attack would be made north of the Meuse. In contrast, another Belgian, General Dujardin, concluded in 1905 that the left (or north) bank of the Meuse was actually the only region suitable for major strategic operations. As for General Maitrot, he thought in 1911 that 'the possibility of an attack by the left bank of the Meuse – in other words a large-scale movement by way of Brussels – should be dismissed once and for all'. He added: 'We do not believe the English will intervene.'[11] The only common element in these magisterial statements is that none of them was able to state exactly how far north the German right wing would extend. The uncertainty meant that such intuitions were not particularly different from Joffre's own thinking at this stage.

* * *

In 1914, France had Britain and Russia as allies. The alliance with Russia was well developed, for a military convention had been signed in 1892. It was strengthened in 1899 and 1906, and the French and Russian Chiefs of the General Staff met regularly. Joffre went to Russia in 1913 to attend the Russian manœuvres and to hold discussions with both the Chief of the General Staff, Gilinsky, and the Commander-in-Chief of the Russian army, Grand Duke Nicholas. The Russians undertook, in the event of a war with Germany, to begin operations a fortnight after the start of mobilization.[12] That seemed early enough to pin down about one-fifth of the German strength and to reduce the German pressure on the Western Front by the same amount.

Top-secret conversations had been held with Britain. Much work had even gone into the question of the strength and nature of the British intervention on the Continent. At the 9 January 1912 meeting of the Supreme National Defence Council, Joffre reckoned he could count on six divisions of infantry and two of cavalry being available on the Continent about a fortnight after mobilization. Agreement was reached on the positioning of the British troops:

suitably near the coast and on the left of the French dispositions. Detailed studies were carried out by the staffs and could be put into immediate effect when the time came. But nothing had actually been signed and the British undertaking remained dependent on a vote in the Houses of Parliament, which was by no means a foregone conclusion. The neutrality of Belgium was fundamental to what Britain would decide to do. If France was the first to violate that neutrality, or if it merely gave the impression that it intended to do so, it would be irrevocably abandoned by the British to its fate.

Joffre obtained an important political clarification about the French government's position regarding Belgian neutrality. On 21 February 1912, a meeting was held at the Ministry of Foreign Affairs.[13] Those present included Poincaré, who at the time was the President of the Council of Ministers; Millerand the Minister of War; Delcassé the Minister of the Navy; Paléologue the Director of the Political and Commercial Affairs Division within the Ministry of Foreign Affairs; Joffre the army's Chief of the General Staff; and Aubert his naval counterpart. Joffre made a long statement, during which he said:

> In the event of a war with Germany, the plan that is most likely to produce decisive results involves launching a vigorous offensive right from the outset of operations, in order to knock out the enemy's organized forces at a single stroke.

Joffre added: 'It would be most advantageous if our armies were able under any circumstances to enter Belgian territory south of the line between Namur and Liège.' He even suggested taking the precaution of securing the British government's backing. Note that he spoke about entering just the territory south of the Sambre and Meuse – this was the same region through which he believed the German army would direct its attack.

Poincaré pointed out, politely but firmly, that they had to be sure a 'plan of this nature would not cause England to withdraw her support from us'. In short, the French army was not going to take the offensive through Belgium unless the enemy had already done so himself. Indeed, the French would go one step further, and carefully ensure that the concentration areas of their army did not even give the impression that they intended an offensive in Belgium. The situation at the start of 1912 therefore seems clear: Joffre wanted to take the offensive and to launch it through Belgium. But since the French government wanted to avoid getting into a no-win situation that would endanger the likelihood of the British joining the war on its side, it could not let any of its forces pose even a distant threat to Belgium.

Paradoxically, Britain was conducting military conversations with Belgium at this same time, but these remained bilateral talks. In 1919, Field Marshal French wrote about the pre-war period: 'Belgium, however, remained a "dark horse" up to the last, and it is most unfortunate that she could never be persuaded to decide upon her attitude in the event of a general war.' French was convinced – or so he claimed in his book *1914* – that the German attack would come in the far north of Belgium: 'Personally, I had always thought that Germany would violate Belgian neutrality, and in no such half measure as by a march through the Ardennes, which was what our joint plans mainly contemplated.'[14]

* * *

Joffre intended the offensive, but that in itself was neither an aim nor an objective. We must be clear in our minds about the definition of the word 'objective'. In Staff College parlance, it means 'the end of the trajectory'. In other words, it boiled down to the question: why attack? There were two possible answers: either to destroy the German army, or to take Berlin – or indeed both. Joffre never gave a clear-cut answer, except perhaps privately. He probably intended, at the start of the war, simply to fight an *offensive battle*, leaving the rest to be decided by the outcome.

This raises the related problem of the operational plan, which was to be put into effect once the concentration was complete. Joffre always denied that he had ever had a *written* operational plan. When he was giving evidence to the Briey Commission after the war, he claimed that no plan had existed.[15] Later, in his memoirs, he repeated what he had told the commission, explaining that: 'The operational plan can be made only by taking into account events and the information that arrives during the course of operations.'[16] He added: 'In my view, therefore, the concentration had to be regarded as an initial disposition of our forces that would make it possible to implement any operational plan.' Joffre, when questioned on the same subject by the Briey Commission, replied: 'It was a plan held in our heads, but not committed to paper.' Not only did the members of the commission – and many subsequent historians – refuse to believe him, it has even been implied that the written evidence was deliberately destroyed.[17] That, however, is most unlikely to have happened, not least because it would have been impossible to ensure that every scrap of evidence disappeared, not to mention any witnesses. Something always survives such attempts to wipe clean the record. Further support for the idea that no written operational plan existed can be found in the many arguments that raged at the Staff College, at the Centre for Advanced Military Studies and in the military press of the time about the need to draw up a campaign plan that would be carried out after the plan of concentration.

These disputes revolved around the concept of the 'preconceived idea', which was all the rage at the start of the twentieth century. Langlois, for example, declared: 'No preconceived idea – instead, probe everywhere, and make an all-out thrust against the point where the fighting has revealed the enemy is weak, avoiding the point where he is strong. In order to do this, keep very strong reserves in hand.'[18] Similarly, Foch wrote in his Staff College course: 'It is impossible to decide with any certainty on an operational plan that extends beyond the first battle.' The simple truth is that Joffre himself had no preconceived ideas either. He had no geographical objective and adopted a campaign plan only after the first battles. As he himself wrote: 'In short, I was limited to an opportunistic approach, intending to exploit events ... once the outcome of the first days of the war had become clear.'[19] There is every reason to believe him.

Of course, this does not mean that Joffre lacked a general idea at the back of his mind. Indeed, the idea was a prevailing one. As always, Foch put it best when he said: 'We must go to Berlin, by way of Mainz.' Napoleon had gone to Berlin in 1806, von Moltke the Elder had come to Paris in 1870, so why should the French not return to Berlin? It made sense to go via Mainz, for the Moselle valley offered the easiest way of reaching the Rhine from the French frontier, even if alternative routes to Berlin did exist, for example by crossing the Rhine near Strasbourg.

Nor does the absence of any disclosed operational plan mean that Joffre had neglected to plan the direction of his attack. Indeed, that was the purpose of the *Directives for the concentration* of Plan XVII, which we shall examine in Chapter 5. We can be reasonably sure, therefore, that by the time the war broke out the top brass all knew the outline of what they had to do, even if an operational plan is most unlikely to have been committed to paper. (The members of parliament were another matter, particularly the 'backbenchers' – the Deputies knew practically nothing.) Evidence to support this view can be found in a letter that Galliéni wrote to Joffre in 8 July 1913. At the time, Galliéni commanded the 5th Army, which was the army nearest the Belgian frontier. 'After the French armies have been concentrated', Galliéni wrote, 'they clearly need to arrange for their offensive operations [etc.] ...'. This indicates the members of the Supreme War Council knew that the French army would take the offensive after it had been concentrated – or, to be more precise, that it would seek to fight an offensive battle.

The French army was to fight this battle with all its available strength – or as Joffre wrote: 'No preconceived idea except a determination to take the offensive with all the assembled forces.'[20] The phrase 'all the assembled forces' meant there would be practically no reserves (in the sense of troops kept back in reserve). This was another topic for debate before the war. Were reserves needed and, if so, for what purpose?[21] General Cardot gave his opinion in his usual, colourful language: 'Why keep a general reserve – or any other reserve – when you intend a decisive attack, when you have decided on a great onslaught? That makes no sense – it's rank stupidity, ineptitude.' For good measure, Napoleon was quoted: 'Even one battalion could be enough to win you the victory, if you release it from reserve.' This was the same justification that Joffre gave for intending to commit the whole of his forces. (However, the reality of a situation tends to be more complex than surface appearances. In the event, Joffre kept some divisions in reserve, even if only a very few.)

* * *

The German army's strength caused much concern, especially as it was growing ever stronger. The French kept a close eye on the way the *Reichstag* passed various laws that continually increased the German army's numbers. The garrison towns of the units were known. The organization of the forces was fairly well known, as was the number of their component units. The strengths of the companies, battalions, regiments, divisions and army corps were roughly the same as in the French army. The organization into Active army, Reserve, *Ersatz*, *Landwehr* and *Landsturm* was also known.[22] Joffre did some calculations and apparently concluded that the two sides in the western theatre were evenly balanced overall, with about thirty army corps on each side. But important structural differences existed, for more than ten of the German corps were reserve corps. The French had no reserve corps, but only reserve divisions. They could claim to be evenly balanced with the Germans only if two divisions were taken to be equivalent to a corps, but in terms of command and control this was not strictly true.

Moreover, Joffre had little or no information about the Germans' concentration, and even less about their operational plan. The French General Staff tried to shed some light on a future conflict by drawing up an intelligence-gathering plan covering its various stages, starting with the period of mounting tension before the start of hostilities, followed by the deployment of the covering force, the concentration of the armies and then the engagement. Despite subsequent criticisms, this was actually an excellent intelligence plan, and it shows how much attention was paid to the problem of Belgian neutrality and its possible violation. It is all the more astonishing, therefore, to find that the plan failed to produce any results, as we shall see in due course.

The General Staff took a gamble on which it seemed to have little chance of being wrong, but the result was a whole series of miscalculations. The staff officers reckoned that the Germans would not commit their reserve units to action in the first line, for it was an article of faith in the French army not to use their own reserve units in such a way. Indeed, General Michel had been dismissed by Messimy in 1911 after advocating a sort of amalgamation of reserve and active units. The French high command – along with some politicians spanning the spectrum from the Right all the way to the Left-of-Centre, if not further – thought that the reserve units would be unsuited to fighting in the first line until they had become war-hardened by first-hand experience of conflict. These units were composed of men who had left active service a long (or fairly long) time before and since then had received few or no periods of refresher training.

Naturally enough, the French command assumed that the Germans shared its own stance on the use of reserve units. In fact, the Germans themselves confirmed this assumption – or at least they had confirmed it in the past. For example, an article by von Schlieffen published in 1909 included the statement: 'The *Landwehr* and the *Landsturm* (the Territorial army and the Territorial army reserve) can be counted as part of the nation's military strength only to a very limited extent and in special circumstances.'[23] But the situation changed, as we shall see when we examine the Three-Year Law, and by 1914 the Germans no longer heeded Schlieffen's clear-cut opinion. This was the second surprise of the war – the first having been the wide outflanking movement by the German right wing – and it very nearly caused the French army to be defeated in the opening four weeks.

Joffre knew little more about his potential allies than he knew about the Germans. In particular, none of the information he had about the Belgians indicated that he could rely on them taking part in the war. Indeed, General Wilson, who made the preparations for the arrival of the British troops on the Continent, feared that the Belgians might actually contemplate joining the Germans in the event of a war between France and Germany. On the other hand, it became more and more likely that the British army would be committed, and the Russians had lost none of their resolve – as Joffre was able to see for himself during his trip to Russia in 1913. Since Italy would definitely remain neutral, Joffre would be able to withdraw forces from the southeastern frontier of France, although these units would be summoned to take part in the fighting only after the start of hostilities.

No unity of command existed. This was a particular problem in the north, where the greatest difficulties were likely to occur. There was no means of coordinating the action of the British, French and Belgian armies, even though this was exactly what the British and French wanted to prepare before the war. Since such mistrust prevailed, everything had to be improvised after the start of hostilities, using liaison officers who did not always know much about the situation. One of these officers was Colonel Huguet, the former military attaché at London, who had helped to negotiate the British army's intervention on the Continent. Huguet played an important role, but his knowledge was patchy. His British counterpart with the French 5th Army was Edward Spears (he was knighted in later life). Spears found it just as difficult to deal with Lanrezac, the commander of the 5th Army, who was no anglophile. Athough a degree of information was exchanged between the allies, coordination was sometimes non-existent.

Joffre always kept in mind the problem of Belgium. The Centre for Advanced Military Studies held a map exercise between 13 and 29 February 1912, based on two French armies opposing 'enemy masses moving westwards through the northern region of Belgian Luxembourg, which were reported to have reached a front between Namur, Dinant and Rochefort'.[24]

Another exercise on the same theme was supposedly held in the spring of 1914 under Galliéni's direction, but I have been unable to find any documentary evidence to confirm this.

General Micheler's personal reminiscences formed the basis of a book published after his death.[25] He dwelt at length on his memories of the Centre for Advanced Military Studies in 1912, and recalled that 'the invasion of Belgium was regarded as certain'. He mentioned another exercise directed by Galliéni, which aimed at transporting an army held in reserve near Paris to the region of Maubeuge. Micheler also recalled that when he was Chief-of-Staff of the 6th Corps immediately before the war, there was a TEWT (Tactical Exercise Without Troops) directed by Joffre in the area around Saint-Quentin and Guise, based on a German offensive on the left (or north) bank of the Meuse.

Belgium clearly remained a major concern for Joffre. But perceiving the threat seems to have been less of a problem than deciding how best to parry it. The Operations Department of the General Staff wrote in October 1911 in preparation for a meeting of the Supreme National Defence Council: 'Germany will not hesitate to extend the zone of operations over a more or less considerable area of Belgian territory.' Everybody at one time or another, including the General Staff, foresaw the possibility of an outflanking movement by the left bank of the Meuse, though without being able to say for sure how wide it might be. Nor was any more reliance placed on Dutch neutrality being respected than that of Belgium. The neutrality of Luxembourg was considered worthless, given Germany's obvious economic dominance of that country, including its railways.

We should note one other point. Even if Joffre did not have an operational plan set down on paper, it does not necessarily follow that the General Staff failed to work on one. For example, a document has been found in the French military archives, entitled *Note concerning the operational plan of the North-Eastern Armies*.[26] It was written in the autumn of 1912 by Colonel Demange, probably as part of the development of Plan XVII. It is just one of many such documents, and it is important as it shows that although decisions were not rushed, they were considerably swayed by the determination to take the offensive.

*   *   *

Joffre was now on the point of establishing his plan of concentration in the form familiar to us today. As Castelnau explained, the concentration posed three problems:

> It must not be forgotten that the nearer the frontier we move our base of concentration:
> a) we reduce the distance separating us from the enemy.

b) we cause the first great clashes to occur earlier.

c) the concentration contains within it, in more developed form, the first clues to the dispositions that will be adopted for the initial battle.[27]

On 18 April 1913, the basis of the plan was presented at the Supreme War Council, which was presided over by the Minister of War, *Monsieur* Etienne.[28] The following question was put to the council members: 'Does the council think that a new plan [Plan XVII] should be prepared, based on the information given in the introductory report?' This report was remarkable in both form and content. Sixty-eight pages long, it set out the entire issue. The council's response was a unanimous 'yes', apparently without any of its members having asked questions about the document's contents, for no questions are recorded in the minutes. When criticism arose years later, Joffre was able to emphasize that no dissent had been voiced at the time – not even about the appropriateness of the concentration in the event of a German offensive through Belgium.

In the end, the following disposition was adopted. It took into account the three problems explained by Castelnau. Four armies (the 1st, 2nd, 3rd and 5th) were distributed from the Swiss frontier to Hirson on the Belgian border, and the British army could potentially extend the disposition up to the Sambre. That left the 4th Army, which remained further back, ready to support either the 3rd or the 5th Army as required. Within the sectors occupied by the armies, each army corps was arranged in depth in two lines, with a couple of days' marches separating the lines. (A day's march represented a distance of around 20–30km.)[29] The army corps were pushed as near as possible to the frontier, so they would have less distance to cover when they launched their attack and also so they could prevent the enemy from occupying French territory.

Months of preparatory work followed. Every unit received a mobilization diary that specified in minute detail not only what it had to do, but also where, how and with whom. The use of the railways would ensure units were in place in good time, and these so-called 'marches' by train required the compilation of entire files of detailed documents. The loading and unloading of trains had to follow a strict schedule and needed special platforms. Joffre emphasized the fact that the railway network available to him in 1914 gave him much more flexibility than before, and made it possible to make some last-minute changes. Only since 1912 had this greater flexibility existed, and in the event it allowed him to slip the 4th Army in between the 3rd and the 5th after he learned of the German attack on Liège.

Plan XVII was a good plan, even though it has come under all sorts of criticism. It was drawn up with remarkable precision, and here we can see Joffre the engineer once more, completely mastering all the technical data connected to the problem. He disposed his armies so they had a whole range

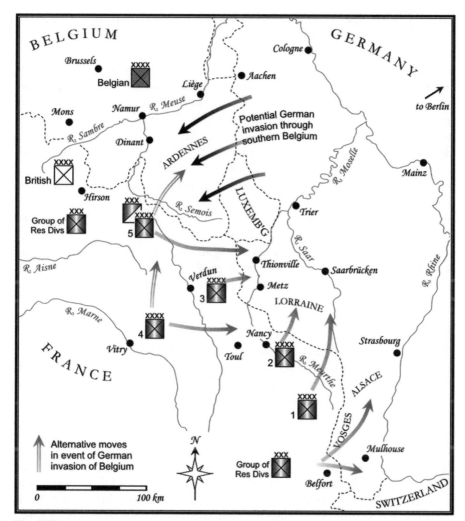

Plan XVII.

of possible options available to them and could respond to any hypothetical engagement. They could take the offensive, perhaps towards Belgian Luxembourg, or perhaps on either side of Metz and Thionville in the direction of the Rhine. Alternatively, they could adopt the defensive in order to repel an invasion of France. The French dispositions could be completed by Army W (the British army) being put in place on the left wing.[30] In theory, it would then be possible to oppose a German invasion through Belgium, provided the Germans did not move too far to the north – in other words not too far north of an axis running roughly through Liège, Namur and Maubeuge. No French plan of concentration had ever arranged its units so far north.

Could Joffre have chosen different dispositions for his armies? Given the focus on an offensive battle, the answer is a clear-cut 'no' – unless, that is, he had been authorized to enter Belgium as soon as war broke out, without waiting for the German army to violate Belgian neutrality. If Joffre had been permitted to do this, he would have held the initiative and could have set the pace of the campaign. But as it was, he had little choice except to do as he did, since he had insufficient strength for covering the entire 600km of France's frontier with Belgium and Germany. He might, of course, have concentrated his forces further back from the frontier, but that would have left French territory wide open to invasion and entailed abandoning any idea of taking the offensive. His plan was a middle-of-the road option, a good compromise that enabled him to respond to many possible eventualities. It may not have been inspired, yet in the eyes of his critics no plan would have been deemed inspired unless it won the war bloodlessly in just three weeks. Two key uncertainties remained. First, would Belgium defend itself and, if so, how? Second, would the British army be at the rendezvous, at what date and in what strength? Nobody knew the answers to these questions until the war actually began.

Fortifications

Plan XVII, and the offensive action that followed on from it, ended in failure. As a result, Joffre was criticized for not having remained on the defensive, in the way that the previous plans had ordained to a greater or lesser extent. Many Frenchmen at this time still placed their trust in Séré de Rivières' fortifications, and they were quick to make their views known both during and after the war. Even today, devotees of fortifications continue to praise Séré de Rivières' immense work. His system was unprecedented, and transformed France – and even Algeria – into a besieged fortress.[31] So the question they ask is why Joffre did not favour a defensive concept based on these permanent fortifications. Two generations of politicians and historians have debated this question, and it ultimately boils down to a much simpler issue. Was Joffre justified in taking the offensive, with the aim of fighting an offensive battle – followed, in the event of a victory, by more ambitious objectives? (This is the aim we can infer from the plan of concentration.) I suspect that those who put their faith in fortifications would answer with a flat 'no'.

Yet the same question of whether the offensive was justified has never been considered with respect to the German army. It is simply taken for granted that Germany as the aggressor had no option but to take the offensive, and that France as the victim had to defend itself. Many authors, such as General Négrier, consider that 'the army of a parliamentary republic is not, and can not be, an instrument of the offensive.' History has shown that Négrier's remark is generally valid as far as democracies are concerned, so long as it is amended to read 'an offensive instrument for starting a war.' Be that as it may, what war aim should a republic have? Should it allow an aggressor to pocket the gains of his aggression and get away scot-free? If, on the other hand, the republic regards such an outcome as unacceptable, what methods should it use to remove the threat? The problem with the defensive is that it can never change the situation that produced the war – it simply makes it more entrenched than before.

It was in 1918, while the war was still being fought, that the publication of a book by Fernand Engerand cast doubt on whether the offensive was justified. The book was called *The secret of the frontier*, and championed Séré de Rivières. The chapter entitled 'The 1871 frontier and the spirit of the offensive' should ideally be read in full, but I'll quote a brief extract: 'Defending the country is the army's role and the very reason for its existence, and everything else must take second place.' Another passage sums up Engerand's whole argument:

> I'll repeat the point, for I can not over-emphasize it. The Treaty of Frankfurt, in conjunction with that of 1815, allowed Germany to dominate France strategically and deprived us of the very area we needed for an offensive deployment. Since we were restricted to our 1871 frontiers, we could wage a war of movement on the desired scale only within France itself – and yet deliberately drawing the enemy on to your soil in order to manœuvre against him is taking a big risk. ... Never before, perhaps, has anything more incredible been seen than this blunder, this strategic amateurism. It was the logical result of being dogmatically attached to the offensive for its own sake.[32]

According to Engerand, France had been in a permanent state of military inferiority ever since 1815, and the only thing it could do was surround itself with fortifications and turn its territory into a vast, engineered zone. But the implication is that nothing was changing during this era, that everything was staying the same. What difference did regime changes make, or the formation of alliances, the shifts in public opinion, or the lightning advances that were being made in technology? The world was moving, everything was changing – except for France behaving like a 'dog that has received a beating', to quote General Langlois' memorable simile. I am surprised that Engerand was so submissive to the ups and downs of history, so doggedly resigned in the face of whatever the enemy or fate might do. It goes without saying that Engerand well and truly tore into Plan XVII and its author – and everything he wrote was later repeated and added to by others.

Between 1920 and 1930, an avalanche of criticism had the effect of confusing Plan XVII with the offensive, which in fact was simply its consequence. Many of the attacks were motivated purely by hostility to Joffre and by deep-rooted political hatreds. Not until the start of the Second World War did the controversy die down, for by then there were more important matters requiring attention. Joffre never answered back.

The most curious aspect of all this controversy is that no one stopped to remember that Joffre was a sapper who had built or improved a number of forts, a former professor of permanent fortification at Fontainebleau, and a former Director of Engineers whose duties had included constructing and maintaining France's permanent fortifications. Why, then, did he not opt for a defensive concept based on fortifications? One crucial problem was that very few of the existing forts, except in Eastern France, had been upgraded with reinforced concrete and with retractable armoured turrets made of cast-iron or steel. Some light is shed on this by the minutes of the Supreme War Council, especially those of its meeting on 2 May 1910, which was presided over by Fallières. Joffre had not been on the council for long, and had not yet been appointed Commander-in-Chief designate. On this particular day, the agenda included the decommissioning of certain fortifications in both the first line – we have already mentioned the example of Lille – and the second line.

Joffre intervened twice in the discussion. His first intervention was to recommend 'keeping in commission only those works that are in a state to put up a long and serious defence'. He added:

> The small, old fortresses such as Longwy or Montmédy – and especially works such as those of Reims, Laon or La Fère – should not be kept in commission. Instead, they should be placed at the disposal of the Commander-in-Chief, who will either occupy or abandon them as he sees fit, and who will be able to use them, if necessary, as points for supporting the field army.

Joffre also called for lightweight equipment to be made, so that existing fortifications could quickly be put into a state of defence when required. Then, in his second intervention in the debate, he stated:

> [I wonder] if such feeble fortifications should really be considered as fortresses, or if it should not instead be up to the Commander-in-Chief to decide to what extent they should be defended, and if necessary authorize the governor to abandon them.

This is on the same lines as what Joffre did five years later – notably at Verdun, where his policy was sensible and simply needed more time to take effect. It was an intelligent approach, for it enabled Joffre to use the fortresses simply when he needed them and only to the extent that it was worthwhile to do so. It explains why he was never likely to draw up a defensive plan based on permanent fortifications.

All that Joffre expected from the forts was that they should protect the putting in place of the covering force at the start of the war. But he was not so dogmatic as to turn his back on every available means, should he need them. He intended to use the outdated fortifications, but he would do so as part of a new concept that saw the existing permanent fortifications being integrated into the lines of defence. The term that began to be used was that of a 'defensive organization', and this concept led during the war to the creation of 'fortified regions'. Shortage of funds meant that the permanent fortifications failed to be upgraded as time passed. This made Joffre even more convinced that they were useless except as part of the defensive organizations that the field armies might find themselves obliged to create.

This does not mean that Joffre overlooked the value of temporary fortifications – in other words, the making of trenches, shelters and machine-gun positions protected by barbed-wire belts. In fact, quite the opposite was true. This becomes clear if we consider the example of the *Grand Couronné* – the heights outside the city of Nancy. These hills had been left unfortified by Séré de Rivières. At the Supreme War Council on 18 April 1913, Joffre asked not that the *Grand Couronné* should be fortified, but simply that surveys should be done in peacetime so that plans could be made for establishing temporary fortifications. He stated that 'the semi-permanent works will on the whole be sufficient to offer the desired resistance to the enemy'. It was around this same time that he recommended the use of mechanical diggers to create trenches more quickly, but it would be the 1970s before the French army was actually equipped with such machines.

Joffre set priorities within the framework of Plan XVII. Nancy, which I have just mentioned, was one priority. Others were the *Hauts-de-Meuse* and – as Galliéni had requested following a tour of inspection – Montmédy on the Belgian frontier. But it took a long time for anything to be translated into action, and come 1914 the defensive preparations available to Castelnau at Nancy were still unfinished and nothing had been done at Montmédy. There were many reasons for this, including the insurmountable reluctance of the French army – officers and men alike – to dig fighting positions. This was a reality that had to be kept quiet, since the French army could not be admitted to be less than perfect.

It is completely false, therefore, that Joffre was opposed to any defensive preparation of the ground whatsoever, despite the allegations made by devotees of fortification. But as an engineer, he instinctively sought what we today would call the best cost-effectiveness. The hard fact of the matter was that in 1914 permanent fortifications used up scarce resources and produced very dubious results.

*   *   *

We have accepted that seeking an offensive battle was justified, provided the overall circumstances were right. But was this condition satisfied? To answer the question, we need to jump forward in time and consider what happened during the opening weeks of the war. The French wanted to fight an offensive battle on the Franco-German border. In August 1914, they tried to do so in the direction of Belgian Luxembourg with their 4th and 5th Armies, only to be roundly beaten. The German offensive met the same fate. It involved an outflanking manœuvre through Belgium extending far to the north of the Meuse. Initially, it was more successful than the French offensive, but it then became bogged down between Verdun and Paris. By October 1914, the German front had solidified above the Aisne river, and the so-called 'Race to the Sea' was in full swing.

Did this mean that every offensive from 1914 onwards was doomed to fail? The fact is that until 1918 all offensives failed – that is to say, fell short of obtaining decisive results – no matter which of the various national armies fighting the war carried them out. It is easy enough to find explanations with the benefit of hindsight, and various reasons can be identified. But the most relevant point in my view was the difference between the tempo of attack and that of defence. In 1914, an attack was made at the speed at which an infantryman could walk: a maximum of 20–30km a day, and much less when the enemy was known to be present and it was necessary to deploy and place artillery in firing positions. But defence was based on the speed of the railway: when reinforcements were required, it took little more than a day to shift the leading elements of an army corps from Verdun to Paris. At the same time as the attack was wearing itself out, the defence grew more robust – and the stronger the defence became, the faster the attack petered out.

Except if one side had a marked superiority of numbers, no lasting breach could be made in the other side's dispositions unless there were exceptional circumstances such as surprise. But if surprise was to work, it had to have an immediate impact. The Germans tried to achieve surprise in August 1914 by marching through the centre of Belgium, but they failed because in doing so they over-extended their lines of operations – in other words, there was too great a distance from their base of operations to their objective. Despite the forced marches, their manœuvre took too long. This gave Joffre enough time to change his dispositions, and enabled him to create Maunoury's army after 25 August by moving units from Alsace to Picardy. The German 1st and 2nd Armies had effectively attempted (without realizing it) what Grand-maison advocated, but they had set off from too far away to be successful. A case can be made for arguing that the Germans failed precisely because of their wide outflanking move through Belgium.[33] I will not go as far as adopting the philosophy mocked in Voltaire's satirical novel, *Candide*, that 'all is for the best in the best of all possible worlds'. Nevertheless, there are some grounds for thinking that what the Germans gained on the one hand with this manœuvre they lost on the other.

None of these considerations was fully grasped in 1914. But Joffre – 'the stationmaster', as Driant referred to him – was aware that a revolution was underway in the use of transport not simply for concentrating forces but also for their operational manœuvres. This was transforming the situation. Furthermore, the Centre for Advanced Military Studies was beginning to realize how railways could make the redeployment of forces more flexible. As we have seen, railways had already made it possible in Plan XVII to shorten the time needed for the concentration and to carry out last-minute variations such as the insertion of the 4th Army between the 3rd and the 5th.

The failure of Joffre's offensive actions could not have been foreseen, and their outcome is no reason for denying that they were initially justified. There was no reason for Joffre to reject the principle of an offensive battle. Neither the balance of forces, nor the terms of France's alliances, nor the problem posed by Belgium stood in the way. Nor did the shortage of heavy artillery, for this was unlikely to be a major problem during what was expected to be a short-lived war of movement.

The one major uncertainty was the professional skill of the troops and their officers and NCOs. More than forty years had passed since the defeats of 1870. The keenness of the men was beyond any doubt, and the updated military studies taught at the Staff College and the Centre for Advanced Military Studies seem to have provided Joffre with high-quality staffs. The unknown factor was the tactical competence and leadership skills of the commanders of small and medium units up to divisional level inclusive. It was probably this that the *Field service regulation* was intended to perfect. If only enough time had been available for the regulation to have an impact before the start of the war, and if only training camps had been developed where it could have been practised. The operational quality of units ought to have benefitted greatly as a result.

Joffre had good reasons to opt for an offensive battle, which he could have developed, in the event of success, into a strategic action. Never since 1871 had the international situation been so favourable to France. The country had managed, through its system of alliances, to erase the potential impact of the superiority Germany enjoyed in almost every sphere – demographic, industrial and, more generally, economic. The Continent of Europe was perpetually troubled by disputes that seemed irresolvable, and peace proved ever-elusive. But if France sought an offensive battle – and if it won that battle and transformed it into a strategic action – it could potentially regain its lost provinces and establish a new balance of power between itself and Germany, for that was the ultimate aim.

The French political authorities had not explicitly desired this offensive battle. But since they were too timid to provide any leadership, they simply stuck their heads in the sand and let things be. All the evidence suggests that they knew exactly what the soldiers intended, and simply washed their hands of it. They must have known what was going to be done, even if they were unaware of the details of how it would be done. To be fair, we must recognize that it was impossible to achieve a political consensus. What decisions could the politicians have taken in the atmosphere of that time? During the early part of the 1900s, following the Dreyfus Affair, an unbridgeable abyss existed between the ideas of the Socialists on the one hand and those of the parties on the Right and the Right-of-Centre on the other. In these circumstances, it is difficult to see how any national defence policy might have been agreed that was capable of establishing geostrategic concepts and maintaining them in the long-term. Yet such concepts should have remained above political squabbles, and unaffected by them.

From the time of Joffre's appointment, and even slightly earlier, it was the soldiers who took charge of France's defence. They decided on a policy and implemented it in a determined and consistent way – even though that policy should have been defined and led by parliament. This reversal of roles resulted in an eclipse of parliament that lasted until 1916. When parliament finally ditched Joffre in 1916, it was rejecting not simply the Joffre of the war years, but also the Joffre of 1911–14.

In German eyes, France had broken the sort of balance that existed in Europe by voting for the Three-Year Law and by forming alliances that were basically directed against Germany. This was no mere illusion on the part of the Germans. When they learned after the war that Joffre had intended to violate Belgian territory, just as they themselves had done, they did not fail to accuse France of duplicity. In France itself, the forces on the Left, particularly the Socialists, alleged that a series of governments had followed an aggressive policy against Germany, and claimed that these governments bore a share of the responsibility for the war. Poincaré was readily accused of militarism, and many Socialists always referred to him as 'Poincaré-the-warmonger'.

It remains for us to see which offensive or offensives were possible and to examine what they were meant to achieve. We shall do so in Chapter 5, which covers the Battle of the Frontiers.

Chapter 4

Preparing for War

The reserves

Before addressing the Three-Year Law, we need to discuss the reserves and be clear in our minds about how to define that term, since it can mean several different things.

Let's start by explaining the word 'reservists'. Every year, a conscript army received a large proportion of the men from a specific class, or age category, that had become liable for military service. At the same time, it released recruits from the previous class or classes who had reached the end of their period of service. Reservists were trained men who had left the Active army, but who remained subject to military obligations for a period whose duration I shall explain in due course. At any given moment, therefore, the French army included both the Active army – the barracks army, to use Jaurès' deliberately insulting term – and the Reserve army.

Yet the word 'reserve' can also refer to a body of active troops temporarily placed in reserve while the action developed – or one that was intended to reinforce another unit already in action. (To make matters more complicated, the unit that was already in action might itself be a reserve unit, in the sense of being composed of reservists.) When I talk about the use of the reserves, I will usually be referring to the use of reservists following mobilization.

The Active army was organized into armies, army corps, divisions and brigades. But the reservists were effectively just individuals who had returned to their civilian jobs after 'fulfilling their military obligations', and no peace-time organizational framework existed for receiving them, except the so-called active 'cores'. When war was declared – or at the time of mobilization shortly beforehand – the reservists might be used in two ways. The first was to add reservists to active units in order to bring them up to their full war strength.[1] The second was to create units composed almost entirely of reservists. These reserve units did, however, contain active 'cores' composed of active officers and NCOs who could give some experience to units that might greatly need it, depending on how long ago their men had completed military service.

In France, the Active army was traditionally regarded as far more effective than the Reserve army. There was simply no way that the latter – even those of its units composed of the youngest men – could equal the cohesion and training of the Active army. In theory, there were meant to be periods of training to keep the reservists up to scratch, but in practice the men were rarely assembled because of the expense involved – the number of occasions can at best be described as inadequate. Those units that were composed entirely of reservists (apart from their active cores) required mobilization centres to put them on a war footing. At these centres, weapons and equipment could all be found in one place. Units were created by forming an extra, reserve, regiment for an active regiment, and then grouping these reserve regiments together to form higher formations.

At the time, the bulk of the infantry equipment consisted of the men's uniforms, backpacks, ammunition belts and personal weapons, although some machine-guns were starting to appear. Matters were somewhat more complicated for the cavalry (the horses were supplied partly by requisitioning) and also for the artillery, which likewise needed horses, at least for the field artillery.

Providing enough officers and NCOs for both units and staffs was more difficult. Generals commanding brigades or larger units needed more personnel on their staff in direct proportion to the size of the unit. The problem was that the French army was short of officers and NCOs, and increasing their number was one of Joffre's preoccupations. The shortage caused several problems, and one of the most important was that it ruled out the creation of reserve corps as was done in the German army. None of the French plans of concentration, except at the end of the nineteenth century, included the use of reserve corps. The most that Joffre could do was follow the example set by his predecessors and create groups of reserve divisions, as we shall see in due course.

At the time that Joffre took up his post, the French army was run under the recruitment system of the Two-Year Law. The law had been passed on 21 March 1905 and changed the Freycinet Law on the army's recruitment, which dated from 15 July 1889. The 1905 law reduced the period of active service to two years, but compensated for this by ruling out the many partial or complete exemptions that were contained in the 1889 law. The justification given for ending these exemptions was that it was on the grounds of equality.

In 1889, there existed not just the Active army and the Reserve, but also a Territorial army and a Territorial army reserve. This made a total of four categories, and every Frenchman served for a variable number of years in each successive category. The total duration of military obligations in 1889 was twenty-five years: three in the Active army, ten in its Reserve, six in the Territorial army and six in the Territorial army reserve.

After 1905, the total duration of military obligations remained twenty-five years, but the length of active service was reduced by one year, and this was balanced by increasing the length of service in the Reserve from ten years to eleven. A big effort was planned to improve the quality of the reservists, especially by obliging them to take part in two manœuvres, each lasting four weeks. The General Staff did some calculations and reckoned that the abolition of exemptions would ensure the total manpower remained on much the same level as under the Freycinet Law.[2] The planned changes to the training even offered hope of seeing an overall improvement in the French army's quality in the event of mobilization.

But the 1905 law soon fell short of its ambitions. The two periods of manœuvres were reduced from twenty-eight days each to twenty-three and seventeen days respectively. The Territorials would do nine days instead of thirteen, and – as Colonel de Gaulle subsequently pointed out – there were many obstacles to actually assembling the men.[3] Agricultural work, elections and personal convenience resulted in the periods being postponed or cancelled. In 1907, as many as 36 per cent of the men who were summoned failed to turn up.

Despite these problems, the fact remained that military obligations lasted for twenty-five years. This meant that twenty-five classes (annual age-groups) were available at any one time, making a theoretical total of around 5,000,000 men. Although the figure is just a vague estimate, it does give an idea of the scale. This was clearly a considerable mass of potential soldiers, but manpower alone is not enough to make an army. The men have to be equipped and armed, and need officers to command them. Furthermore, their vigour depended on their age, and in 1910 life expectancy at birth was just fifty years.

It was over the problem of the reserves that the major differences emerged between Right and Left. The Right tended to focus on quality, whereas the Left thought more in terms of quantity. The ideas of 1789 lived on in the national consciousness, along with the notion of the nation-in-arms involving the mobilization of the entire population. In 1870 there had been much talk of making a 'torrential sortie', in the hope that numbers and enthusiasm would be enough to break the German blockade of Paris.

Only a few Socialists were sitting in parliament in 1905. But within a few years they became more numerous and constituted a new political force that could not be ignored. Naturally enough, they turned their attention to the army, and in 1910 Jaurès made a name for himself with his book *The new army*.[4] As Jaurès pointed out, the problem of national defence had an alternative solution. France in a way had created the conscript army in 1798. The soldiers who fought the Revolutionary and Napoleonic wars were raised by a form of conscription that was significantly different from what it later became but had some similar aspects. Following 1815, France maintained a sort of semi-conscript, semi-professional army.[5] Then, after being defeated in 1870, it imitated the Germans and gradually reverted to a conscript army. The 1905 law instituted a system of conscription that for the first time was truly egalitarian. This was the start of the model of compulsory military service that continued in France up until as recently as 1996.

In contrast, some other countries, which were just as keen on the idea of the nation-in-arms, preferred to entrust their national defence to militia. Switzerland was one example. The concept was that of the citizen-soldier defending his land against aggression. Its antecedents could be seen in the soldier-settlers of Ancient Rome who had guarded the Empire's frontiers against Barbarian incursions, holding a sword in one hand and a plough in the other.

In France, the Left-wing politicians took up this notion of the citizen-soldier. They recognized the necessity of national defence, but were loathe to entrust it to generals whom they were bound to distrust. The generals were assumed to have reactionary, and often clerical, sympathies. They were seen as potential leaders of *coups d'états*, and recent history had shown that a military coup was a distinct possibility. To the Left, it seemed that the institution of a French version of militia was the best way of resolving an apparently unsolvable problem. In fact, they wanted to abolish the Active army altogether and create a National army composed exclusively of reservists. This was where the word reservist changed its meaning, resulting in frequent misunderstandings. The traditional concept was that the reservist supplemented the active soldier, but the Left saw the reservist as being the one and only defender of the nation.

Jaurès' hefty book (it was more than 550 pages long) strove to build this 'new army'. It was a difficult task, for with Germany's economy and population both growing strongly, the German army was becoming larger every year. A little thought should have shown the impossibility of France building the new army at this time, since the international situation made peace so unstable. Some of the more clear-sighted Socialists reckoned that it would take fifteen years to set up the new system. It was a perfect illustration of how politicians do not always live in the real world. This was not exactly the best time to replace a tried-and-tested organization with one that had yet to prove itself. In Jaurès's defence, it must be stressed that the hostility between France and Germany had existed for forty years and that a favourable time had never existed. Furthermore, the political mood was dominated by the confrontation between politics and religion to such an extent that people joked about the French government's military concerns being limited to 'invading the Vatican and besieging the faithful'. National defence – and its main instrument, the French army – were second only to education as an ideal battleground for this never-ending internal strife. How on earth could the men of this time have examined matters calmly and dispassionately?

What did Jaurès advocate? He proposed an army composed of thirteen reserve classes, summoned every two years for periods of what the author called 'brisk manœuvres'. Young men would receive a special military education between the ages of 10 and 20 years, in order to prepare them for military training. This education would be followed by a six-month training course in recruit schools (rather than within military units). The citizen-soldiers would keep their uniform and equipment, and if they lived in the frontier zones they would also keep their weapons.

But Jaurès's book had little to say about the practical organization of such an army. Anything the least bit technical, such as engineers, railways or the telegraph, was left unaddressed. Jaurès dwelt on the wholly defensive character of this army and made no effort to hide his ideological prejudices, as can be seen in this insulting extract:

> The generals chosen in advance to command armies [when war breaks out] are set apart from those armies, and are just lavish furnishings for the salons of Paris – furnishings that fade in the artificial light. They lead the life of lazy oligarchs, and nothing prepares them for the big clash, the crushing responsibility for which is soon going to fall on them out of the blue. Their artificial and empty attitude spreads downwards to all the officers.[6]

In contrast, Jaurès set out what he hoped would be the result of his plan:

> ... throughout the entire army will circulate the same spirit – the sap of a generous and noble land. The citizen masses and their officers will be in complete harmony, and it really will be the nation-in-arms that protects its own independence ...

At the end of his book, Jaurès included a proposed law, consisting of eighteen articles that summarized the new organization he hoped would be adopted.

Some years later, as we shall see, Jaurès took up these ideas again in a legislative counter-proposal and tried to have it passed during the parliamentary debates, in place of the government's bill.

The Three-Year Law

When Joffre asked for the Two-Year Law to be changed, he did not do so out of delight or a sudden, militaristic whim. Legrand-Girarde, who prepared the new law with him, wrote: 'The truth is that Joffre was hostile to the plan, or at least accepted it only because he had no other option.'[7] Various other pieces of evidence suggest that this was probably true. It is interesting to follow the discussions of the Supreme War Council of 4 March 1913.[8] At 2.10pm that day, all the council members met at the Elysée palace, along with Briand (the President of the Council of Ministers) and Etienne (the Minister of War). Each member had received a long briefing note setting out the plan, supported by some statistical data extracted from the General Staff's archives. The President of the Republic, Poincaré, presided over the discussions – this was most unusual – and he stated from the outset that 'the council has been convened to discuss matters of exceptional importance'. Matters were then addressed in order. Five questions were asked. The first, which Poincaré termed the 'preliminary ruling', was: 'In view of the German measures, do we need to try and increase our military strength, and our covering force in particular?' (The role of the covering force was to guard the frontiers and cover the army's mobilization and concentration.)

What was the rationale for increasing the army's strength? Joffre set out the reasons why he was asking for more men. The steps that Germany had taken in 1911–12, or had announced for 1913, would raise its Active army to a strength of 850,000 men. Since Germany had such a vast pool of potential conscripts available, it did not need to make any changes to its recruitment law. It deliberately refrained from conscripting all its available manpower, in order to limit the expense. It therefore had available a surplus of men and could adjust its strength to suit its financial resources. Under these circumstances, the German army no longer needed to mobilize, and could 'overrun our covering force and throw the detraining of our troops into disorder'. If the French wanted to ensure their mobilization proceeded smoothly, they would have to make their covering force strong enough to protect the frontier. Joffre reckoned that eleven divisions (five-and-a-half corps) were needed, at full wartime strength, which meant at least 200 men for each infantry company.

As for the other active units, in the interior of the country, it was vital that they had at least 150 men to a company. This would ensure that when the supplementary men (reservists) were added on mobilization there would be an average of three active soldiers for every two reservists. Joffre emphasized that the increase in numbers would not change the *overall* numbers of troops after mobilization. (In fact, this was not completely true. A system of three years of active service would leave a surplus of about 50,000 men. This surplus would be used to increase the number of artillery batteries, and to make it possible to meet other needs that might arise, such as the engineers.)

Poincaré and Briand foresaw arduous parliamentary debates on this issue. They – particularly Briand – asked what steps the Germans had taken to increase their military strength. Joffre thereupon handed over to Pau, who was probably more capable of explaining the matter, for Joffre was never comfortable when it came to speaking off the cuff. Pau started with the Treaty of Tilsit and with the events of 1815, and set out a long, detailed and well-informed account of what would now be called Prussian militarism and its various manifestations in German military laws. He concluded: 'An army constituted on this basis is a first-rate offensive instrument and is ready for use at any moment.' This was no exaggeration.

The cavalry posed another, specific problem. The Two-Year Law appeared to have demonstrated the impossibility of training cavalrymen in under three years so they were capable of the duties of that era, including taming young horses. This was a genuine constraint and not simply an excuse. It influenced the discussions, especially as the Germans had decided on three years of military service for the cavalry and certain other arms, whereas it was two years for the rest of their army. France could not accept falling progressively behind Germany. In the end, the council voted by a show of hands. Its answer was a unanimous 'yes': it was indeed necessary to try and increase France's military strength.

But how was this to be done? There were various possible solutions. The first of them was Jaurès' plan, which was described concisely and fairly impartially in the briefing note. It was rejected, primarily because it was purely defensive and so was not fit for purpose: 'It professes faith in the effectiveness of the Hague Convention, and asserts a stubborn desire for the Nation to confine itself to a passive defence no matter what might happen, since the enemy's territory is considered sacrosanct.' The minutes of the meeting contain no record of any of the council members contributing to the discussion. In fact, Jaurès' proposal may not even have been discussed at all – it was probably just put aside by tacit agreement.

The second solution was the so-called system of 'consecutive reservists'. This was a plan that had previously been put forward by a Deputy, *Monsieur* Clémentel. It consisted of calling up each of the reserve classes for one month every year, which would increase the number of soldiers under arms while also improving the quality of the reservists. But this solution, too, was rejected, for various reasons connected with the complexity of having to provide the usual training for the new conscripts while also dealing with the reservists.

The third solution was Pédoya's plan. General Pédoya was the Deputy for the Ariège and subsequently became the President of the Army Commission in the Chamber of Deputies. He had a plan to which he was deeply attached. He proposed a twenty-seven month term of military service. This meant that at least two conscript classes would be under arms at any one time, if 1 July was set as the induction date and 30 September as the release date. The plan was rejected owing to the difficulty of adapting it to the constraints of training. The idea of a twenty-month term of service was also rapidly dismissed.

The discussion then turned to the fourth solution, which proposed a three-year period of service. This found favour with all the members of the council, as well as with the politicians, and the plan was adopted unanimously.

The possibility was also raised of setting different lengths of service for different arms according to their various requirements, as was done in the German army. Joffre rejected this solution for the sake of equality. The use of North African and 'black' troops was discussed, but in terms of numbers they were just 'spare change' and an inadequate solution to the problem at hand.[9] Interestingly, many of the council members contributed nothing to the debate, or at least nothing that was reckoned worth minuting. Whereas Joffre, Pau and Michel had much to say, Castelnau, Chomer, Marion and Galliéni remained silent.

The subject of voluntary enlistments sparked much discussion. They had been included as one of the provisions in the 1905 law, and were really a way of finding men who might subsequently improve units' cadres (their central core of officers and NCOs). But General Legrand, in his role as *rapporteur*, provided the figures for enlistments from 1901 to 1912. The number of enlistment agreements had dropped from 19,000 to 13,000, representing a fall of 30 per cent. Those who enlisted had a poor reputation. Inspection reports were quoted, which were scathing: 'Two-thirds have enlisted only for the bonus, and once inducted they commit serious offences and end up spending their time in prison.' Pau added: 'Men suitable for enlistment are not exactly plentiful.'

Various other solutions were discussed, such as restricting the use of soldiers for labour. In an article, Patrice Mahon wrote:

> The captain in command [of a company] is required to provide men for fatigue duties or to act as waggon-drivers, clerks, labourers, secretaries, orderlies and cooks. The lieutenant finds that his men miss their training, their classes and their theoretical instruction. They disappear from his platoon so completely that for most of them the two years of military service are reduced to no more than six months of training.[10]

Conscripted armies have frequently experienced this problem, even if it later became far less tolerated.

Briand, who was always thinking warily about the forthcoming parliamentary debates, remembered that the Senate and Chamber of Deputies had passed the Two-Year Law in the belief that it was going to provide sufficient numbers of troops. The government would now have to explain why this no longer held true in 1913. The Supreme War Council also considered whether exemption from conscription should be granted to men who came from large families. It rejected the idea of increasing to thirteen years the period of service in the Reserve of the Active army.

The soldiers and the politicians who were in power were therefore agreed: parliament had to be confronted. This was a most daunting prospect and the outcome was far from a foregone conclusion. Since Briand fell from power, it was his successor, Barthou, who had to defend the proposed law. The issue pitted two groupings against each other: the so-called Moderate Republicans against the Radicals allied with the Socialists. Joffre and Pau attended the debates in the Chamber of Deputies and the Senate as the government's representatives. Their presence angered some members of parliament and encouraged them to be more extreme than usual in the hope of sparking off an incident. Joffre kept his cool, but Pau struggled to remain calm. The debates began on 2 June 1913 and lasted for seven weeks.

Jaurès in particular returned to the attack. On 17 and 18 June, he gave a speech in which he called for 'the national army and the popular army', while exalting the reserves and accusing the government and General Staff of imitating German militarism.[11] What he thought of the proposed law can be summed up by a statement he made in the Chamber of Deputies: '[It is] an abominable law, disastrous for France, an attack on democracy and an attack on the peoples of the world.' He was even more virulent at this time in the newspaper *L'Humanité*, with his demand 'to repudiate, wreck and condemn this law of reaction and humiliation, this law of ruin and defeat, this law that has jeopardized both the nation's defence and the Republic's efficacy, paving the way to every external disaster and internal trouble.' People weren't exactly into understatement in that era. The general tone of Jaurès' speech was the same as that of his book *The New Army*. Some of his comments turned out to be premonitory – they were about the Germans launching an invasion through Belgium, and about France's alliance with Russia being fragile. But they were hardly any more far-sighted than many remarks made by other people at that time, for they were based on the same sources, namely what had been written by German authors, especially General von Bernhardi whom we have already mentioned.

Several of Jaurès' observations about the long term were more interesting. He showed that Germany's population and birth-rate would enable it to mobilize ever greater numbers of trained soldiers whenever it wanted. Its birth-rate was roughly twice that of France, and the demographic imbalance between the two countries effectively made the problem impossible to resolve. Perhaps the only point of interest in Jaurès' speech, therefore, was to show that the Three-Year Law could be no more than a stopgap measure, and that it would be necessary to come up with something else. No administrative machinery, however clever or sophisticated, can obtain replacement soldiers if they simply do not exist.

Many speakers gave their views, and it would be tedious to follow all these fairly stormy debates. Numerous members of parliament came up with ideas, suggested amendments or made counter-proposals. In the heat of the discussion, some extreme statements were made. Chautemps, a young Socialist Deputy, brazenly described Joffre as a 'recalcitrant general', and exclaimed that 'the Three-Year Law will make the army passive, half-witted and ready to do anything at the bidding of commanders who hate the Republic.' Another opponent of the law, Brizon, claimed it was 'a surprise attack by reactionaries ... a reactionary General Staff and top brass who want a compliant army.' In the country at large, a wave of protest condemned the infamous law. Led by Anatole France, 360 academics and authors signed a petition to 'preserve the nation's honour, stop the military panic'.

What everyone forgot was that the army's purpose was war-fighting. Instead, it simply became a political football. Nobody stopped to consider the simple question of what was in France's best interests – and in those of the Republic. Joffre made three interventions in the debates.[12] The first was to decline to confirm that he had said words that were attributed to him. The second was to stand in for Pau on the spur of the moment and to read what he would have said. The third and final intervention was to correct some inflated statistics about the German army.

The law was conclusively passed in the Chamber on 18 July 1913 by 358 votes to 204, and in the Senate a few days later by 244 votes to 36. The Senate, being much more conservative, was easier to win over. The terms of the law were more or less in line with what Joffre wanted, except for a few changes such as reducing the length of service for conscripts who came from large families.

One possible way of implementing the the new law was to summon the conscript classes of 1912 and 1913 to do their military service, while lowering the age of the summons from 21 to 20, and at the same time keeping the 1910 and 1911 classes in active service for longer. But this suggestion had to be abandoned, and the 1910 class was released in October 1913. The upshot was that three classes were serving under the colours when war was declared – those of 1911, 1912 and 1913 – but the latter two were still only partly trained.

One major problem connected to the Three-Year Law was the need to build barracks. About 200,000 extra men now had to be accommodated, fed, cared for and trained. The budget for the engineer arm had to be increased, but the construction could not be carried out at the same speed as the law was implemented. Regiments therefore found it difficult to comply with their new obligations, and it did not help that some units moved to a new garrison. Local authorities also complicated matters, and the problem of building new barracks was still a major headache in 1914.

Despite all the discussion about the reserves during the debates, little had been said about how they were actually to be used. Obviously, it was known into which units the reservists would be absorbed – they would fill up the numbers in active units, and also form reserve divisions – but the way they were to be used was not addressed in detail. In contrast, the basic issue that divided the two political camps was crystal clear: the reserves were trusted by the Left, and distrusted by the Right.

General Pau had this to say about the problem of the reserves when he spoke in the Senate as the government's representative:

> The reserve divisions of Plan XVII are better organized, provided with better cadres and better led. We can reasonably expect them to become capable of carrying out certain missions alongside the active troops ... [missions] that until now would have been entrusted to them only reluctantly, especially at the start of the war.

This was eminently sensible. Yet what was really needed in such cases was a thorough analysis of the problem in order to try and provide the basis of agreement on how to solve it. Interesting though it is to note the absence of such an analysis, I can hardly say that it comes as a surprise owing to the political opposition.

*   *   *

The Three-Year Law was a victory for Joffre – but a precarious victory that could be nullified. The coalition of Radicals and Socialists hoped to reopen the issue as soon as possible, and the forthcoming elections of May 1914 seemed to offer a favourable opportunity. The campaigning focused on issues closely linked to the problems of national defence (and of income tax). The elections were won by the men on the Left, especially the Socialists. Those who opposed the Three-Year Law now had the upper hand, and two successive governments that refused to repeal it were brought down by the Chamber of Deputies. If the war had not broken out within a matter of weeks, the law would probably have been repealed sooner or later, given that it was so unpopular in France.

None of those who had opposed the bill expressed regret afterwards. A final piece of 'collateral damage' was that the debates 'vaccinated' Joffre for good against parliament's excesses. These few weeks in the middle of 1913 certainly help explain his reactions when parliament subsequently tried to interfere in what he regarded as his business.

In connection with the Three-Year Law, I should mention Joffre's patient and determined work to improve the lot of the officers and especially the NCOs. The Two-Year Law had depleted both the numbers and the quality of the NCOs, and a new infusion of energy and vigour was now needed, for these men had a vital role to play in the French army's preparation for war. Despite overt opposition in parliament, Joffre managed to improve their pay significantly, with the size of the increases being in inverse proportion to seniority of rank.

This increase in the quality and quantity of NCOs helped to ensure that reserve units had at least a basic level of supervision. The Infantry Cadres Law, passed on 23 December 1912, was intended to give reserve units larger cadres of active officers and NCOs.[13] Each active regiment was to have another three field officers and six extra captains, while each reserve company was given six NCOs instead of two. Joffre's concern that reserve regiments should have adequate cadres also caused him to reduce the number of battalions within each reserve regiment from three to two.[14]

When the Supreme War Council met on 18 April 1913, it abolished one brigade of each of the active corps, and added a two-battalion regiment of reservists to each active division. These changes were likewise designed to improve the cadres of the remaining units. During the meeting, the council members debated the matter fully and so we can see what expectations were placed on the reserves, and what value they were thought to have. Galliéni, for example, stated: 'Any step that limits the use of reserve troops is a good one.' Only Michel, who still stuck to his views of 1911, opposed the majority view of the council.

What was the state of the French army by the summer of 1914? To use a modern-day expression, it was 'fit for purpose' – at least in terms of numbers. The initial application of the Three-Year Law made it possible to achieve the intended goal. Infantry companies in the covering divisions now had a standardized strength of 200 men, while those in the divisions in the interior of the country had 140 men (instead of the planned 150). On 1 August 1914, France had 800,000 men serving under the colours.[15] This represented an increase of more than 200,000 men compared to what the number would have been if the Three-Year Law had not been passed. Another 2,800,000 men were added during mobilization between 2 and 15 August. The total came to 3,600,000 men, of which 2,800,000 were directly involved in the operations that followed.

We also need to compare French and German manpower. It is difficult to make reliable comparisons without either becoming bogged down in detail or making misleading assumptions about what can be deemed equivalent in the two armies. Unit strengths were more or less the same: for example, an infantry company in both France and Germany contained 250 men when at full war strength. Yet we would hardly be justified in simply totting up the number of divisions, taking no account of whether they were infantry, cavalry, reserve or Territorial divisions. We must also confine our comparisons to those theatres where the French and German forces confronted each other, namely the North-Eastern theatre.

Once France finished mobilizing, it had twenty-one army corps, all of them active, which were deployed between the Belgian and Swiss frontiers.[16] In addition, it had around ten reserve divisions, some independent divisions and about ten cavalry divisions, making in total the equivalent of another fifteen army corps. The German army opposed this force with thirty-six army corps, thirteen of which were reserve corps. (These statistics include only those units in the North-Eastern theatre.) Overall, the Germans had a slight numerical superiority, but this in itself did not mean much. What counted was to have the advantage of numbers at the right time and the right place.

We now need to examine which conscript classes supplied men to which units. In France, the reservists who were used to fill up the active regiments came from the four youngest classes, and were therefore no older than 27 years. In the reserve regiments, each company contained only twenty active soldiers, along with 230 reservists from the 1903–6 classes (maximum age 31 years). The other classes, composed of the oldest men, remained behind in the depots.

In the German army, the active companies contained reservists with a maximum age of 26 years, while the reserve units contained men (reservists and *Landwehr*) no older than 30. These figures need to be treated with caution. A single year's difference might not seem significant, but it meant that the French strength was either increased or deducted by as many as 200,000 men at a stroke, and the German strength by double that number.

It also has to be remembered that the Germans did not use their reserve corps in 1914 in the same way as the French. This sparked much controversy within France. I have already quoted what General Pau thought: essentially, he was saying that reserve units could not be used in the same way as active units without first going through a period of being hardened in war. I have also mentioned the Supreme War Council's discussions about this issue on 18 April 1913.

As far as I can tell, the Germans initially intended to use their reserve corps in the same way as French. But they then refined their thinking, and were thereafter prepared to use their reserve corps in the first line as if they were active corps, contrary to what the French General Staff expected. (The terms first and second lines should not be taken too literally. They were the terms used at the time, but in today's language the distinction was between high-intensity and low-intensity combat.)

The German change of mind on this issue had important consequences. By reducing the depth of their dispositions in this way, the Germans were able to make the theatre of operations wider. In the previous chapter, I emphasized the sheer scale of the theatre, and this was something that affected both sides. If the Germans launched a vigorous offensive immediately after hostilities broke out, they would be able to turn and envelop the wing of the opposing forces.

This enveloping manœuvre was the central element of the Schlieffen Plan, and it was the manœuvre that the *Großer Generalstab* used in 1914.[17] This greatly surprised Joffre, but some respected authors soon claimed that the way the Germans used their reserve corps had largely been forecast by the French intelligence services. Indeed, the intelligence services had actually concluded in a report in May 1914: 'To sum up, the reserve corps are intended to be used in active operations like the active corps, and under the new mobilization plan they have become a more homogenous instrument than before and have better cadres ... .'

Yet the German reserve corps contained less artillery than the active corps. Moreover, saying that the reserve corps were going to be used in active operations was not the same as saying they would be used in the first line. Simply occupying a piece of ground is an active operation, but it does not necessarily involve fighting in the first line. Joffre's memoirs contain no explanation as to why he ignored the intelligence about the Germans' intentions while he was developing Plan XVII. Perhaps he did so because of an ingrained prejudice about reserve corps, or perhaps he misinterpreted the evidence, or was simply convinced he was right.

The fact remains that, as Joffre himself stated, he still believed as late as 25 August 1914 'that the Germans were engaging only active corps in their offensive operations'.[18] I am unconvinced by the excuse that confusion was caused by reserve corps being numbered the same as the active corps formed in the same district. If anything about the German reserves was known at all, it really ought to have been that piece of information. It seems that the German active and reserve regiments were also numbered similarly, but since the Germans found the addition of the letter R sufficient to distinguish their reserve regiments, surely the French should have been capable of working it out.

*   *   *

What conclusion should we draw from this? First and foremost, even if the Three-Year Law was Joffre's only claim to fame, he would have deserved France's gratitude. Let's imagine how the start of the war would have unfolded if the law had never been passed. The French army would have been too small and too inferior in quality. Even if it had been deployed differently and had possessed a more realistic operational plan than the one that was actually put into effect, it was likely to have suffered crushing defeats. The miracle of the Marne would never have occurred.

The controversy about the reserves was primarily a symptom of the political confrontation between the Left and the Right, set against the background of disputes over religion. After the war, the controversy intensified and became embellished. Some generals were perfectly aware of the truth of the matter, but cynically accused Joffre of having disregarded the reserves – either by giving them secondary tasks or by leaving them in the depots. It was always the same generals making these criticisms. Regnault was one. Another was Percin, who did not exactly distinguish himself at Lille in 1914 and was caustically referred to in Right-wing newspapers as 'the cooking pot that is never seen in the fire'.

Joffre was able to point out that he had actually used more reserve divisions than his predecessors: twenty-five rather than twenty-two.[19] But this merely provoked the retort that since he had reduced each reserve regiment by one battalion, he used a smaller total of reserve battalions than his predecessors: 300 instead of 396. This tortuous argument by Joffre's critics amounted to mere hair-splitting. He had come to the decision that twenty-five slimmer divisions were better than twenty-two larger ones. That decision may have been right or wrong, but I personally believe it was right. Throughout the war, all the combatant nations tended to take Joffre's approach. Even though smaller divisions had less combat capability, they could be used more flexibly.[20] The problem was that many Frenchmen continued to regard the proper use of reserves as a dogma no less sacrosanct than the Holy Trinity. Ideologues regarded the argument as a reaffirmation of their profession of faith. The unruly generals who drew inspiration from these ideologues saw it as an opportunity to take revenge on Joffre, a man who had never belonged to their exclusive circle and whom they refused to accept as one of their own.

All of these critics forgot that manpower alone was not enough. An operational unit also needed weapons and equipment, along with motor transport since horses soon became inadequate. Anyone who claimed to believe otherwise was either an ideologue who was never going to listen to reason, or was one of those men living in the past – lost in nostalgia for the age of oil lamps and the splendour of sailing ships, to use one of General de Gaulle's memorable phrases. Parliament's parsimonious allocation of funds for the army probably had its most serious consequences when it came to the reserves. Frenchmen wanted reserves that were armed, trained and provided with proper cadres, but they were reluctant to pay for them and came up with all sorts of good reasons for avoiding the call-up.[21] When the French army was mobilized in 1914, it depended heavily on these reserves. Out of the total of 1,643 infantry battalions that existed once the army had completed its mobilization, as many as 957 were newly formed. The proportion of newly-formed artillery batteries was also high, at 672 out of 1,527. After 1915, the subtle distinctions between active troops, reservists and men of the Territorial army no longer had any real meaning.

Heavy artillery
I have reserved the rest of this chapter for considering the other problems that Joffre faced in preparing for war. But I have no intention of going into every single topic, for there are too many of them and some are of little interest. Instead, I shall concentrate on the only really important one, namely the shortage of heavy artillery.

I'll start by considering the Ministry of War's budget, for nothing could happen without it. The budget was voted by parliament, but the politicians who did the voting never admitted afterwards to feeling any guilt over the attitudes they had adopted. In the closed parliamentary sessions held during the war, and again after it was over, they all loudly claimed that they had granted everything the soldiers had requested. Of course, they were hardly going to say anything else, for they had no desire to be held at all responsible for controversial matters such as the heavy artillery.

There is no need to go into the details of how the budget was prepared before being put to the vote, for it was a fairly complex process. The key point – bizarre though it may seem – is that the draft budgets considered by the Deputies had been negotiated exclusively between the Minister of War, the directorates (I shall explain in due course what they were) and *ad hoc* parliamentary commissions. This meant that the General Staff's funding requests ended up being changed, and the Commander-in-Chief designate was unable to do much about it. After 1911, Joffre and the General Staff were more involved in the budget's preparation, but the Directorate of Financial Control, which was directly under the Minister's authority, continued to play a role that exceeded its remit.[22] For example, Alexandre has described what happened when he went and asked Financial Control for its opinion on a pay increase for NCOs who re-enlisted: 'The two financial comptrollers unanimously thought it was madness to pay the NCOs more than what they were likely to earn in civilian life, based on their age and skill-set.'[23] Not much has changed since then: similar remarks could be heard just a few years ago, using practically the same words.

It is true that spending increased regularly from 1912.[24] But in some areas it had fallen behind, and the adverse effects of this time-lag were not made good. Indeed, they were compounded by the greater expenses resulting from the Three-Year Law. The Ministry of War's budget in 1914 was around 1,000,000,000 *francs*. When combined with that of the Ministry of the Navy, it accounted for as much as 30 per cent of the overall budget. Intelligent men were rightly concerned about this tapping of the nation's wealth, especially as it had been ongoing for several years.

Let's return to the artillery. When war was declared in 1914, the French army had just five regiments of heavy artillery. They were concentrated at army level – one regiment for each of the five armies. As is always the case when resources are in short supply, the heavy artillery was concentrated at the highest practicable level. Resources are decentralized only if they are plentiful – such as the 75mm gun, which could be found at both divisional and army corps level.[25]

What was the reason for this shortage of heavy artillery? In order to ascertain whether Joffre was to blame, we need to go back and examine the situation when he was appointed in 1911. At this time, the German and French artillery differed significantly. A German army corps had a total of 160 guns and howitzers, and their calibres were 77, 105 and 155mm. In contrast, a French army corps had just 120 guns, and all of them had a calibre of 75mm. At this stage, the French heavy artillery was concentrated in seven elements at army level. (It was not until 1913 that the five heavy artillery regiments were created.) These seven elements contained a total of twenty-one *groupes*, or 'brigades', which meant that in the event of mobilization each army corps could be strengthened by a brigade of two heavy batteries. But since a battery consisted of only two artillery pieces, each army corps had just four pieces of heavy artillery, and that was simply absurd. All of these pieces were 155mm quick-firing Rimailho howitzers of the 1904 model. They could fire six rounds a minute and were equipped with the same recoil-absorption technology as the 75mm gun.

But there was another dimension to the situation, for France actually had two types of artillery at this time. Besides the field artillery and its 75mm guns, there existed the fortress or siege artillery, which was sometimes called foot artillery. The latter type was produced and put into service in fortresses following the construction of Séré de Rivières' defensive system. It could be used either to defend or to besiege a fortress, and was mainly equipped with so-called 'long-barrelled' guns designed by Colonel de Bange. They were long-barrelled 120 and 155mm guns, with a range of 8 or 9km. They were rarely moved, for they had to be installed on a platform, and although this platform could be dismantled it weighed as much as 6 tonnes. Ten hours were needed to prepare a battery position in accordance with the strict rules that governed its construction, and the same amount of time to dismantle it. These siege artillery pieces did have the advantage of a hydraulic brake linking the gun carriage to the platform, and this enabled them to fire around one shot a minute.

The siege artillery was unable to accompany an army in movement. That was the main argument deployed by opponents of heavy artillery. But they failed to see that the constraints on the mobility of these pieces were in the process of being mitigated by technological advances. Colonel de Bange produced some even heavier pieces as part of the same programme: 240mm guns, and 220 and 270mm mortars.[26] The fortresses still had some older guns, such as de Bange 80 and 90mm, and Lahitolle 95mm pieces. In 1914, these older guns were used to arm Territorial divisions intended for either sieges or field operations – and some of these guns were still in service as late as 1917.

In all, the fortress and siege artillery consisted of more than 3,000 guns with a calibre of at least 120mm.[27] The sheer number of these pieces explains the attitude of many generals and senior officers who thought that different types of gun should be kept separate, and that each branch of artillery should be assigned its own particular pieces for carrying out its specific mission. In other words, the argument ran, heavy guns were for fortresses, while light guns were for the field army. After all, there were plenty of cannon available.

One of the perverse effects of permanent fortifications was to make people think in terms of separate categories. They found it impossible to escape from this burdensome mindset, which delayed the birth of the French heavy artillery. If the war had not broken out, the concept of permanent fortifications would have continued to flourish for a long time. This can be clearly seen in the fact that the fortress or siege artillery was on the verge of being modernized on the very eve of the war.

Many artillerymen had serious doubts about the need for more cannon. Percin wrote: 'I adamantly oppose any increase in the artillery, whatever the circumstances. We have enough artillery. The Germans have too much. Let's leave them to get tangled up in their megalomania for cannon.'[28] General Langlois, another expert we have already met, wrote: 'Firepower can not dislodge good infantry from a strongpoint.' He added: 'Artillery is ineffective against defenders who are sheltered by walls or protected by trenches.' The high command was just as divided. It had an obsessive fear of burdening the army's columns on the march, and tended to shy away from the logistical problems of having to supply ammunition for a mix of different calibres.

I'll make the point right away that the shortage of heavy artillery had no major impact on the operations during the opening weeks of the war of movement. The 75mm gun, on the other hand, proved outstandingly successful and single-handedly retrieved some extremely critical situations, as is clear from reading the German reports. In fact, until 1915 the shortage of 75mm shells was more of a drawback than the shortage of heavy guns. General Baquet, the Director of Artillery, said as much and as a result was called a 'criminal' by Clemenceau, as was Baquet's colleague, General Sainte-Clair Deville, who had helped design the 75mm gun.[29] It was only when the troops were dug in that the need was felt for howitzers with a sufficiently large calibre – and not until 1917 was the deficiency really made good.

The 75mm had a rate of fire of up to fifteen rounds a minute in actual battle conditions. It was practically an automatic weapon and was marvellously effective against troops in the open at ranges up to 6,000 or 7,000 metres. But very long ranges were avoided, because it was not possible to observe where the shells were falling and to make the necessary adjustments for accuracy. The ideal range was reckoned to be 3,000 metres, since at that distance the gun could be aimed directly by using the sights, almost like aiming a rifle. Artillerymen were slow to accept that they could fire further than this, and in order to do so they had to work out a way of observing their fire.

The 75mm was a remarkable gun, but had two drawbacks. The first was that the explosive charge of its shell was too weak to shatter hard structures. The second was linked to the flatness of its trajectory. The high muzzle velocity of the projectile gave it a very flat trajectory and therefore prevented it from reaching a target that in military parlance was 'masked'. It was impossible to hit a valley floor, for example, or any target that was behind an ordinary hill, even though these tasks were well within the capabilities of the German guns from the very start of the war.[30]

The 120 and 155mm de Bange pieces had the same drawback of a flat trajectory, only they fired a much heavier shell. The 155mm fired a 40kg shell, while the 120mm used one that weighed about 20kg. What was needed, therefore, was an artillery piece that was mobile (at the start of the war, that meant being pulled by teams of horses). Its shell had to be an acceptable compromise between its weight and its effectiveness. Above all, it had to be possible to give the gun enough elevation to deliver plunging fire. A gun that could fulfil these conditions was called a howitzer.[31]

*   *   *

It was during the meeting of the Supreme War Council on 19 July 1911 that Joffre stated his views about the artillery issues that were the main points on the agenda. (Michel was still Commander-in-Chief designate at this stage, but held the post for only a few more days, as it was during this session that he found himself isolated over the question of the reserves.) The first issue was deciding whether it was appropriate to equip the artillery with a field howitzer. Some generals, including Michel, expressed doubt about the wisdom of this step. But the council approved it, and considered the context of the equipment and the way the howitzer batteries ought to be formed, though without reaching a firm conclusion. Joffre said that he wanted the calibre of the pieces to be a maximum of 120mm, and this was agreed by the council.

The second issue was the creation of a mobile heavy artillery. After a discussion to which Joffre did not contribute, the matter was deferred, as the council sensibly concluded that the decision depended on whatever solution was adopted for the method of forming the howitzer batteries.

The Supreme War Council re-examined the problem of the artillery on 15 October 1913. It considered the weaponry and organization of the arm. Lengthy discussions revealed a greater acceptance of the need for a heavy artillery. The council decided to create heavy artillery regiments at army level, consisting of both guns and howitzers. But it left open the possibility of reconsidering the army corps level, should enough men and equipment become available.

The council had therefore approved the approach advocated by Joffre. Galliéni had struggled to try and gain acceptance of the principle that allocating the heavy artillery at army level should be just a transitory stage. Galliéni did not favour the creation of heavy artillery regiments and would have preferred the existing organization, with the artillery distributed by brigades, but in the end he swung behind Joffre's proposal.

As a result of this decision, Plan XVII provided for the establishment at army level of four regiments of heavy artillery and one regiment of foot artillery acting as heavy field artillery. Each regiment consisted of four brigades, each of which in turn had three batteries. A battery contained two artillery pieces. The pieces were 155mm quick-firing Rimailho and 120mm Baquet, along with 105mm light howitzers that began to be produced only at the start of the war.[32] The men came from the previously-existing heavy artillery elements at army level, from coastal batteries that were taken out of service (preferably without antagonizing local public opinion) and from the additional manpower provided by the Three-Year Law.

Joffre kept an eye on developments in this field. On 29 May 1912, for example, he asked the Artillery Testing Commission to carry out trials comparing the effectiveness of shells of various calibres.[33] He followed this up on 31 March 1913, demanding to know why these requested tests had not even begun.

Since 1911, therefore, Joffre did much to insist on the creation of a heavy artillery. Although the results by the start of the war were mixed, he could hardly be accused of procrastination. Yet this was precisely the allegation laid against him.[34] He was accused of not having put enough pressure on successive Ministers of War to overcome the obstacles to the development of the heavy artillery at army level.

Joffre's critics overlooked the fact that he ran into a big stumbling block. At this time, there existed twelve directorates (or comparable organizations) under the Minister of War's control. During the 1911 reforms, Joffre failed to win agreement that the directorates should come under his authority. They took no orders from him and some of them were extremely powerful, such as the 3rd Directorate for the artillery and the 4th for the engineers.

Little has been said about the role played by these directorates, and yet it was crucial. Not only did they award all the contracts that were made with private enterprises, they actually made in their own factories most of the equipment required by the armies. They were effectively states within the French State. Even the Minister of War could do little if they were opposed, for overcoming that opposition would have required a continuity in office that was the one thing unobtainable during these periods when there was such a high turnover of ministers. The Directorate of Artillery was a sort of Ministry of Armaments before one officially came into existence. It controlled the design and production not only of artillery equipment, but also of armaments in general and the manufacture of explosives. It had at its disposal many workshops and factories using a State-employed labour force, at locations such as Bourges, Tarbes, Puteaux and Saint-Etienne.

The Directorate of Artillery did not have a complete monopoly over all the stages of producing guns, since private industry – notably Le Creusot – provided roughly manufactured items that were subsequently machined in the directorate's workshops. The almost philosophical dithering about whether or not it was necessary to develop heavy artillery equipment, combined with the perfectionism of the artillery officers (this was a result of their training at the *Ecole polytechnique*), resulted in the various pieces of equipment either being adopted belatedly or not being produced at all. Joffre gave the anthill a bit of a kick by proposing to turn to private industry (Le Creusot again), which at this same time was producing orders from abroad for fairly similar equipment to what the French army wanted to bring into service. The Directorate of Artillery had no desire to lose the near-monopoly enjoyed by the State-run arsenals.

Nor were matters straightforward. By my calculations, no fewer than four different types of howitzer originally saw the light of day between 1881 and 1904. All but one of them were intended for the siege artillery. The first was the short-barrelled 155mm de Bange, mounted on a platform. Then came the short-barrelled 155mm Baquet, which was basically a failure. The 155mm Rimailho followed in 1904. Finally, an improved version of the short-barrelled 155mm de Bange was produced in 1912 with the platform as an integral part of the artillery piece, so the platform was transported with the gun without being dismantled. Of these four different types, only the Rimailho was a true heavy field piece. It alone performed satisfactorily, notably in terms of its rate of fire. The impression I have is of a process based heavily on trial-and-error in the absence of any clear-cut decisions. It is clear that the Directorate of Engineers was too focused on permanent fortifications to embrace the century with any great desire for change, while the Directorate of Artillery was too convinced of its own excellence to do so.

Some other steps were taken that made it possible early in the war to compensate for the shortage of heavy field artillery. They may seem small steps, but they were simple to put into effect. The first gave a degree of mobility to the 120 and 155mm de Bange guns belonging to the siege or fortress artillery. There were 3,000 or so of these guns sitting idly in the artillery parks of the forts that they were supposed to arm.[35] They were not howitzers, but the weight of their projectiles made them potentially much more destructive than the 75mm. The problem was finding a way of moving them without minimizing their advantages. There had to be a way of dispensing with the cumbersome platforms, while still being able to put the guns in firing positions without making the process of aiming them too complicated.

Part of the answer was an Italian innovation, the *rotaie a cingolo*. These special caterpillar tracks were officially adopted in France from 1913. Consisting of articulated blocks clamped around the wheels of artillery pieces, they increased the surface area that was in contact with the ground and hence made it possible to move the pieces across unfavourable terrain. As an added bonus, the blocks acted as a brake limiting the recoil of the piece, and this simplified the process of aiming. Consequently, the ballistic performances of the long-barrelled 120mm were little different from when it was mounted on its platform equipped with a hydraulic brake. Some long-barrelled 120mm guns were even grouped into batteries towed by tractors. Three of these batteries existed at the start of the war. This was the first appearance in France of motorized artillery, though at this early stage it was known as mobile artillery.

The de Bange guns could have been improved much earlier by alterations to their carriages. But the Directorate of Artillery took a perfectionist approach and was loathe to bring guns into service if their performance was not going to be entirely satisfactory. Since war was not expected in the next few years, there was no pressure of time and it seemed better to design a piece of equipment that would be sure of proving as successful as the 75mm. Thus, the French army had only about 100 pieces of modern heavy artillery in 1914, compared to the German total of 700.

* * *

When all is said and done, Joffre had three years of hard work to his credit. He had undertaken many reforms, although a shortage of time and money prevented him from seeing all of them through to fruition.[36] His critics pass lightly over this period,[37] in order to play down the solid progress he achieved. He incontestably put France in a much stronger position for confronting the impending storm.

There were two Joffres: the pre-war Joffre and the wartime Joffre. Detractors have deliberately ignored the actions of the first, while vilifying those of the second. There was, of course, more of the engineer in the earlier Joffre. Yet in order to belittle the subsequent, wartime general, critics have had to overlook the pre-war years – years during which the engineer demonstrated exceptional organizational skills in difficult circumstances.

Chapter 5

Battle of the Frontiers

I'll start by saying something about the enemy. In August 1914, the German army had both a plan of concentration and, unlike the French, a *written* operational plan. This was the famous Schlieffen Plan, revised and corrected by von Moltke (known as 'the Younger' to avoid confusion with his uncle, the von Moltke who had led the German armies in 1870). I have no intention here of going into the details of the Schlieffen Plan, since readers who want to know more can consult the reams of pages that have been written about it. The plan had been modified several times, and in 1914 it envisaged a main thrust consisting of a gigantic envelopment north of Liège, sweeping round the French army's left wing. This thrust would be carried out by two armies, the 1st and the 2nd, or a total of twelve army corps, six of them being reserve corps (not including cavalry units). The initial versions of the Schlieffen Plan, at the start of the century, contemplated a much more modest turning move, to the south of the Meuse and along it – somewhat along the lines of what Joffre expected. It will be noted that the German strategic think-ing was in a different class to that of the French. The Schlieffen Plan, even after its modification by Moltke, showed a perfect mastery of what today would be called operational planning.

For diplomatic and dynastic reasons, Moltke – unlike Schlieffen – wanted to avoid crossing the protrusion of the Dutch province of Limburg, which meant that the space available for the passage of twelve army corps was especially limited. Hence the German forces had to be echelonned in depth, with the active corps preceding the reserve corps, and this helps explain why the French took so long to find out what was happening. The limited space also justifies the Germans in capturing Liège as early as possible so as to use the east-west communication routes, for Liège is an important crossing point of the Meuse by both road and rail. A glance at a map shows that the city lay a mere 30km or so from the German frontier and for this reason it was subjected to a sudden attack on 4 August before the Germans had completed their concentration. Indeed, they did not complete their concentration until around the 13th, and it was the 18th before their northernmost armies began their march. This is important since it meant that no intelligence could reach Joffre until then, except from a secret agent or from Belgian sources. Sending Sordet (the commander of the French cavalry corps in Northern France and Belgium) so far from the French frontier was out of the question.

The other German forces were deployed, in a somewhat similar manner to the French, along the joint frontier. From south to north, the left wing – which was the weakest – consisted of the 7th and 6th Armies, while the other five were echelonned further north as far as Aachen. The 7th and 6th did not have offensive missions, but Moltke expected French attacks in Alsace and Lorraine. These two German armies were simply to counter and pin down the opposing forces in that sector – their missions would evolve later on.

Joffre's headquarters

I'll now turn briefly to the *Grand Quartier Général* (GQG) – the operational staff that established itself at Vitry-le-François on 4 August. At this date, it was a slim organization. Composed of some fifty officers, it was located more or less at the centre of gravity of the French deployment, in such a way that the liaison officers could reach the front and return in a single day. It basically consisted of four *bureaux* or departments: 1st, Personnel; 2nd, Intelligence; 3rd, Operations; and 4th, Department of the Rear Zone, or logistics as we would say today. Each department was run by an officer ranked colonel or above. Joffre had the support of a chief-of-staff (Belin) and three assistant chiefs-of-staff (including Pellé and Berthelot), who had overall responsibility for the four departments. GQG was not a group of selfless men, and its officers should not be seen as perfect. None of them had the slightest real experience of staffwork during a European war. Yet despite the calamity that soon descended on them, they withstood the storm and did wonders. Some years later, Joffre quite rightly paid tribute to them. As I have already said, though it needs emphasizing, the French army – in common with every other army – lacked the slightest experience of running organizations of this sort, which had to command 2 million men extended along a front of 400km (a distance that was soon almost doubled).

These brilliant officers, although highly-intelligent and academically-accomplished, were too young to have had the least operational experience, except perhaps a few colonial ventures. Had this been otherwise, it might have been possible to inject a bit of realism into the initial conduct of the conflict. We can only regret the absence of a veteran whose experience of 1870 would have been useful – Castelnau would have been more suited to remaining at GQG instead of becoming commander of the 2nd Army. (In all probability, Joffre was against the idea, lest his supremacy was undermined.)

Another problem was that the means of communication did not match the extension of the front. Numerous mistakes and inaccuracies in the conduct of the war, and during the Battle of the Frontiers in particular, can be explained by the communication difficulties. The delays were always long – too long. From the moment when a report reached GQG and the time when an order was sent in return, several tens of hours might elapse, and in the meantime the situation might have changed so much that the reply was no longer valid. Communications within divisions and army corps were barely any easier. A division, about 15,000–20,000 men strong, moved along one or two axes, and the head of the column might be some 15km in front of the tail. Sending an order or report this distance, using a despatch rider on horseback, took several hours at the start of the war. Lateral communications were no easier. Later, the problem would be resolved as the motor-car became commonplace.

Telephone and telegraph stations, which by necessity were spaced-out, were provided along the lines of march by using the existing civilian networks. Almost every French village had a telephone at its post-office, but the system was still inefficient and was a far cry from our modern communication networks. The military telephones were most inadequate in both number and quality, and the length of wire was allocated parsimoniously.

* * *

We have seen how the intention behind Plan XVII was to 'take the offensive'. This desire was expressed in Febuary 1914 in the *Directives for the concentration*:

> The action of the French armies will take the form of two main operations, which will develop:
> - One on the right, in the terrain between the forested massifs of the Vosges and the Moselle downstream of Toul.
> - The other on the left, north of the line Verdun-Metz.
> These two operations will be closely connected by forces operating on the *Hauts-de-Meuse* and in the Woëvre.

The missions of the various armies were then set out: the 1st and 2nd Armies would operate between the Rhine and the Moselle, and the 5th Army north of the line Verdun-Metz, while the 4th would remain in the second line ready to move up to either north or south, and the 3rd would connect the 5th with the 1st and 2nd.

Each of the armies was aware of what it had to do, but did not know its objective. They had to attack, in one or more directions expressed in terms of particular features of the terrain, such as towns, rivers or mountainous massifs. No clear missions at this stage, but there was reason to hope that further information would arrive once the concentration was complete, especially as Joffre expected much from his intelligence-gathering plan.

One piece of evidence is puzzling. Back in February 1912, when Joffre asked permission to make an offensive through Belgium (during the meeting at the Ministry of Foreign Affairs), he set out at length the reasons for his request. Furthermore, in his memoirs he quoted what he said almost in full.[1] Briefly, the justification he gave for authorizing the passage through Belgian territory was the multitude of difficulties presented by the natural obstacles and fortified barriers that were arrayed along the Franco-German frontier, including the entrenched German camps of Metz and Strasbourg, the forested massifs of the Ardennes and the lakes of the Dieuze region. In reading it, you get the impression that no offensive action was possible anywhere except through Belgium. His conclusion was: 'Neither in Alsace nor in Lorraine will we find terrain favouring a decisive offensive.'

So why, little more than two years later, did he hurl his armies in the very directions that he himself had stated to be unfavourable terrain? How had the situation changed to make feasible in 1914 what had been so difficult in 1912? Naturally, we may suspect him of having exaggerated in the meeting at the Ministry of Foreign Affairs, and it was sound tactics to try and influence the decision in this way. Nevertheless, the difficulties of the routes have been noted by many commentators since before the war.[2] Joffre never explained the contradiction – it was left to Berthelot to declare one day that, if they wanted, they would fight everywhere.

According to Recouly, Berthelot also explained why Joffre wished to take the offensive:

> Moral, as much as military, reasons induced Joffre to hurl his troops forward. He feared that the memory of the terrible defeat of 1870 ... might exert too much influence on our generals and soldiers alike, perhaps on the soldiers less than on the generals. It was necessary to destroy this fantasy, this legend of German military superiority over the French.[3]

Also justified in this way was the local offensive against Mulhouse (the first attack undertaken by the French army, even before the concentration was complete), to which I shall return in due course. This would explain why the terrain limitations did not carry much weight when set against the intention of giving battle. Moral reasons (that's what I'll call them, in line with the vocabulary of the era and that of Berthelot) weighed more heavily on Joffre than the military reasons. Yet it's a pity he did not express himself more forthrightly about these military reasons, a phrase that implies such things as intent, plan and objective – everything, in short, that we do not clearly understand.

We would at least like to know what Joffre had in mind. From what we can tell, he conceived the following operational plan shortly after hostilities had begun, but before the concentration was finished. The plan took into account what he had learned about the German offensive, and this was how he explained it after the war to the Briey Commission:

1. Carry the war beyond the nation's borders.
2. Direct the main attack through Luxembourg and Belgian Luxembourg with the 3rd and 4th Armies, threatening the communications

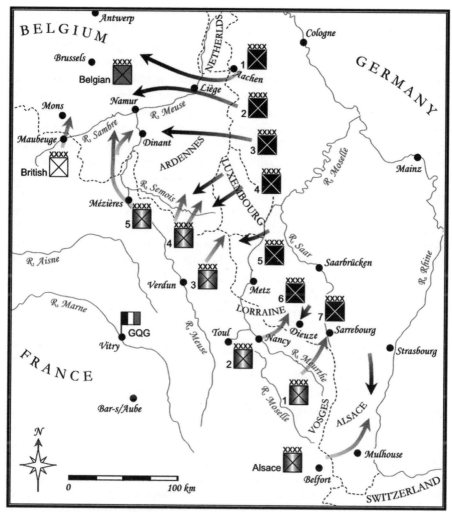

The first moves, mid-August 1914.

of the German armies that were crossing the Meuse between Namur and the Dutch frontier.

3. Make a secondary attack between Metz and the Vosges with the 1st and 2nd Armies to prevent the enemy from falling on the flank of the previously-mentioned armies.

4. Finally, with the Army W (the British army), Belgian army and 5th Army, to delay and block the westward march of the German armies by taking up dispositions on their flank, between the Meuse and Sambre, based on the entrenched camps of Namur, Antwerp and Maubeuge.

Be that as it may, on the morning of 7 August the French 7th Corps entered Alsace. This operation was a preliminary move. It sought to boost morale by giving public opinion what it wanted – a victory, and not just any victory, but one gained in Alsace. The move was intended at the same time to prepare the way for the subsequent offensive. Yet the man in charge of the operation, General Bonneau, does not seem to have understood his mission properly. Whereas Joffre saw it as an initial offensive flourish, Bonneau apparently thought in terms of merely pushing forward the covering screen. Mulhouse was occupied and then abandoned within forty-eight hours, to the stupefaction of the French population, which had been prematurely filled with enthusiasm by the capture of the city and its loud trumpeting by Joffre, who had splurged on an order of the day.

The situation was about to become clearer. Everything suggests that after the German assault on Liège, Joffre felt confirmed in thinking that the Germans were attacking along the Meuse valley. He reckoned that he now had enough information to make his intentions more specific. On the morning of 8 August, he sent *General Instruction No. 1* to the armies. Nothing is more unreadable than these headquarters documents, so I shall simply quote its basic points, rather than reproduce it in full. There are two key sentences, the first of them at the start: 'The Commander-in-Chief's intent is to seek battle with all his forces united, and with the right of his general disposition resting on the Rhine'. The other sentence is the conclusion: 'They [the army commanders] will immediately take preparatory steps likely to facilitate the offensive and make it overwhelming.' Note the two expressions 'seek battle' and 'make it overwhelming'. The first conveyed Joffre's intention unambiguously, but the second was unfortunate, for it encouraged many corps and divisional commanders to make a headlong charge, with consequences that soon became clear.

General Instruction No. 1 was perfectly in line with the *Directives for the concentration*. The 1st and 2nd Armies were to attack in Alsace and Lorraine. The 3rd Army had a double mission: either to operate to the north, or to counter-attack a German offensive coming from Metz–Thionville. The 4th Army was to insert itself between the 5th and 3rd, and to attack between the Argonne and the Meuse. The 5th Army also had a double mission: either to counter-attack a German offensive between Mouzon and Mézières, or to cross the Meuse between those two points.

Uncertainty in Belgium
We need to consider the circumstances in which the battle took shape. Joffre explained in his memoirs that he saw no drawbacks in promptly ordering his right wing to attack, but added that he was much more inclined to wait in regard to his left wing on account of the shortage of information about the German army, the delay to the British army and the limited capabilities of the

Belgian army. He still lacked a key piece of intelligence on which to base his manœuvre – the German army's order of battle, in other words the arrangement of its concentration areas and its directions of attack. (He totally discounted the possibility that a German army might remain on the defensive to await the French attack.) Hence the Intelligence Department counted and recounted the German active army corps.

At least Joffre knew where he stood with the British army. Its landings were well under way, although its commander, Field Marshal Sir John French, stated that it would not be ready for action until 20 August at the earliest – and instead of the expected six divisions there would be just four, along with some cavalry brigades. Joffre had also received some good news from Russia, where the mobilization was proceeding as planned. The Russians had re-affirmed their promises of a swift offensive around 15 August, in accordance with the pre-war agreements.

I shall briefly consider the Belgian army and examine how the French forces might have been able to support it. The Belgians actually made an official request for France's help, which was rather ironic given their earlier policy of invariably turning down French and British offers of military co-operation. But regardless of what Poincaré might promise, there was little Joffre could do short of changing his deployment – and only an emergency could justify resorting to such a step. He therefore contented himself with sending Sordet's cavalry corps. Its squadrons rode through Belgium, mostly south of the Meuse, wearing out both their men and horses without achieving anything.

Joffre was inevitably accused after the war of having sacrificed the Belgians. But since the Belgians had turned down any military talks before the war broke out, they had actually sacrificed themselves and no one else could be blamed. Joffre had wanted to include the Belgian army in a united Belgian, British and French front, but his attempts had come to nothing. The Belgians were completely crushed by the Germans and fell back on Antwerp, which had always been their national fortress. At the same time, they still sought to protect Brussels, but that was obviously beyond their strength.

Lieutenant-Colonel Brécard was Joffre's liaison officer with the Belgian army at Louvain. He subsequently related what the Belgian Chief-of-Staff told him:

> If the army is unable to hold on to the position it currently occupies, it will withdraw on Antwerp. Public opinion in the country fully supports the army fighting to avenge the wrong done to Belgium, but it would not understand why the army should undertake an offensive operation alongside the French army.[4]

In other words, the Belgians were summoning the French army to help them, yet were reluctant to fight alongside it. This sounds like one of those tall stories the French tell in order to poke fun at the Belgians, but unfortunately it was for real. Indeed, it was typical of the way that operations unfolded in this region, and all the parties contributed to the situation. The French began looking over their shoulder at Paris following the failure of their advance on Mainz, while the British kept one eye firmly on the Channel coast and the Belgians were intent only on seeking refuge in Antwerp. Joffre apparently wanted to counter the German offensive by trying to unite all the available forces under centralized control, but any such attempt was doomed to failure by this lack of coherence. After the war, intelligent men such as General Mordacq pointed out that the two sides were almost equal in numbers, even though the Germans were using their reserve corps in the first line. Yet this numerical balance did not prevent the Allies from being defeated piecemeal, as a result of their inability to reach agreement with each other before the war.

The information coming from Belgium remained sparse and confused for a fortnight. As we have seen, Liège had been attacked on 4 August and nearly captured by surprise. Since then, it was unclear whether the city was wholly in German hands, or if the forts of its entrenched camp were still holding out. In fact, Liège's final fort fell only on 16 August. What the Belgian field army was doing remained equally unclear, despite the presence of Brécard, who was doing what he could. Joffre's critics argued after the war that the German attack on Liège made it obvious that the main thrust of the German army lay north of the Meuse. Yet this does not necessarily follow. The Germans might have had several motives for capturing Liège, such as seizing control of the many communication routes of the Meuse, or neutralizing the city's entrenched camp in order to prevent threats emerging from it, perhaps against a flank.

More than twenty days elapsed from 4 August until GQG was correctly informed on the 25th about the substantial nature of the German forces north of the Meuse and about the presence of their reserve corps. This intelligence failure is hard to understand. The necessary information could have come from at least three sources: the French, Belgian and British intelligence services. But the French services seem to have been unforthcoming,[5] and the Belgians knew practically nothing despite being ideally situated on Germany's doorstep. The British intelligence services already had a deserved reputation for competence, but they were just as ignorant as the Belgians – or possibly they just kept quiet about what they knew. In any event, it was the French who helped supply information to the British War Office, rather than the other way round.

No convincing explanation has ever been provided for the information vacuum during this crucial period. All that can be said is that no French agent, and no agent working for the French, managed to penetrate the inner sanctum, the *Großer Generalstab*. No German officer or diplomat was 'turned'. This shows just how thoroughly the Germans managed to preserve secrecy.

It's easy enough to blame GQG for having failed to guess the reality of the situation, and easy for all of Joffre's critics to exclaim that the situation had been crystal clear and that they would have acted differently had they been in the shoes of the slow-witted Commander-in-Chief. The snag is that no evidence exists to support such claims. No archive document explicitly records any clues that might have revealed the German manœuvre or the *Schwerpunkt* – the focal point – of their right wing. Joffre the engineer had no desire to change his plan, which he had spent a long time thoroughly polishing, simply on the basis of information that was largely guesswork. A more inspired commander might have acted differently, but would have been basing his decision on his inner conviction rather than on reliable intelligence.

What some people call obstinacy is seen by others as perseverance. The difference between the two lies in how the commander evaluates the situation. His dilemma is always the same: whom or what should he believe? A fairly rational man, such as Joffre, waits for statistics, dates and actual occurrences. Someone who is more intuitive, on the other hand, lets his intuition give meaning to the information he holds, however fragmentary that information might be. This is why it is so important to realize that during the period from the declaration of war right up until the time the German offensive finally began on 18 August, practically no information arrived from Belgium's frontier with Germany except about what was happening at Liège.

Seeking battle

I shall rapidly run through the main phases of the Battle of the Frontiers. A distinction is usually drawn between the offensive in Alsace and Lorraine involving the 1st and 2nd Armies; the Battle of the Ardennes with the 3rd and 4th Armies; and the Battle of the Sambre (also known as the Battle of Charleroi) and Battle of Mons fought by the 5th Army and Sir John French's army in Belgium. The outcome was that between 20 and 23 August, the French and British armies started to retreat, and they stopped only when they fought the Battle of the Marne from 6 to 10 September 1914, which forced the German armies to fall back.

Much has been written about these actions, so I shall not go into the detail of how they unfolded. But we should note that it was not until after the war that the French army's Historical Branch was able to finish working its way through millions of written documents, orders and reports in order to unravel the tangle of events. Distinguishing between intentions and actual actions was not always easy, and this was seen during sessions of the Briey Commission in 1919. Several generals, who had been in command of armies or army corps, were surprised by some of the others' testimony. The ensuing spats delighted the Deputies who were on the commission, including its president Maurice Viollette, as it provided them with more ammunition with which to attack Joffre and GQG in petty acts of revenge along the lines of 'I told you so'.[6]

At 9.00am on 13 August, Joffre issued *Special Instruction No. 5* to the commanders of the 1st and 2nd Armies, ordering them to take the offensive. The concentration was complete and Joffre felt ready, on his right wing at least, to launch the operation that he had been planning for so long. The operation was to start on 14 August. The orders specified that the enemy 'will be attacked wherever he is found', and that the 1st Army would halt north of the line Sarrebourg, Haselbourg, Obersteigen. The 2nd Army would support the northward offensive of the 1st by attacking towards a front between Dieuze and Château-Salins with its righthand corps. Joffre demanded that his subordinates were 'to seek battle', as in his order of 8 August.

What exactly is the meaning of 'to seek battle wherever the enemy is found'? Joffre's instruction amounted to ordering an advance, rather blindly, and then leaving his army commanders to move relentlessly forward, use their initiative and break any resistance they ran into. No precise objectives were given – just a line that had to be reached. The only explanation I can think of (and it is no more than a possibility) is that Joffre expected a straightforward occupation of territory, an 'offensive march' as he called it in his instruction, involving the reduction of just a few, perhaps isolated, points of resistance.

At the same time, the commanders of the 3rd, 4th and 5th Armies received *Special Instruction No. 6*. Similarly, this was not an operational order. It simply specified what movements needed to be carried out, with a view to a possible encounter with the enemy around 15 or 16 August. In other words, it was another case of 'seeking battle'. The 3rd Army received a complex mission, since it had to be ready either to come to the assistance of the 4th Army further north, or to operate eastwards in the direction of the entrenched camp of Metz, from where a German army might debouch. The 4th Army was to push its main body to a front between Sommauthe and Dun-sur-Meuse. As for the 5th Army, the head of its main body was to be 8–10km behind the Meuse, in front of Mézières and further upstream. 'Before attacking, it will wait until the enemy has engaged a large part of his forces on the left bank. Speed should be used both in mounting the attack and in conducting it after it has begun.'[7] Joffre was therefore preparing to launch an offensive to the north-east, towards what he thought was the belly of the German forces, but had yet to issue the formal order to unleash it. Nor had he stated his intention, although it was clearly to cut the German armies into two parts.

Lanrezac, the commander of the 5th Army, was deeply worried that the Germans would turn his left flank. On 14 August, he went to see Joffre and the operational heads of the General Staff, Berthelot and Pellé, in order to share his concerns. He had no more positive information about the German manœuvre than they did, yet his intuition told him that the Germans were going to decend along the left bank of the Meuse and that he, Lanrezac, was in danger of being unable to oppose them unless he extended his left wing sufficiently far to the north-west. It was on this occasion that GQG and Joffre gave him the notorious reply: 'We have the feeling that the Germans have nothing ready on that side.'

With hindsight, it is perfectly natural to condemn GQG for being blind or short-sighted. Yet at this stage Joffre still knew nothing specific about the German manœuvre and – since he insisted on making decisions only on the basis of hard facts – he could hardly have given Lanrezac any other answer than the one he did. Admittedly, he should have chosen a better form of words than 'have the feeling', for by using that particular phrase he was simply replying to Lanrezac's hunch with a hunch of his own, and he thereby gave the misleading impression that he shared Lanrezac's intuitive style of thinking. The incident had an unfortunate side-effect, since it was natural for people to assume that a Commander-in-Chief who so obviously lacked flair was likely to be equally deficient as a strategist. Joffre's 'feeling' severely damaged his reputation, and to make matters worse his dismissal of Lanrezac several days later was widely seen as a petty act of revenge by an incompetent commander against a more gifted subordinate.

On 15 August, a German reconnaissance tried to capture the crossing of the Meuse at Dinant. GQG received misleading information about this attack, which was reckoned to have been made by an entire army corps. This mistake actually had a beneficial effect, for it prodded the staff into starting to realise what was actually happening. The result was that Lanrezac obtained permission on that same day, 15 August, to push his forces to the north-west. GQG seemed to be adapting, as far as it could, to the various pieces of information it was receiving, which on the whole substantiated each other. At the same time, the French dispositions (3rd and 4th Armies) had to be adjusted so as not to leave gaps that might be exploited by the enemy.

Staffs were obsessed with the danger of being outflanked, and that made army commanders acutely cautious about their wings. Many withdrawals during the war resulted from concern that a unit needed to fall into line with its neighbour.[8] Anxiety about flanks were one reason for Lanrezac's troubled relations with Sir John French. The two of them were barely speaking to each other, and when they did it was always by proxy, using liaison officers as go-betweens. Bristling with hostility, they kept an eye on each other and were constantly ready to make accusations that one of them had fallen back without giving any warning. This friction within the Allied armies was another of the crosses that Joffre had to bear at this time.

* * *

Now let's return to Alsace and Lorraine. On 11 August, Joffre had created an Army of Alsace under the command of General Pau, whom Messimy had recalled to active service. The Army of Alsace was actually a deception: it was intended to pin down German forces in Upper Alsace. It began its advance at noon on the 14th, moving along the Belfort-Mulhouse road. On the 19th, it reached its objective, Mulhouse, which French troops entered once again. General Pau intended to veer round to face north and advance up to a line between Colmar and Neuf-Brisach, with his right resting on the Rhine. By the 20th, the Army of Alsace was level with Colmar, but it then halted on that line on the 20th and 21st as the 2nd Army was now in increasingly serious difficulties. Joffre sent an order to retreat, the French abandoned Mulhouse for the second time on the 24th, and the Army of Alsace's main component, the 7th Corps, left the area to form part of what was to become the 6th Army on the Allied left wing.

The 1st Army, commanded by Dubail, started its offensive as planned on the morning of the 14th. (It was to the 1st Army that the Army of Alsace was attached.) Opposite the 1st Army were some reliable German forces and, in particular, the entrenched camp of Strasbourg. The army attacked in the general direction of Sarrebourg and Saverne, while its right wing guarded the flank in the Vosges level with Sainte-Marie-aux-Mines. The action was difficult because of the terrain, which consisted of fairly high mountains with some densely-wooded areas and a few narrow roads and tracks. The battle was confused and swung back and forth with frequent attacks and counter-attacks. It ended on the 22nd with the French units returning to their departure positions astride the Meurthe. This was the result of the 2nd Army having fallen back after being defeated at Morhange, and is a further example of the concern about keeping units aligned.

The 2nd Army had been supposed to head eastwards, then turn north and attack on the front between Dieuze and Château-Salins, heading in the direction of Saarbrücken. But it faced the German 6th and 7th Armies under Crown Prince Rupprecht of Bavaria, which operated jointly against both the 2nd and 1st Armies. After a heavy defeat at Morhange, the 2nd Army poured back on Nancy. Catastrophe nearly followed, but the Germans failed to take Nancy. The city's fall would have been a hard blow for the French, close on the heels of their second abandonment of Mulhouse. Castelnau almost abandoned Nancy to its fate, but managed in critical circumstances to restore the situation on the *Grand Couronné* – the fortified heights that dominated the city.[9]

In September 1913, the Supreme War Council had made plans for defensive lines to be established on the *Grand Couronné*. Not much had been done by 1914, though Foch had done some work there with his 20th Corps. In the event, the defences proved enough to enable the troops to cling on, and Nancy never fell. Rupprecht launched a pursuit of the French, in the belief that they were already beaten. He hoped to penetrate through the famous Charmes Gap and link up with the German 1st and 2nd Armies that were descending through Belgium. Instead, he suffered a bad defeat on the Mortagne river on 25 August. Yet the fighting, far from ending there, continued into the beginning of September and during the Battle of the Marne.

The counter-offensive by the German left wing was actually an improvisation and did not form part of the Schlieffen Plan. It instead enhanced the plan by seeking to trap the French armies in a pincer movement between a northern prong in Belgium and a southern prong in Lorraine. Moltke had been persuaded to make this change by the successes the Germans had gained since their initial clashes with the French. But many commentators argue that the Germans should have stuck to the original plan, for if they had managed to transfer at least part of their 6th and 7th Armies to their right wing, they would have had the additional strength they needed on the Marne.[10]

* * *

It is time to interrupt our account of the battle for a moment, in order to return to Joffre. His initial attempts to explain the setbacks he had suffered give us our first substantial insight into what he was thinking. On 13 August, he sent a message – it was telephoned to the Minister of War – in which he stated:

> In some respects, the results have fallen below our expectations. The blame lies solely with the commanders. I have already taken action by removing an army corps commander and two *généraux de division* from their posts.

This marked the start of the *limogeages*, or 'dismissals'. General Bonneau (the commander of the 7th Corps at Mulhouse) had the unenviable privilege of being the first to climb into the tumbril of dismissed generals, and if Messimy's recommendation had been heeded it would have conveyed them to the execution post.[11]

Three days later, Joffre issued a note to his army commanders, in which he pointed out the lessons that needed to be learned. By this stage, the French army had fought just a few engagements, notably the entrance into Mulhouse on the 8th. Only the initial lessons of the campaign could therefore be drawn when Joffre wrote his note, but he already found the failings of the troops and some of their commanders glaringly obvious. Here are some extracts from what he wrote:

> There is no wish to destroy the élan that is the main reason for success. It is important, however, to wait for artillery support, especially when it is a matter of taking entrenched positions. The troops must be prevented from dashing into the open where they are exposed to enemy fire. At no time must generals lose control of the action. The infantry should not simply make a direct, frontal attack against the enemy; it instead needs to

start investing strongpoints and outflank them if it is able to do so. As much artillery as possible should be employed right from the start of the action. ... Courage and élan are not enough to ensure final victory – it is also necessary to learn endurance, and this entails making sure the troops are not prematurely worn out either on the march or in action ... .

Joffre also pointed out: 'Attacks that are prepared more carefully will have all the more impact and be altogether less bloody.' The fact that he needed to issue this reminder is surprising, for it is the very ABC of infantry combat, and everything he was insisting on could already be found in the 1913 regulations. This demonstrates the incompetence of the mid-level commanders and points to an almost total lack of instruction and training of the troops in what not to do on the modern battlefield, as well as indicating an absence of the routine that should govern their training. That the generals might 'lose control' of an action says much about the lack of cohesion of the units in question. The only orders received by some units were: 'Fix bayonets. Forward, march!'[12] Attacks were launched unthinkingly, almost as a reflex action, without taking the enemy into account, examining the terrain or bothering with artillery preparation – indeed without bothering to ensure any coordination at all with the artillery. Such attacks failed everywhere with officers and men being mowed down while still unaware of what was happening and often without having seen a single German. Nothing seemed to have changed much since 1870. War was still fought in the same way: move in column, deploy into a line of skirmishers, with bugles blowing and the flag to the fore, and charge with fixed bayonets without even knowing the enemy's exact location. It was during the first weeks of the war that the French army suffered its worst casualties. During the Battle of Morhange, for example, some units were hurled into an attack across 2,000 metres of completely exposed slopes, with results that can be imagined. Fire-support was neglected, and machine-guns were left behind on the grounds that they burdened the columns and that there was no time to bring them into action. The French simply reacted to events, instead of taking decisive action of their own.

Lanrezac

It is time to return to the French left wing, where the 3rd, 4th and 5th Armies were operating. The 5th Army was finally moving up to the Sambre, where it halted with a view to taking the offensive. Apart from a few skirmishes with German cavalry detachments, it remained unengaged until 21 August – some ten days after it had completed its concentration – and so, although reorganized, it was still undamaged. Lanrezac now had the British army under Sir John French on his left flank, and was given the freedom by Joffre to choose the right moment to unleash his offensive. On the 21st, he issued a preparatory order for his army corps commanders to hold themselves in readiness.

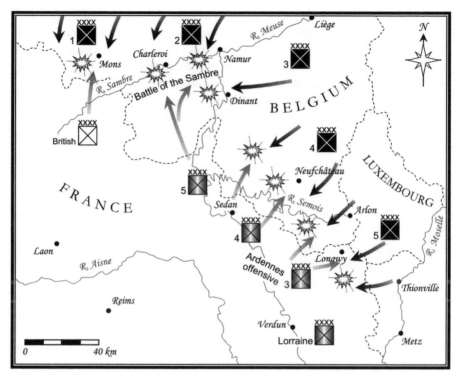

Battle of the Frontiers, end of August 1914.

GQG had every right to expect Lanrezac to cross the Sambre. Yet instead of doing so, he came up with excuses for staying where he was and for wasting time establishing a defensive line south of the river (a line that only General Franchet d'Esperey's 1st Corps actually began to dig). Lanrezac later wrote in his book that he intended to take the offensive and cross the river on the 23rd. Yet he made no attempt to secure the north bank of the Sambre, despite knowing that the German 2nd Army under von Bülow was on the move in front of him, about one day's march north of the river. He reckoned that the terrain made such a venture too difficult, and the 5th Army was in an awkward posture on its right flank, which faced the German 3rd Army under von Hausen. (Even so, by using the 1st Corps to protect that flank it was probably doing so with an unreasonably large force.)

The Germans made up Lanrezac's mind for him and attacked.[13] This resulted in the Battle of the Sambre, in which the French were defeated and some of their army corps, notably the 3rd Corps under General Sauret, were routed. The battle was a series of rather obscure actions in which the French were thoroughly hammered, which was the usual outcome during these early stages of the war. So chaotic was the engagement that it is difficult to follow what happened and to separate out the various actions. Post-war accounts of the battle were often written to try and vindicate Lanrezac, but have simply made the sequence of events even more complicated. The fact remains that in the evening of the 23rd Lanrezac gave the order to withdraw, apparently without even informing the British, with whom his relations had been appalling ever since the start of his meeting with Sir John French at Rethel.[14]

Later on, the storm of hostility directed against Joffre caused Lanrezac's retreat from the Sambre to be reinterpreted. It was portrayed as an operation that saved the 5th Army and thereby secured victory for France by making possible the Battle of the Marne. (The credit for winning the Marne was, of course, attributed to Galliéni.)

Battle of the Ardennes

We now return to the 3rd and 4th Armies commanded respectively by Generals Ruffey and de Langle de Cary. Their task was not an easy one, for they had to launch an offensive to the north-north-east through Luxembourg and Belgium Luxembourg. It fell to them to unleash the strategic offensive that Joffre had been planning and refining for so long. On 20 August, Joffre decided to begin the operation. The 3rd Army stood between Verdun and Luxembourg, while the 4th Army was on its left, extending along the frontier up to the Meuse.

De Langle de Cary was authorized on the 20th to begin moving forward, in order to ensure he would be able to debouch in due course over the Semois river for an advance on Neufchâteau. His 4th Army was the largest of the French armies and contained as many as seven army corps, which reflected the fact that it was entrusted with the main offensive. It made only preliminary movements on the 21st, as the initial hope was that the German armies advancing from east to west would continue their progress and become even more exposed to a flank attack. It was on the 22nd that de Langle began his offensive. His entire army was deployed more or less along a single line, though with its corps staggered progressively rearwards. All these corps failed in their attacks. By the evening of that same day they were flowing to the rear, and some of them (including the 17th Corps) were doing so in disorder. Although de Langle hoped to advance again on the 23rd, he was obliged to face up to reality and give the order to retreat. GQG continued to misjudge the enemy's strength and failed to grasp what was happening. It reckoned that de Langle was opposed by just three German corps, whereas he actually faced slightly more than an army.

As for the 3rd Army, it likewise had orders to move off to the attack on 22 August. Its offensive was complicated by the presence of the entrenched camp of Metz on its right wing. The potential existed for a threat suddenly to emerge from this camp – namely the army of the Crown Prince of Prussia, who was impatient to play a role worthy of his military ambitions. In order to watch the routes out of Metz, Joffre created a short-lived Army of Lorraine.

(Built around the reserve divisions of General Paul Durand, and commanded by General Maunoury.) In the event, the 3rd Army fought a series of disjointed actions in which its corps were thoroughly drubbed. It was then obliged to fall back and its commander, Ruffey, was soon dismissed.

'Where are we going?'

At 9.05am on 23 August, Joffre telegraphed the Minister of War:

> It's now up to the men responsible for implementing the plan. They have to exploit this [numerical] superiority. The question is therefore a question of quality – quality of the commanders and quality of the troops – and above all a question of carrying it out with perseverance.

Berthelot said much the same thing, using similar words: 'The players are in place; now it's up to the men responsible for implementing the plan.' Unfortunately, this made it seem that GQG was washing its hands of the outcome of the operations. Berthelot's brief remark was held against Joffre and repeated by countless critics even while the war was still in progress. The words were poorly chosen. They were reckoned to be typical of the sort of comments that were heard at a wargame and they were open to being misinterpreted. Some men were predisposed to believe (or had particular motives for believing) that the staff saw no difference between pre-war manœuvres and the actual war. They accused the staff of refusing to accept responsibility for the bloodshed it caused.

Yet there is another, perfectly simple explanation for Berthelot's remark. Joffre stated in an interview with the newspaper *Le Matin* on 11 September 1912:

> The commanding general's role will be practically over once he has brought the armies that are due to take part in the action to the desired point in the firing line. The role of the colonels and captains will begin once the first rifleshots have been fired.[15]

We can now understand Joffre's conviction that he was powerless to do much more once the opposing armies met. He genuinely did believe that it was then up to the 'men responsible for implementing the plan'.

By 24 August, the various French offensives had collapsed and there was nothing else to be done except face up to the consequences. GQG recognized that retreat had become unavoidable and ordered it along the entire line between Verdun and Amiens. Joffre wrote in his memoirs: 'By the morning of the 25th, it was clear that the strategic manœuvre we had been preparing since the 18th was ending in complete failure.' That was putting it mildly. In ten days, Joffre's plans had come to naught – rarely has an army been so completely beaten. As Charles de Gaulle wrote: 'Joffre saw his plan collapse, his information turn out to be wrong and his orders become invalid.'[16]

The morale of the French troops quickly deteriorated. The further down a soldier was in the hierarchy, the less he knew about what was happening. When the French armies began withdrawing, the troops and junior officers knew they were retreating, but lacked an overall view of the situation – often they did not even know what neighbouring units were doing. 'Where are we going?' exclaimed Lintier, a gunner who was retreating with his 75mm gun. 'We know nothing and are too tired to think or even to feel afraid.' He added in due course: 'Are the French still in Belgium and in Alsace? ... If only we knew the truth, whatever it might be!'[17]

Every eyewitness account says the same thing, with just slight variations. General Xardel wrote in his diary:

> We were kept in the most complete ignorance ... for weeks on end. The government and the General Staff seem to have concealed even the slightest news from us, doubtless because they had nothing to boast about. They seem to have deliberately prevented us from knowing whether the enemy had invaded France – as if wanting to know was a crime rather than the most natural desire.[18]

Even if we make allowances for Xardel's argumentative tone, which was typical of him, it remains striking that he – a brigade commander – was almost as much in the dark as his men.

It is now time to consider some post-war views about the military qualities of the soldiers and the high command. I shall start with Spears, whom we have already met. This is what he wrote in *Liaison 1914*:

> There is no doubt that the fearful losses of the French and their lack of success in so many encounters, in spite of great gallantry, [were] attributable largely to faulty training of the troops and to a complete misapprehension on the part of the officers of the conditions of modern warfare.

De Gaulle experienced these August actions as a young officer and described them superbly.[19] Unfortunately, it is impossible to reproduce five whole pages of his text, and so I will content myself with a short extract, but I encourage you to read the full version in his book:

> All of a sudden, the enemy's fire became aimed and concentrated. Every second intensified the hail of bullets and the thunder of shells. The surviving men lay down and were pinned to the ground in the midst of the screaming wounded and the unobtrusive corpses. ... In the blink of an eye, it seemed that all the courage in the world would be unable to prevail in the face of this fire. ... Whilst the infantry dashed to the attack, the artillery went into position. But even though the artillerymen were diligent, they still needed time to find locations for the guns and also for

the horses and those personnel not required at the batteries, to set up observation posts and to establish communication links. In any case, what were they to fire against, when all they could see of the enemy were faint flashes from guns in well-covered positions? ... Those on the scene at the time had just one thought: 'This is absurd.'

* * *

Joffre was going to have to explain why his armies had been checked. At 9.00am on 24 August, he sent a message to Messimy: 'The evidence can not be ignored. Despite the numerical advantage that had been ensured for our army corps,[20] they have not shown in open country the offensive qualities for which we had been given reason to hope by the earlier, partial successes.' He added: 'The fears that the previous days inspired in me about the offensive capabilities of our troops in open country were confirmed yesterday, with our general offensive suffering a conclusive check in Belgium.' Joffre still seemed convinced that he enjoyed the advantage of numbers, for he had not yet identified the German reserve corps, even if he had a pretty good idea of the active corps.

It is curious to read these extracts. They are further indications that the reality of the situation was only just beginning to dawn on Joffre. Yet he ought not to have been as completely ignorant as he seems to have been. His three years as head of the French army had given him plenty of time to gain an inkling of the actual state of affairs. The inspectors of the Supreme War Council – future army and army corps commanders – had often lamented the gaps in the soldiers' training, even if they were rather vague about what those gaps were. Similarly, it had been necessary to remove some senior officers after the Grand Manœuvres in South-Western France in 1913, before the word *limogeages* was coined to describe such dismissals. The official report on these manœuvres, following which General Faurié lost his command, stated:

> The troops lack both training and discipline. ... The inexperience shown by the officers would have had fatal consequences in an actual campaign. ... Commanders do not strive to carry out the missions assigned to them with the energy and liveliness that are essential for success.[21]

Now, in mid-campaign, Joffre was going to take corrective action. On 24 August, he issued the following note. It was in line with what he had already written on the 18th, and was drafted by the Operations Department and then signed by him:

> The infantry and artillery are not closely coordinated when attacks are carried out: ... the artillery must prepare the attack, while the infantry must be held back and unleashed only at a distance from which it will definitely be able to reach its objective. Whenever attempts have been

made to throw the infantry into the attack from too far away, before the artillery fire has taken effect, the infantry has come under machine-gun fire and suffered losses it could have avoided. ... The infantry seems to be unaware that it needs to organize itself in action for the long-term. Throwing large and dense units into the line exposes them at once to the enemy's fire, leaving them decimated and exposed to a counter-attack ...[22]

Once again, the key point was the need to 'hold back' the infantry. On the 27th, a further note was issued, this time concerning the artillery. It began:

Army commanders will once more call their troops' attention in the most emphatic way to the *absolute*[23] necessity of ensuring complete liaison between the infantry and artillery. So far, this liaison has not always existed. The infantry has attacked over-hastily, while the artillery has often gone into action in a slow, hesitant and limited way. Most of the losses incurred by our infantry have resulted from this fundamental mistake .... [24]

Only around three weeks into the war, therefore, did Joffre remind his sub-ordinates of the need for less costly tactics. You may want to read what he had to say about this in his memoirs, where he elaborated on the frequency with which such deadly mistakes were made within his armies.[25] He omitted to mention the problem of what is now known as friendly fire. Percin claimed that several tens of thousands of men were killed by their own artillery during the Battle of the Frontiers – and he was possibly right, given the artillery's lack of liaison with the infantrymen when the latter set off to the attack.[26]

The army commanders repeated Joffre's instructions and added to them. Franchet d'Esperey, who had just taken over command of the 5th Army, wrote on 5 September in his preparatory order for the Battle of the Marne: 'At the start of the engagement, the attack should be carried out by strictly limited numbers of infantry, supported by all the artillery. The bulk of the infantry is to go forward only after the artillery has opened the way for them.' In other words, an army commander was having to inform his troops on the very eve of action how to fight.

Castelnau made the same points on 27 August, in his *General Instruction No. 4*. Similarly, Ruffey wrote on the 23rd from his command post at Damvillers: 'Bayonet charges can not be permitted in the situations where they have usually been made up to now.' As it happened, the French officers, NCOs and soldiers soon adapted of their own accord.

The extracts I have quoted are bound to cause readers some bewilderment. As far as I know, this is the only time commanders have fought a war by belatedly explaining what should have been done at the start. The French army is depicted by Spears as a sclerotic army that had neither learned anything new, nor forgotten any of the outdated basic knowledge and skills to which it had clung for so long. It lagged far behind the doctrine professed by Grandmaison and the 'Young Turks', who were regarded as just a bunch of intellectuals.

Capitain So-and-so, or Lieutenant Such-and-such, who had mostly been promoted from the ranks, knew nothing of the 'Young Turks'. Chief Warrant Officer Someone-else did not even know Grandmaison's name. As for the reservist lieutenant .... Unfortunately, these were the officers who fought the war. Each successive set of regulations passed over the French army like water flowing off a duck's back. The army was tactically offensive – but not methodically so, for that would have required too much seriousness. Instead, its offensiveness was an instinctive reaction. Practically all that soldiers were taught in their regiments was how to skewer an opponent in between two sessions of close order drill. The French army got a high from the offensive: it was 'hooked' on it. Probably nothing could have forced it to change, except a dreadful detoxification resulting in tens of thousands of deaths in a month – and even then the cure remained incomplete.

It was a price that had to be paid. Giving an exact figure for the losses is difficult, though not because of any lack of time to hone the calculations during the 100 years since the war. The problem comes with trying to specify what the word 'losses' entails. Obviously, it includes the fallen, but what about mortally wounded men – what was the cut-off date after which their death should be deemed to be from natural causes? Some of the wounded, of course, were injured more than once. As for the vast numbers of the missing, they include men of whom nothing was known but whose fate has sometimes been gradually ascertained. For example, it is clear that many soldiers took a direct hit from a shell and their remains were naturally absorbed into the ground. Some prisoners never returned as they died in captivity. Nor did all the sick recover.

Several statistics have been published in an article by Lieutenant-Colonel Larcher, and the following are the key ones for the start of the war.[27] According to its medical branch, the French army lost 216,000 men in August 1914 and 238,000 in September, including sick and prisoners. Never again were the losses so high, not even in 1916 during the Battle of Verdun, nor in 1918 at the time of the final German offensives. The conscript classes of 1911 to 1913 – these were the classes that were serving with the colours in August 1914 – lost between 24 and 30 per cent of their numbers during the war.[28] The year 1915 also took a very high toll, notably during the *grignotages* (the attritional 'gnawing away') and the Champagne offensives. Other statistics reveal that 10 to 11 per cent of officers were put out of action (killed, wounded or missing) in August 1914 alone.

On the other hand, the German army suffered almost as badly. Its army corps were bled white and left behind up to two-thirds of their strength.

In the prestigious Guard Corps, for example, no more than 12,000 men remained out of 36,000.

* * *

Who was to blame? The responsibility seems to be shared by many people, and it is unclear which of them should be the first to be tried in the court of history – if, that is, someone or something ought to be put on trial at all. (As you can imagine, that would not have my support.)

Once the war had been unleashed, it was impossible to subdue. But since we find the death of the first fallen soldier just as shocking as the mass slaughter that followed, where should we draw the line? Above what level should the losses be reckoned to be unacceptable? It is precisely this dilemma that makes it imperative for a strong civil power constantly to assess the nation's interests and to decide what action to take. The civil power is responsible, using its own evidence and information obtained through all the channels at its disposal, for saying when the cost of victory is in danger of becoming greater than that of defeat. Yet nobody was prepared to consider this question in 1914.

Who, then, was to blame for the bloodshed? I shall mention the culprits in no particular order and without claiming to have compiled an exhaustive list.

Was the country to blame? Yes, at least because of its illusions. The overwhelming majority of the population no longer had any personal experience of war, and did as it was told by its leaders. It was fond of the army, yet detested military service, especially three whole years of it. It was ready to fight, yet rebelled against any discipline. It firmly believed it knew everything there was to know about the profession of arms, even though it had never learned anything. It was convinced that its righteous cause would be enough to ward off machine-gun bullets. It believed that French intelligence and dash would easily prevail over the ponderous Teutonic methods. In any case, it had been told that the great new international brotherhood of Socialism would avert the war by uniting the people of all nations in a common destiny. Jaurès for one was convinced that this would happen.

The politicians? They were certainly to blame, above all because they had never managed to agree on what we might call a concept of national defence. All of them, on both Right and Left, supported or denigrated the army for purely ideological motives, without stopping to think that they were thereby helping to pave the way for the coming catastrophes.[29] They split the officer corps into two hostile tribes – two political camps – and thereby undermined the cohesion of the corps as a whole.[30] An officer's chances of promotion might depend on which political party he supported, rather than on his own worth. The danger from Germany from obvious, yet the politicians' mental outlook in the face of that threat was childish. The offensive was the preserve of the Right, they claimed, while the defensive was equated with the Left. The defensive was Republican, and the offensive reactionary. If only life were that simple!

Should the Commander-in-Chief be blamed? Joffre bore a share of the responsibility, for although he did not encourage the glorification of the offensive, he failed to rein it in. Nor, as we saw in Chapter 2, did he ever state clearly – until after the event – that the offensive had 'requirements'.

What about the various theorists, stubbornly attached to their dogmas? They were undoubtedly responsible, particularly Foch, who fired up his listeners with enthusiasm for the offensive. Compared to Grandmaison, Foch exerted more influence and over a longer period of time. He sometimes failed to draw a line to prevent his words from being taken to extremes, and his thinking was slow to evolve in response to the realities of the war. Yet he grasped, perhaps before the others did, that it was essential to avoid the mistake of doing anything just for the sake of doing something. Besides, there was a confusing side to his personality: whenever he asserted something, he almost immediately added a qualifying statement in an opposite sense. As a result, it is often possible to find a statement from Foch supporting whatever argument you happen to favour. Foch, in his own way, was one of the ideologues of the war – in stark contrast to Joffre.[31]

The 'high command'? Yes, it was certainly to blame. Embroiled in its immature disputes, it proved unable to agree on a sensible course of action and it failed to focus enough on the soldiers' training. It produced lofty theories instead of taking solid, practical steps. A bit of fresh air was needed to blow away all the cobwebs in the barracks.

The officers further down the hierarchy? The primary responsibility for training lay with the colonels in command of regiments, but they only went through the motions of being involved. It was left to the subalterns and NCOs to do the actual business of repeating for the umpteenth time the exact same lesson that they themselves had learned many years before.

Throughout this period, the engineer in Joffre prevailed over Joffre the general. This might seem surprising, as it is usually assumed that the general dominated the engineer. Yet it is noticeable that Joffre stuck to the plan – the engineer's plan – even though another possible solution existed. This alternative involved entering Belgium between 15 and 20 August, in order to bypass the Ardennes and enter the easier terrain of the regions north of the Sambre and the Meuse. It would have been too early for the British army to take part in the advance, at least in the initial stages. But this alternative option had some key advantages: the problems imposed by the terrain were reduced, the earlier diplomatic constraint regarding Belgian neutrality no longer applied, and the German army began its advance only on the 18th. Such a manœuvre would have been truly stunning and is what Joffre the general could have decided to do, had he taken precedence over the engineer. As it was, Lanrezac, de Langle de Cary and Ruffey spent ten days or so idly waiting for the order to engage. Joffre has been accused by his critics of all sorts of rash actions, and yet he actually seems to have been meticulously cautious, doing his best to base his decisions only on reliable and cross-checked intelligence. The problem is that neither he nor his Intelligence Department knew what he should be looking for – or rather, he believed he knew full well what he was looking for, and that may have prevented him from looking elsewhere.

It is now obvious that Joffre's determination to go and seek battle was a mistake – at least on the left wing. This has, in fact, been clear ever since the immediate aftermath of the war. Joffre lacked two pieces of intelligence, which actually amounted to just one piece since they were so closely linked: the scale of the outflanking move that the Germans were making through Belgium, and the fact that they were using their reserve corps in the same way as active corps. But it would be wrong to hold this against a man who had used his intelligence to think carefully through the problem and who *believed* he had collected *all* the information he needed before making his decision. We should also note that the left wing remained on the defensive until Joffre reckoned he had enough information to remove any lingering doubts about the distribution of the German active corps. As for the operation on the right wing, it certainly helped to relieve the enemy pressure on the French left wing, despite its flawed execution. Lastly, we should note that Joffre never expressed any self-criticism.

In any case, did Joffre really did seek battle? He may have done so in Alsace and in Lorraine, but not in the north – in Belgium or Luxembourg – where he was actually content to await the German offensive before counter-attacking. This resulted in the opposing armies colliding on the Sambre and Meuse in what is known as an encounter-battle – and that type of battle is even more difficult to conduct than an offensive or defensive action, since it opens up the possibility of a whole range of surprises. The fact remains that the operational orders or the directives issued by GQG will not be remembered as models to be imitated. They were full of vagueness, omissions and mistakes, and hardly made the operation more efficient.

Needless to say, everyone who had a grievance with Joffre welcomed the setback. (Incidentally, it was a setback suffered not by Plan XVII itself, but by the operational plan or at least by what passed for an operational plan.) Among those who welcomed the setback were generals who had been dismissed, politicians, Joffre's opponents and competitors, mediocre men of all sorts, and there were plenty of them in an army whose officer corps was politicized and growing older. The paradox is that although Joffre was criticized for his supposed mania for the offensive, he in fact retreated for around ten days. Nevertheless, he did so in an orderly manner, with the intention of making possible a reorganization of his armies, and even as he fell back he was looking out for the opportunity for a fresh engagement.

Chapter 6

Joffre and Galliéni

This is one of those stories that start happily, only to end in tears. Neither of the two protagonists appears in a favourable light, although this is particularly true in the case of one of them. Their relationship turned toxic during the two years between 1914 and 1916, not simply because of the circumstances but also because of the deliberate actions of their cliques of supporters.

Galliéni

Galliéni was no second-rater. Conscious of his abilities, he could be rather scornful of the political world with which he felt little affinity, and he often had a superiority complex regarding his peers, whose careers had been very different and much less spectacular. Lyautey, who had served with him at Tonkin and on Madagascar, always claimed that six months of colonial service were more valuable than an entire career spent on the French mainland. This was unkind on Lyautey's comrades, but Galliéni both agreed with it and did not trouble to keep his opinion to himself. The 'mainlanders' were equally obsessed by the issue, and looked down on the 'colonials' as just a bunch of jovial clowns who had opted for an easy and exotic life.

Galliéni had served almost without a break in the colonies, including Indo-China, the Sudan and Madagascar, and was one of the men who forged the French colonial empire. He had much in common with the landed gentry of long ago: he laid down the law and imposed peace and prosperity without tolerating the slightest departure from what he considered to be his civilizing mission, in the sense in which that was understood at the time.

Strong, unbending and very independent, Galliéni was used to exercising command a long distance away from his superiors and from political supervision, which he regarded as more of a hindrance than a help in his successive posts. He gave free rein to his subordinates, whom he carefully picked, and quickly won their respect. He was esteemed throughout the French army, despite being reckoned a bit eccentric, but he often clashed with the Staff College, which he accused of being mentally blinkered, and this helps explain the avalanche of criticism he directed against GQG some years later.

Since Galliéni was away on his colonial campaigns, he avoided becoming embroiled in the political controversies that affected the army at that time. Although a Republican, he was rather moderate and greatly admired Gambetta. Compared with his fellows, he was less intent on revenge against Germany since his colonial career had given him a broader horizon.

Furthermore, he came from South-Western France, and through family connections (Gheusi) he was quite close even to Jaurès, even if the two of them
had opposing views on many military issues such as the use of the reserves.

Galliéni liked to dispense advice, and there was an offended *prima donna*
side to him, which grated with people. Often exasperated when his primacy
was not universally acknowledged on each and every occasion, he readily
retreated into contempt for the other party if he had failed to convince them.
After the Battle of the Marne, he gradually became convinced that he was
surrounded solely by rivals or incompetents, be they soldiers or politicians.[1]
Rightly or wrongly, he believed that he knew what had to be done and was
being prevented from doing it by Joffre, GQG, the government and parliament. In reality, he was also impeded by his own sickness and indecision, but
his sense of powerlessness continued to worsen right up until the end.

The story starts happily, with Joffre serving under Galliéni's orders on
Madagascar. He arrived on the large island on 1 March 1900 and left for Paris
in October 1901. He returned to France glowing with success, having earned
an exceptionally brilliant commendation from Galliéni and the stars of a
général de brigade. Having come back to the island in 1902, he sailed for
France for the final time in the spring of 1903. As well as being a general
officer, he was now a commander in the Order of the Legion of Honour. His
proudest achievement was fortifying the harbour of Diego Suarez. From
Galliéni he gained a further, particularly laudatory, testimonial of satisfaction,
a testimonial that was remembered and was brought up again some years
later.[2] Joffre's promotion to *général de brigade* had been on 12 October 1901,
and Galliéni wrote some private reports – at least three to the Minister of the
Colonies, to whom he was answerable – in order to advance the interests of
his *protégé*. Joffre was the right man![3] Without Galliéni's help, he would
certainly have become a general, but perhaps not so soon. Appointed when
just a few months over the age of 49, he was the youngest brigadier in the
French army.

The two men's careers did not cross again until 1910, when Joffre joined
the Supreme War Council, to which Galliéni had belonged since August
1908. Then, in 1911, as a result of the vacancy created by Michel's resignation, Joffre was appointed Chief of the General Staff and Commander-in-
Chief designate of the Armies of the North-East, with Galliéni's blessing and
possibly his support.[4] Galliéni had apparently been offered the post himself,
only to refuse it for two reasons: he had only two-and-a-half years left until
his period of active service came to an end, and he had urged Messimy to
dismiss Michel. At any rate, that was what Messimy stated in his memoirs.[5]

Whatever the truth may be about the events that led to Joffre's appointment, it remains most likely that Galliéni turned down the post. Nevertheless,
by helping one of his former subordinates – a colonial like himself – to secure
the responsibilities of the Commander-in-Chief, he could count on wielding

Joffre at his desk at GQG.

ench soldiers at rest. Over
00,000 of them lost their lives
a result of the war. Joffre
s reluctant to visit hospitals,
case it left him incapable of
dering further offensives.

French troops in a primitive trench in the early stages of the war.

By the time of the Battle of Verdun in 1916, the French infantry had been equipped with helmets and had more sophisticated defensive systems.

he French army relied on the famous 75mm gun at the start of the war, but suffered from its ortage of modern heavy artillery following the onset of trench warfare.

heavy artillery piece. This long-barrelled 120mm de Bange gun has special caterpillar tracks fitted its wheels to make it more mobile.

The Senate's Army Commission, 1916. Its president, Georges Clemenceau, is seated third from the left. Also present is one of Joffre' most tenacious critics, Paul Doumer (sitting o the far right, at the end of the table). Seated to the right of Clemencea are two members of th government: the Minis of War, General Pierre Roques (on the far left and the President of th Council of Ministers, Aristide Briand.

(*Below left*) Lieutenant-Colonel Emile Driant. Both soldier and a Right-wing politician, he had beer elected to the Chamber of Deputies in 1910 and fell at the start of the Battle of Verdun in February 1916. His warnings about inadequate defences at the front helped inflame relations between Joffre and Galliéni.

(*Below right*) Clemenceau with a group of British and French officers. He became President of the Council of Ministers in November 1917. He was fluent in English.

General Joseph Galliéni. One of France's foremost
colonial administrators, he initially fostered Joffre's
career, but later became a bitter and resentful enemy.

General Maurice Sarrail, probably
photographed in Salonika in late
1916. He and Joffre loathed each
other, but his Left-wing views meant
he had influential political support.

General Charles Lanrezac. He was removed from command
of the 5th Army on the eve of the Battle of the Marne. As
one of the most prominent of the dismissed generals, he
became a figurehead for Joffre's critics.

Joffre was accused of having disarmed Verdun's forts, but their usefulness has been exaggerated. This is Fort Douaumont, seen from the air on 19 May 1916.

Inside Fort Douaumont after its recapture by the French in October 1916. This casemate has been smashed open by a 420mm shell.

...offre on a visit to the ...erdun sector during ...e battle. On the right is ...eneral Philippe Pétain, ...e commander of the ...d Army, who was ...trusted with the ...efence.

Joffre decorates one of the heroes of the Battle of Verdun, General Maurice Balfourier, the commander of the 20th Corps.

Joffre as coalition commander. British, French, Belgian, Russian, Italian and Serbian representatives are all present at this Allied conference held at GQG, at Chantilly, in March 1916. On the far left of the front row are General Edouard de Castelnau and the Commander-in-Chief of the British Expeditionary Force, Sir Douglas Haig.

(*Below left*) Joffre (second from right) with the President of the Republic, Raymond Poincaré (far left)
(*Below right*) A train brings Joffre back from a visit to the Verdun sector in spring 1916. He is accompanied by two of his closest assistants: General Pellé (left) and General de Castelnau (centre)

some sort of moral authority over him by virtue of having placed him in his debt.[6] It might be thought astonishing that Galliéni and Joffre accepted such a situation. The only possible explanation is that they reckoned it would be transitory, and that they could foresee no clash likely to threaten their hitherto untroubled rapport. Besides, Joffre's candidacy offered such advantages in political terms (as we have seen in Chapter 1), that any other consideration was pushed to the background. Even his request to have General Castelnau as his assistant gave the political Right something it could regard as a compensation.

Life continued until the summer of 1914. The two men got along amicably despite being at odds over a handful of points, notably the appointment of certain generals. Galliéni favoured candidates (such as Gérard, another veteran of Tonkin and Madagascar) who were not necessarily Joffre's. Yet this was just the usual friction of everyday life – the background noise to a peaceful cohabitation that lacked any major clashes. When Joffre and Galliéni met, it was more often when they passed each other during their usual morning routine of horse-riding in the *Bois de Boulogne*, the wood on the western side of Paris, rather than in the course of their professional duties.

Since they were so different from each other, there was practically no chance of them meeting off-duty. No personal chemistry or affinity existed between them. Galliéni was cultured, a lover of literature, and made a point of 'bathing his brain' (as he put it) for at least an hour a day. He spoke German, Italian and English to various degrees of competence, and published several books about his colonial experiences. Joffre, on the other hand, gave the impression of being a boor, with no interest in anything outside his profession. He was dull and clumsy and incapable of holding a conversation of the sort adored by Parisian fine society, full of witty remarks, trivialities and the latest gossip. In contrast, Galliéni was brilliant and elegant. Poincaré was always impressed when he met him, and did not stint on his praise, as this brief extract shows:

> [Millerand] was accompanied by General Galliéni, whose height, slim and elegant appearance, and handsome military uniform [etc] … . I found him unchanged since I had last seen him: the same determined and penetrating gaze from behind his eternal binocle, the same methodical mind and sober, precise speech.[7]

Whereas Galliéni seduced people, the deadly serious Joffre surprised them. So the proconsul of Madagascar did not have much in common with the man who had become better known as the railway builder of Kayes than as the conqueror of Timbuktu. It is difficult to imagine men so starkly different, and yet the fortunes of military life had caused their paths to cross and was to turn them into antagonists.

They saw each other whenever the Supreme War Council met,[8] yet it was noted that Galliéni said little during these council meetings – he apparently did not utter a word during some of them.[9] Joffre in his memoirs was lavish in praising his former superior's performance during map exercises or in the autumn grand manœuvres. This was generous of him, but not necessarily accurate. The 1912 Grand Manœuvres, in which Galliéni was opposed to General Marion, did not show Galliéni in a particularly brilliant light, even if he managed to 'capture' his opponent. Indeed, the German military attaché reckoned he was just hesitant and indecisive. When Galliéni retired, the Supreme War Council assembled for a luncheon at which Joffre (who had hoped that his former superior's term of active duty would be extended), showered him with praise.[10]

Galliéni lost his wife to illness while he was in retirement at La Gabelle near Saint-Raphaël. Immediately afterwards, he was recalled to duty by Messimy right at the start of the war. He came and established himself at Paris on 2 August 1914, to take on the duties of *ad latus*.[11] He had, in fact, been chosen as Joffre's successor as Commander-in-Chief, should that become necessary. Joffre himself had requested this, and it was in keeping with his earlier wish for an extension to Galliéni's term of active duty.

Galliéni had therefore returned and had gone up a step in the process. But within weeks the first of the wartime causes for misunderstanding exploded. Galliéni really did seem to hope he could join Joffre at GQG. Naturally, Joffre refused. It is a bit surprising that Galliéni could have thought he would more or less share operational control. He was too well aware of military habits and customs to have thought for a single moment that he could be involved in the decision-making. He himself would never have tolerated sharing the least bit of his authority, either at Madagascar or elsewhere in his many, varied campaigns. A two-headed military staff has never been seen and probably never will. Galliéni, incidentally, did not mention the matter in either his memoirs or his diaries.

Messimy seems momentarily to have had the same idea of seeing the two men in partnership. He gave Galliéni an office at the Ministry of War to enable him to keep track of operations as far as was possible from the sparse information GQG was willing to share. On 14 August, Galliéni went to GQG, probably at the request of Messimy, who wanted to know more details. But Joffre barely saw him, sensing as he did that the *ad latus* would be an instrument for allowing politics to influence military operations, which was something he was set against at all costs. It is highly likely that, for the first time, Galliéni felt rather put out by his reception from his former subordinate.

As France's situation worsened during August – particularly after the 20th – the question of Paris arose. The Military Governor of the city, in command of its Entrenched Camp, was none other than General Michel who had been given this sinecure after his resignation in 1911. In wartime, the proclamation of a state of siege gave the Military Governor full civil and military powers. It is true that Paris was unlike other fortresses, since it was the seat of the executive and legislature. Nevertheless, the first and foremost duty of the Governor (whose role was clearly defined by the *Instructions on siege warfare* of 1909) was to put his fortress in a state of defence.

A plan for defending Paris existed and had been painstakingly refined during the previous years. But the city's Séré de Rivières forts had never been modernized and, to use a phrase of that era, had become 'bomb-magnets'. As for the older, detached forts of 1840, they had been turned into depots or magazines, even though plans existed to site some guns in them. But contrary to general belief, there was no longer any role for either of these two belts of forts, nor for the continuous inner ring of fortifications. Instead, the defence of Paris depended on 500 guns dispersed in exterior batteries, and on an outer defence line measuring about 200km in circumference and consisting of trenches, some concrete redoubts, and belts of wire (as yet this was not always barbed wire). Only after mobilization and the proclamation of the state of siege could all the battery positions be installed and the trenches dug. It was impossible to prepare the terrain beforehand in peacetime because of the obligation to respect private property, and as a result everything had to be done in a hurry.

The defence was entrusted to Territorial troops (four divisions and one brigade), although it was not until 15 August that they were at their posts. When the situation became worrying after the Battle of the Sambre, the Minister of War, Messimy, suddenly realised that Paris would come under threat within a matter of days. Yet still the work of putting the city in a state of defence dragged on. There were many reasons for this, and rather than going into the details we need simply to note that the unfortunate Michel was a convenient scapegoat. Since Messimy had no more respect for him now than he had in 1911, Michel once again lost his post following a stormy meeting. Messimy approached Galliéni, who accepted the vacancy and was appointed Military Governor of Paris on 26 August.

A second disagreement between Joffre and Galliéni soon occurred. When Galliéni took up the Military Governor's duties, he was under the Minister of War's orders and not Joffre's. In view of the paucity of resources he had available for defending Paris, he appealed to Messimy for help, but Messimy had no troops at his disposal unless he asked for them from the Commander-in-Chief. From the very outset, Galliéni requested as many as three active army corps, or six divisions, a total of slightly more than 100,000 men.[12] Yet he could hardly fail to be aware of the French army's overall active strength in 1914. It amounted to just forty-six active divisions. Demanding 16 per cent of France's best troops, merely for them to wait idly around Paris, was simply bizarre. Joffre was reluctant to comply, for he had no wish to immobilize forces when he had too few of them as it was. Galliéni's demand – which he had made as a condition for accepting his appointment – naturally calls into question the extent to which he understood his mission.

Galliéni was no revolutionary. After returning from the Sudan, he entered the Staff College in 1889 after a special exam and grew comfortable with the existing, conventional concepts with which he was familiar. After 1870, his military abilities were tested only against the indigenous bands he encountered during his colonial expeditions, and these were in an altogether different league from the German army. It is true that as Military Governor of Paris he had to implement someone else's defence plan, yet he made no changes to it. He also stuck to the constraints of the regulations that were in force: the *Instructions on fortress duties* and the *Instructions on siege warfare*. As late as February 1915, he was still complaining that the Germans were failing to play by the rules when it came to attacking fortresses. Joffre in his memoirs reproached him for failing to understand the problem posed by the defence of Paris and for the purely static nature of his notions, even if his dispositions complied with the very letter of the regulations.[13] Joffre himself had a different approach, for he wanted to defend Paris 'in the open country, with the field armies'.[14]

Galliéni was now busy at Paris trying, as the French armies retreated, to speed up the work of making the city's Entrenched Camp ready for defence. But he could do no more than try, for he ran into the same difficulties as his predecessor, who had actually worked harder and more effectively than Galliéni claimed. What Galliéni achieved in the period between 27 August and 6 September was much in line with what Michel had done, and no clearcut innovation or change of pace can be detected. Galliéni did only marginally better than Michel, and if the German armies had tried to storm Paris with a sudden and immediate attack around 4 or 5 September, they would have succeeded easily. Yet neither Galliéni nor his predecessor were to blame for this critical situation.

Meanwhile, Joffre tried to gain time by giving up ground, and prepared to return to the offensive as soon as he could. To make such an offensive possible, he began on 25 August to form a new army on his left wing (in due course it became the 6th Army). He did this by taking units from his right wing in one of the first examples of railways being used operationally to alter a strategic situation.

Galliéni still did not have his three active army corps. But on 2 September, Millerand (Messimy's replacement as Minister of War) wrote a letter putting the new 6th Army at the Military Governor's disposal. At the same time, Millerand granted a request Joffre had made the previous day for the Entrenched Camp of Paris to be placed under him in his capacity as

Commander-in-Chief.[15] This masterstroke seemed to content both Galliéni, who now had an army at his disposal, and Joffre, who absorbed the Entrenched Camp into his command, along with all the troops inside it.

Hence Galliéni had his field army, but he must have been taken aback to find himself subordinated to GQG. The Minister of War's letter of 2 September specified: 'The Entrenched Camp of Paris is to be placed under the orders of the Commander-in-Chief of the Group of Armies of the North-East under the conditions set out by Article 144 of the *Regulation on the handling of large units* and by Article 151 of the decree on fortress duties.' Galliéni was now well and truly under the Commander-in-Chief's orders, and no attempt to twist the wording or analyse the contents of Articles 144 and 151 could change that fact. (The two articles were just a reminder of the restrictions on the use of the garrison.)

From this moment, Galliéni had a double role. He commanded the Armies of Paris as well as a fortress – and no ordinary fortress for that matter. It was a difficult situation, especially as he was also in charge of the civil services and was almost wholly responsible for every aspect of daily life in the vast sprawl of Paris and its suburbs, which must have contained something in the region of 2.5 million inhabitants.

We should note an interesting point. In the wake of Galliéni's appointment and his subordination to Joffre, the two of them exchanged a considerable number of official letters, which were generally supplemented by unofficial ones. The latter are interesting because of what they reveal about the true nature of relations between the two men. Galliéni always began his unofficial letters with the salutation: 'My dear Joffre'. In the military, a polite salutation such as this is only ever used by a superior to his subordinate – this holds true both today and in the past. So Galliéni's use of this brief phrase is revealing, even if it was probably done unconsciously. It means that in his mind Galliéni was still on Madagascar and was once more Joffre's superior, and that explains a lot. As for Joffre, he used the salutation 'my dear comrade', which can be decoded as meaning: 'I consider you to be my equal.' Joffre would never have dared to write 'my dear Galliéni' – and yet he, if anyone, would have had the authority and justification to do so.

Battle of the Marne
Then came the Marne. Who won the battle? In 1914, Joffre was regarded as the victor, but doubts set in from 1920 and by the 1930s it was Galliéni who received the credit. The vigour with which his supporters sang his praises was exceptional even in that era, when moderation was unknown. The pomposity of their language exceeded all bounds, as a few lines will show:

By thrusting his sword into the momentarily exposed flank of von Kluck's Germans, Galliéni – breaking the theoretical rules of war and the principles taught in military academies – triumphed over uncertainty when it was about to lose everything, and tipped the scales of victory as they hung in the balance.[16]

The arguments between Galliéni's and Joffre's supporters have continued right down to the present time, even if nowadays they tend to incline increasingly in Joffre's favour.

We have two ways of trying to understand what happened while this battle was being fought. The first is the traditional one of going through the archives and trying to work out who did what: the orders and reports that people wrote, the telephone calls they exchanged, the messages they sent and received, and the meetings they held. This is a slow and systematic method. It is indispensable in some respects, yet we are bound to be misled if we rely on it alone. If we are to get anywhere near the truth, we must take into account all the many elements that form the background to the battle. This is why we need the second method, which consists of using these background influences to shed light on our subject and thereby compensate for the limitations of a history that is based solely on dry, factual evidence. It then becomes possible to see things from a broader and clearer perspective, correcting mistakes and contradictions. So let's now examine some of these background factors.

We'll start with the personalities of the key decision-makers. Galliéni was hyperactive and, what's more, hyper-reactive: he was one of those men who act and react instantly. Joffre was much calmer, a man of few words who found chatting repugnant. He took plenty of time to make decisions, never rushing but turning all the facts of a problem over and over in his mind before issuing orders. His decision-making process was a very modern one, with his officers freely giving their opinions about operations and often disagreeing with each other. Many eyewitnesses have described Joffre sitting astride a chair, not saying a word himself yet listening to the officers of his personal staff and of the Operations Department. Once a decision had been taken about what was to be done, however, the entire staff adopted it as its own. Joffre's well-known abhorrence of using the telephone was a result of his determination not to be harassed by someone impatient to get his way, or someone who wanted to tip him into replying off-the-cuff without having had a chance to consider the matter. Joffre rarely made a decision without having studied a written document. He always took a broad view of the situation, but once he had made up his mind he never changed it.

Joffre and Galliéni had distinctly different responsibilities. The staff of the Entrenched Camp of Paris was concerned only with Paris up to the exterior limits of the camp (a radius of about 30km from the Eiffel Tower). Galliéni was responsible, to a certain extent, for the fate of Paris, but it was the fate of France that Joffre had in his hands. This is what Joffre meant when he said after the war that he did not know who had won the Battle of the Marne, but

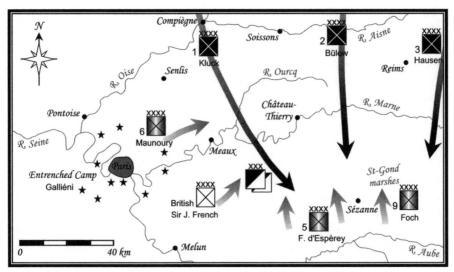

Battle of the Marne, beginning of September 1914.

that he knew full well who would have been blamed for losing it.[17] Galliéni's mission was simply to remove the enemy from the neighbourhood of Paris, but Joffre had to drive them right back to the frontiers and inflict a defeat on them. On 5 September, on the very eve of the battle, Joffre sent a personal note to the Minister of War: 'The struggle that is about to commence might have a decisive outcome, but it might also have the gravest consequences for the country should it end in failure. In order to gain the victory, I am resolved to commit all our forces to the full, without holding any back.' It was Joffre, not Galliéni, who wrote this note. Indeed, Joffre was the only person who could have written it, because of the nature of his responsibilities.

Five armies – soon to be six and then seven – were arrayed along the immense front that stretched from Verdun to Pontoise and even further west, as far as Rouen. These armies had at least as hard a fight as the one that raged in front of Paris. But Galliéni knew nothing of these other fights. Indeed, he could know nothing of them, because he was given little or no information about them and because there was no reason for him to be kept informed about them.

The role that Paris played in the defence of France was overestimated in both 1870 and 1914. In 1870, the Government of National Defence remained at Paris, while sending a delegation under Gambetta to Tours and then Bordeaux. The French spent the rest of the 1870 war trying to break the siege of Paris. They failed to realize that the besieged city, cut off as it was from all communications with the provinces, could no longer fulfil its role as the capital and seat of the government. It had ceased to have any military value and retained only symbolic importance.

In 1914, the Germans were expected to act in exactly the same way as before and lay siege to Paris (unless they attempted a bold, improvised assault on it). But in contrast to what had happened in 1870, the French government took the more sensible step of leaving Paris directly for Bordeaux on 2 September. This meant that should the capital fall, it would have far fewer immediate, practical consequences, regardless of however much symbolism the city retained.[18]

The whole of the subsequent controversy is ultimately based on a single question. On 4 September, did Galliéni commit the 6th Army on his own initiative along the north bank of the Marne towards the Ourcq river, or was it Joffre who initiated the manœuvre? If there was any difference at all between the moments when the two men made up their minds, then it was a matter of just a few hours. The argument about this point soon became mired in controversy, with all the contenders basing their case on pieces of written evidence that were either incomplete, erroneous or non-existent, and on telephone conversations between the chiefs-of-staff and the generals – conversations that either nobody else heard or everyone forgot.[19] Some commentators have even conjured up mysterious documents that were supposedly amended or spirited away from the archives before the end of the war, yet nobody has ever managed to prove that this really happened. Captain Lyet has written one of the best analyses of the problem, and his solidly-based arguments are convincing. He concludes that it was Joffre who was the first to reach the decision (though by just a few hours), and that posterity should therefore regard him as the victor. It would take far too long to go through the many arguments, but you can find them in Lyet's book, although unfortunately it is now fairly difficult to obtain a copy.[20]

Yet is it really necessary to dissect Joffre and Galliéni's actions in this way? The answer is no, and there are several reasons why this is the case. To start with, it was Joffre who was in command and not Galliéni. During those first days of September, nothing that happened within the Army Zone was done without the Commander-in-Chief giving either his formal approval or at the very least his tacit agreement. (The Army Zone also included Paris after 29 August.) No one was more jealous of his authority than Joffre. No army ever has more than one commander: there is no place for any other decision-maker however exalted in status. Even though Galliéni knew this full well, he could not accept it. Yet if the roles had been reversed, he would surely have been more imperious with Joffre than the latter was with him. Galliéni would never have tolerated a rival in any of his various colonial posts. Anyone unwise enough to show the least desire for independence would immediately have been sent back to France by the first boat.

It might be objected that Galliéni at least forced Joffre's hand. In fact, even this is unlikely. Joffre would never have risked launching an attack if he had not already loaded the odds as far as possible in his favour, and in particular if he had not had the green light from the 5th Army. Galliéni claimed, through the writings of his circle, that he had to persuade Joffre several times to attack north of the Marne. But Galliéni was simply mistaking Joffre's prudence for procrastination. Lieutenant-Colonel Bugnet has this to say on the matter: 'Joffre listened to his subordinate's views, was slightly influenced by them, weighed up his arguments, saw them in their wider context, as he alone was in a position to do, took them into account, and decided to a certain extent to follow them.'[21] This is a perceptive assessment – and we should particularly note the use of the word 'subordinate'.

Joffre had to ponder whether the 5th Army was capable of taking the offensive, and consider what it meant for Foch who was fighting in the Saint-Gond marshes and clinging desperately to the ground he held. But Galliéni was unaware of this. Franchet d'Esperey, who had just taken over command of the 5th Army from Lanrezac in awkward circumstances, answered Joffre's query by informing him that he would be ready to resume the fight on 6 September. This was what tipped the balance in favour of the decision to attack. Hence Franchet d'Esperey's role at the start of the Battle of the Marne was at least as important as Galliéni's.

Joffre confessed afterwards that he regretted not having unleashed the counter-offensive a day later, on 7 September, as had initially been planned. This would have given the Germans time to become more tangled up in the trap.[22] The various reasons that induced Joffre to give the green light for the 6th rather than the 7th must have included the insistent pressure from Galliéni and his decision (in line with GQG's wishes) to push the 6th Army eastwards on the 5th.[23] In fact, Joffre's diehard supporters have even claimed that Galliéni's impatience nearly caused the offensive to fail, and it is true that Maunoury experienced some difficult moments on 8, 9 and 10 September.

Besides, the Marne was just the most spectacular part of a gigantic battle that flared up between Verdun and Paris. Never before in military history had a battle on such a scale been conducted by a single staff.[24] The fighting on the Ourcq was certainly important, but what happened elsewhere was just as crucial. The Battle of the Marne was above all a Battle of France, and in this battle it was Joffre – not Galliéni – who held the keys to victory. The Germans retreated not solely because they were defeated on the Ourcq, even if that was where their misfortunes began.[25] The prime reason why they retreated was that at every point they were either beaten or left with no option except to fall back. They retreated because they were as exhausted as their opponents, because their lines of communication were dangerously over-stretched, because their losses had greatly reduced the combat value of units that had become mere shadows of their former selves. It was because of all these reasons, and similar ones, that the arrows on the map now faced the other direction – and this owed nothing to Galliéni, even if he did strive for victory at the particular point where he was posted.

The role that Galliéni did fulfil was that of a first-rate fortress commander who interpreted his mission in a broad sense. He certainly grasped the south-eastward shift in the direction of the German armies as quickly as Joffre – or even a bit faster,[26] since he was closer to where it was happening. He also reinforced the 6th Army to the extent that he was able to do so. (The component units of this army had assembled, but had previously taken a hard pounding during the fighting in Eastern France.) Galliéni should of course be applauded for this, even if we note in passing that most generals would have done the same in his position.

It is clear from his memoirs that Galliéni found this period a trial, even though it lasted only around ten days. Praising his own actions, he claimed all the credit for the battle's outcome. I lack enough space to quote everything here, but you'll see what I mean if you read Galliéni's memoirs for yourself.[27] Not only did he find fault with every one of Joffre's decisions, he even twisted his words. I dread to think what Galliéni's supporters would have said and written, if Joffre's memoirs had been equally critical of their own idol.

In contrast, nowhere did Galliéni indicate that he had been under Joffre's orders for several days.[28] Instead, he implied that he was the Commander-in-Chief's partner. His desire to gloss over his subordination is a crucial point in our efforts to understand what happened. If Galliéni was not under Joffre's orders, then everything that was decided and ordered, everything that happened, stemmed solely from his incomparable initiatives, his authority and his talent. He, therefore, was the victor of the Marne and – to borrow a term used in mathematics to conclude a line of reasoning – QED. (*Quod erat demonstrandum* is a Latin phrase meaning 'that's what had to be demonstrated'). QED is precisely what I feel the urge to scribble at the end of Galliéni's memoirs when I finish reading them. Messimy, who had no illusions about Joffre, nonetheless quoted Pierrefeu's comment on Galliéni: 'The man of the miracle could not trouble himself with considerations of seniority.'[29] That puts it in a nutshell: Galliéni the miracle-worker!

Further proof can be found in what Gheusi has written. This makes it clear that Galliéni's coterie of relatives regarded it as the gospel truth that he was not subordinated to Joffre:

> Galliéni, acting on his own initiative and using his authority as Governor, was able to order Maunoury's army to take the offensive, and thereby forced the hand of the Commander-in-Chief, who was set on retreating. But the public did not immediately realize this, since it mistakenly thought that ... Galliéni and the forces in the Entrenched Camp were under the Commander-in-Chief's orders.[30]

This was a total, wishful misunderstanding of what actually happened, and there was nothing innocent about it. The same approach was taken by such men as Percin, Regnault and Legros in their desire for revenge. Galliéni in his heart was as sceptical about Joffre's military competence as these generals had been (or as sceptical as they later became). How could this rough-hewn and unrefined sapper have won the Battle of the Marne, with the assistance of a staff composed of men whom Galliéni regarded as incompetent simply by virtue of the fact that they were qualified staff officers? The fact that Joffre had been Galliéni's subordinate in the past added to the credibility of the opinions that were attributed to the Military Governor of Paris, since it was assumed that Galliéni knew him well. It was at this time that the two men's relationship really turned sour, and the situation was poisoned by their personal staffs and political hangers-on, who deliberately rubbed salt into open wounds.

The fact that Galliéni wrote letters directly to the Minister of War is further evidence that he did not regard himself as the Commander-in-Chief's subordinate. The correspondence irritated and worried Joffre, who asked for it to stop. The problem had begun on 7 September, when Galliéni wrote to the Minister to inform him about the fighting in progress and at the same time gave his version of recent events. Here is an example of what he wrote: 'In the absence of any clear-cut instructions from GQG, I directed this [6th] Army forward to the east, with the Ourcq as its general objective.'[31] Joffre learned what was happening and notified the Minister of War on the 8th: 'The Military Governor of Paris is under my orders and should not be corresponding with the government.'[32] This did not stop Galliéni from continuing to keep the Minister informed about the operations under the pretext that it was 'in a personal and confidential capacity', though the distinction was mere hair-splitting.[33] Rightly or wrongly, the government showed great indulgence to Galliéni and tolerated behaviour that it refused to allow the other generals.

Galliéni's civil cabinet set out to 'break' Joffre, with Doumer taking the lead in these efforts. Poincaré recorded in his memoirs something that Joffre told him in a conversation. According to Joffre, Doumer had informed Foch: 'If I become Minister of War, I'll remove Joffre on the grounds of incompetence and appoint Galliéni as Commander-in-Chief.'[34] Of course, Joffre had immediately heard about this, and he had not forgotten that Doumer as a senator had already tried to ditch him before the war. As for Gheusi, who was thoroughly at home in the Chamber of Deputies, he championed Galliéni immoderately and spent his whole life trumpeting his idol's merits.

Since Joffre had been covered in glory by the victory of the Marne, his camp focused more on defending him than on attacking others. This magnanimous attitude was in keeping with what was expected from a victor, though he did not overdo it. Tardieu in particular took it upon himself to defend his commander's interests. (He was a well-known member of parliament and a reservist officer who served at GQG with the rank of captain after being mobilized.)

On 10 October 1914, Joffre belatedly sent a letter to his 'dear comrade' Galliéni, thanking him for the reinforcements made available from the Entrenched Camp of Paris during the Battle of the Marne. He closed with a friendly and informal expression, by sending 'his faithful and devoted wishes'. This was an astonishing letter, for Joffre could hardly have paid greater or deeper homage. He was practically asking for Galliéni to continue treating him as an irresponsible underling. Perhaps Joffre was developing a complex?

Yet Joffre could also be petty. He waited a full year, until 25 September 1915, before granting Galliéni a citation in army orders for what he had done during the Battle of the Marne – and Joffre was probably prompted to do so by Millerand, who was still the Minister of War. Citations, it should be noted, are awarded by a superior to his subordinate and never the other way round – which is, of course, fortunate! – and the person awarding the citation and the one receiving it are perfectly aware of how they stand in relation to each other in the hierarchy. The contents of Galliéni's citation are completely accurate and yet strangely lacking in warmth: Joffre was going no further than what he felt obliged to say. Galliéni pointed out in his memoirs that he himself had congratulated his subordinate in an altogether different way on Madagascar. That's true enough, but the question that has to be asked is why Galliéni accepted the citation, against advice to the contrary, if he believed he was not under Joffre's orders.

Furthermore, GQG published a confidential document about the Battle of the Marne, which contained no mention of Maunoury's army being formed, nor of the action taken by the Entrenched Camp of Paris and its commander, Galliéni. This may not have been distorting the facts, but was certainly concealing some of them. It clearly shows how the initial arguments were starting to escalate.

In closing our consideration of the Marne, let's quote a man who took an objective view of the issue. When Foch was asked if it was Joffre who had won the battle, he replied:

> Of course, it was his doing. He had made the preparations and he strove to bring it about. ... The Battle of the Marne was definitely a great victory. ... Joffre was the man who was needed.[35]

When asked 'And Galliéni?' Foch replied:

> Galliéni? He said that he thought the moment had come. While Joffre accepted his arguments, he nevertheless took the decision himself.

Spears (whom we have already met) offers another point of view.[36] Interestingly, Spears was even more vigorously outspoken than Joffre's supporters, despite the fact that as a Briton he was unlikely to take any side in French disputes, or at least not in these ones. This is what he wrote: 'General Galliéni in his book (which unfortunately from every point of view he was unable to revise) gives himself, in his anxiety to prove that he was the instigator of the manœuvre of the Marne, a far less fine role than he actually performed.' A bit further on, Spears calls Galliéni's claim 'inadmissible'.

How do you solve a problem like Galliéni?

Following the German retreat, the 6th Army soon reverted to Joffre's direct command, and so Galliéni had nothing to keep him distracted and prevented from dwelling on his own problems. He was left once more with just his Territorials and the Entrenched Camp, where much work still had to be done. On 18 September, shortly after the end of the Battle of the Marne, he wrote to the Minister of War (who was still at Bordeaux), repeating the demands he had made before the recent crisis.[37] He adopted the idea that the number of men garrisoning a fortress should equal the length in metres of the perimeter that had to be defended. This ratio had been generally accepted by staff officers for the past forty years, and for once their figures favoured his line of argument. It soon provides an impressive total, for after a quick calculation Galliéni asked Millerand for as many as ten divisions. (Eight of them were for the three regions of the Entrenched Camp, and the other two for gaps where the fortifications had progressed no further than the drawing board.) Yet these ten divisions, as Galliéni himself explained, were merely for the sedentary garrison. For good measure, he immediately added that Paris should also have a mobile defence force 'so it would be possible to delay an investing army'.[38] This force had to consist of at least three active army corps or six divisions (this was the same number as he had wanted before the Marne). In all, he was demanding more than 250,000 men. That was a lot, and obviously Joffre lacked enough troops to comply with even a fraction of such a demand. Millerand apparently did not even raise the matter with the Commander-in-Chief.

Galliéni complained in his same letter of 18 September: 'Paris is currently treated too much as a bottomless pool of resources, from which those elements most essential for defending it in the event of an enemy attack are gradually being removed.' You can guess who was doing the removing. On 18 October, the Minister of War replied from Bordeaux, going point by point through the long list of demands that Galliéni had appended to his letter. He gave him no reinforcements and explained: 'It will be up to the Commander-in-Chief, who by necessity has all the army corps at his disposal at the present time, to take into account the circumstances and the overall progress of operations in planning how the field armies are to cooperate with the garrison of Paris in defence of the fortress.' In short, Galliéni got nowhere.

The whole business seems rather strange, but can be readily understood if Galliéni was secretly intending to play an independent role in the conduct of operations. His demands included equipment that field armies would find essential, and this is a crucial point since the Territorial divisions and brigades that constituted the garrison of the Entrenched Camp of Paris were sedentary units. Since they were forbidden to go more than roughly one day's march (20–30km) beyond the limits of the Camp, they lacked the first-line transport needed to keep them supplied. Their very composition meant that they were incapable of operating far from their base or of providing for their logistics in the field.

On the other hand, Galliéni would be able to take part in the battle if he had under his control the total of sixteen divisions he had demanded. This was the equivalent of eight army corps or about two armies. He would remain under the Minister of War's orders, who would be easier than GQG for him to manipulate. The front was only 80km from Paris and Galliéni would have the Entrenched Camp as a solid base behind him. Ultimately, he wanted an operational army, for that would give him the means to fight his war and play his part.[39] Gheusi mentioned a dinner at which Galliéni was insistent on his desire to form 'an army of manœuvre, as only this could bring the campaign to a close.'[40] Poincaré recorded a similar remark when he reached Paris on 7 October during a visit from Bordeaux (this was three weeks after Galliéni had sent his letter of 18 September). Poincaré was greeted, as was usual, by Galliéni, who told him during the ensuing conversation that he reckoned the front was too extended for a single command. Poincaré added: 'He seemed to want two distinct armies to be formed, one of which would be placed under his orders.'[41]

Does this demonstrate a deep-rooted desire on Galliéni's part to return to the centre-stage and take the place of 'dear Joffre'? Towards the end of 1914 and until the start of the following year, members of the Army Commissions in both the Senate (notably including Doumer) and the Chamber of Deputies vainly demanded the creation of an 'army of manœuvre' using troops from the depots. Naturally, a general would have been needed to command it.

On 24 September 1914, Joffre wrote and asked Millerand to replace his *ad latus*, Galliéni, with Foch. The latter, Joffre stated, 'has demonstrated beyond any doubt that he is superior in terms of his character and military concepts'.[42] Joffre added that he would 'have him at his side', which was in sharp contrast to what had happened with Galliéni. Millerand and the government accepted, on condition that the decision remained confidential until the operations that were in progress at that time came to an end. In the event, the decision was never confirmed, and it is unclear if Galliéni was even informed about it.

In another letter to the Minister of War, Joffre set out his views about the defence of Paris. He was responding to a letter from Galliéni demanding Territorial units for completing the defensive works. This time, Joffre expressly named Galliéni and gave him a real thrashing. See what you think of it:

> None of the reasons given by General Galliéni seems worthy of atten-
> tion. .... The stronger our line of battle is, the less we have to fear from
> the hypothetical dangers envisaged by the Governor of Paris. .... Every-
> one's post is in action. If the general's needs have changed, he should
> inform me of it and I would do what is necessary to give him satisfaction.

The tone of Joffre's letter is exceptionally dry and unusually vigorous. Some unknown incident – perhaps the first disputes about the Marne – had prob-ably caused this increase of tension between the two men.

On 18 January 1915, Galliéni wrote yet again to Millerand and repeated his complaints: 'It is incumbent upon me to draw your attention once more to the weakness of the Paris garrison.'[43] There is a sense of weariness peeping through. Time was passing and nothing – still nothing – was being done. Galliéni was always well informed about the war, about GQG and about the world of politics, and he brooded over his grievances, which fill page after page of his diary. He was in poor health. He had long been suffering from his prostate, and as his illness worsened he was often obliged to take to his bed. He found it difficult to sleep. His progressive physical deterioration deepened his pessimism, and hardly encouraged him to make more balanced judge-ments about the military and civilian members of his entourage.

What was to be done with Galliéni? He was an immensely popular figure, who was dubbed the 'Saviour of Paris', even though the title would actually have been more appropriate for Joffre. (Despite this, Joffre was not passed over during the round of congratulations that followed the Marne.) Various solutions to the problem of Galliéni were examined, yet none of them came to anything. He was considered for the embassy in Rome. Joffre was asked to find him a post, and said that he was prepared to give him an army command, yet the one he had in mind was the Army of Alsace, which did not in fact exist. Joffre took the opportunity to point out to the President of the Republic that there was no longer any military justification for keeping the Territorial divisions at Paris under Galliéni's orders. This was perfectly true, but raised the issue of how Galliéni's command could be preserved if he was not given any troops.

The end of 1914 and the following year were punctuated by questions about the Military Governor of Paris and his future. Galliéni was clearly the government's problem as much as GQG's. At the start of 1915, the best suggestion that Joffre could think of was the command of the 6th Army, and Galliéni turned that down. Other ideas included sending him to the East, or giving him command of a large Army of the Interior, but nothing happened.

Meanwhile, another dispute was impending. This time, it concerned mili-tary operations. Joffre was keen to block any attempt that the Germans might make to launch a renewed offensive towards Paris, and he therefore asked for a series of positions to be prepared to the north and north-east of the capital. Consisting of trenches and battery emplacements, these positions were not intended to be occupied on a permanent basis, but simply to be defended by the field armies if that became necessary. It was Galliéni and his Territorials who were given the work that GQG wanted done, and unsurprisingly he reckoned that these constructions were an enhancement of the Entrenched Camp's defences. The creation of this defence line, known as the Thérain-Authonne Line, was begun in September 1914 and resulted in a sweet-and-sour correspondence between the staffs. The letters are too long to be quoted here, and we simply need to note that the Minister of War's response was to sit on the fence.

The Entrenched Camp was turned into a sort of training centre for units destined for the front. They stayed in the Camp for unfixed periods of time, and Galliéni received divisions of almost raw Territorials, which he sent off again to the front when requested. This disorganized the work on the defences, but Galliéni persevered in the face of all the obstacles with the help of civilian workers. In 1915, he created three more defence lines. The first ran from east to west between the Epte and Ourcq rivers, and the second from Lizy-sur-Ourcq to Melun. In the summer and autumn, he used the third to seal off the Forest of Sénart to the south-east of the capital between the Seine and the Yerres.

Galliéni likewise proposed to the Minister of War that a further defence line should be built, linking the upper Seine at Melun to the Loire near Briare. Joffre was consulted, but rejected the idea on 15 July 1915.[44] 'It is not necessary to carry out the construction of large-scale works', he stated, asking that the available manpower be allocated instead to the front for digging second-line positions.[45] If Galliéni's defence line had been constructed, it would have completed the perimeter right around Paris, forming an immense redoubt similar to the one that was later planned to seal off Brittany in 1940. GQG regarded all these works with a jaundiced eye: it would have preferred the existing defences to be maintained, rather than see new positions constantly being created and then abandoned once they were finished.

When Viviani's enfeebled ministry fell in the autumn of 1915, Briand took the helm and appointed a soldier – Galliéni – as his Minister of War. Before Viviani left office, he put a quick question to Joffre in Poincaré's presence: 'If we appointed a soldier, whom would you suggest?'

'Dubail', was Joffre's answer.

'What about Galliéni?' added Viviani.

Joffre thought for a moment and then without hesitation replied: 'Yes.'[46]

Thus Galliéni became Minister of War. He wrote to the Commander-in-Chief and conveyed the impression that he had felt almost morally obliged to accept. Throughout his diary, he had been expressing a desire to seek only peace and quiet. But how could he turn down a summons like this, which would enable him to regain the pre-eminence he had lost in 1911? It was a risky move for Briand and the Cabinet, who knew something of the rivalry between the two men. Yet Joffre and Galliéni's disagreements had been concealed long enough for the two of them to unite – initially at least – against their common foes of politics and politicians.

When Galliéni drafted the passage about the Ministry of War in Briand's inauguration speech as President of the Council of Ministers, he made a point of extolling the Commander-in-Chief's merits and praised his 'skill'. Both Joffre and Galliéni tried to support each other and put on an outward show of unanimity. Unfortunately, trouble did not take long to appear. Galliéni was unable to tolerate remaining a mere figurehead minister for any longer than Joffre could stand giving up some of what he considered to be his prerogatives. They themselves were careful never to undermine each other officially, but their close supporters deliberately sought to maintain and fan the quarrel by seizing on rumours and minor comments.

A plan for reorganizing the high command had existed for several months. The need for it had arisen as a result of the way the war was developing, particularly its extension to the Middle East and, with the Dardanelles campaign, to Turkey. Several contrasting solutions to the problem were considered, for the politicians wanted to take the opportunity to regain control over the conduct of the war. If Joffre's command was moved up one level, it would be possible to appoint a chief-of-staff entrusted with the Armies of the North-East. This might even enable Joffre to be removed from the scene, along with – as Galliéni put it with his usual tact – 'his gang: Renouard, Gamelin, Bayle'.[47] Galliéni, of course, was asked for his opinion, and it was part of his role as Minister of War to draft the decree. He took a long time to reply and did not automatically favour Joffre being given the new post on leaving his old one.

The head of Galliéni's military cabinet, Boucabeille (who had served under him at Tonkin), examined the question and concluded that command should be unified in the hands of the Minister of War.[48] Briand disagreed and pointed out that in his view it would be difficult for the Minister to answer questions in the Chamber of Deputies while at the same time preparing the operations. Galliéni decided to accept Briand's decision – 'very gracefully' according to Poincaré. If Galliéni had managed to convince the politicians, he would have wielded full power not just over the administrative aspects of war, but over the actual military operations as well.

A decree appointing Joffre Commander-in-Chief of the French Armies was finally signed on 2 December 1915. Nevertheless, he was clearly aware of the threat that hung over his command, and had no intention of giving up his authority over the Armies of the North-East. On 4 December, an article was published in *Le Petit Parisien*, which for some reason had been passed by the censor. It bluntly stated: 'Direct responsibility for the French front ... is to be entrusted to a new military figure.' This deputy was nearly appointed by decree, which would have left Joffre unable to do anything about it, as it would have been a formal decision by the government. In the event, he had a narrow escape, for the deputy was Castelnau and was appointed to the post by an ordinary 'letter of service'.[49] Yet GQG was naturally convinced that Galliéni lay behind these machinations.

The end of 1915 was a difficult time. The war was dragging on and Joffre's offensives had failed – this was the period of the *grignotages*, the attritional 'gnawing away'. The backbenchers in parliament were worked up about the generalissimo. He for his part was exasperated by the attacks made on him and reckoned that Galliéni, whose health was deteriorating inexorably, was doing hardly anything to defend him. Galliéni was caught between the two sides and seemed to enjoy the political struggles, despite all his protests to the contrary.

*   *   *

Verdun became the next major cause of disagreemement between Galliéni and Joffre. Some officers – they were often reservists – contacted friends who were in politics to alert them to what they saw as GQG's mistakes or failings. These officers wrote not just from Verdun, though for obvious reasons it was Verdun that subsequently drew all the attention. The letters came from all along the front, and drew the attention of politicians – they were always sent to politicians – to such-and-such a sector that the high command had supposedly neglected.[50]

One of these officers was Lieutenant-Colonel Driant, whom we have already met.[51] A graduate from the officer-training school at Saint-Cyr, he was now on the reserve. As the Deputy representing the Meurthe-et-Moselle, he was well-connected politically, especially in the Army Commission (to which he himself belonged) in the Chamber of Deputies. Driant warned Briand that the defences in the Meurthe, Toul and Verdun sector were most inadequate. Trenches, for example, were either too shallow or did not exist at all. Belts of barbed wire were not maintained and there were too few defence lines for defence-in-depth.

Briand sent Driant to see Galliéni, the Minister of War. Galliéni took up his pen and sent Joffre a ministerial letter in which he pointed out: 'Any breakthrough that the enemy achieves under these conditions would call into question not merely your own liability, but that of the entire government.'[52] Joffre felt that he had been slapped – as he himself admitted, though he did not put it quite so bluntly as that – and flew into one of those unforgettable rages that caused GQG to quake. He replied to Galliéni with a myriad of details, quoting orders that had been issued some months previously, and closed his letter as follows: 'But since these concerns stem from reports drawing your attention to flaws in the defensive preparations, I ask you to send me these reports and let me know who wrote them.' Joffre was being over-confident. Unluckily for him, Verdun happened to be exactly where the Germans attacked a few weeks later. As a result, Galliéni was able to portray himself as a clear-sighted man who had realized the weaknesses of the front better than the Commander-in-Chief.

The letter that Joffre had written in answer to Galliéni had pressed him to be an informer – and what's more, to inform on politicians. Obviously, Galliéni did not comply. Instead, he sent Joffre a soothing letter to try and resolve the issue, specifying that the government 'has complete confidence in you'. This was a big retreat from his initial allegation. Yet Galliéni risked seeing Verdun rebound against him as a result of an order he had issued in the first days of December 1915. He had directed that staff officers were to spend time commanding troops, while regimental officers were to gain experience on the staff.[53] GQG spread a rumour that the ensuing turnover of personnel had disorganized General Herr's staff at Verdun, which explained its flawed response to the German offensive. Naturally enough, Galliéni felt he was being targetted.

The atmosphere turned bitter and each side hardened its stance more and more. Joffre's enemies were after his blood and wanted to eject him as quickly as possible. Galliéni, who was tired and increasingly gripped by illness, failed to defend the generalissimo vigorously during the stormy sessions in the Chamber of Deputies. In January 1916, Joffre was relentlessly 'chewed up' by Clemenceau, by Abel Ferry (who bluntly declared that Joffre 'had no military talent') and by Accambray, who were sometimes to be found in the Chamber and sometimes at the front.[54] Galliéni – rightly or wrongly, or perhaps quite simply out of weariness – either did not reply or else did so feebly. The most acerbic attacks in the Chamber's Army Commission came from Accambray and from old General Pédoya. Joffre's supporters were limited to the venerable Freycinet, Briand, Doumergue as always, and to an extent Tardieu, as well as the loyal men of *La Dépêche du Midi* (a regional newspaper for South-Western France) – along with some members of the government who were too timid to go through with dumping the generalissimo, which was what they really wanted to do. Joffre and Galliéni's disagreements continued to grow during the four months from the start of November 1915 to the end of February 1916, and politicians eagerly sought to exploit the gaping breach between the two men so they could use Galliéni in their efforts to rid themselves of Joffre.

The final act was imminent and it came during the meeting of the Council of Ministers on 7 March 1916. On that day, Galliéni, who had made up his mind to leave the government so he could have treatment for his illness, pulled a note from his briefcase and began to read it out. It was an indictment of GQG and its chief, although Joffre as usual was never mentioned by name.

I will not quote the whole text, which readers can find in another of Gheusi's books if they are interested.[55] Galliéni began with several technical remarks about the way the war was being waged and the need to restore the civil power's prerogatives over the military. Many of these points were justified and relevant. It was high time to clarify the respective roles of the civil and military powers, and in particular to reduce the authority that GQG had appropriated when it had taken over areas neglected by parliament. The war could no longer be conducted from Chantilly alone.

In contrast, when Galliéni turned to anything related to military operations – an area that in principle lay outside his remit as Minister of War – he acted as if he was making the case for the prosecution. This is an extract from what he said:

> We must not hesitate to take punitive action when – as has been the case with Verdun – the attitude of some men proves that they have failed either to understand the present war, or to adapt to the demands of the wholly unprecedented events that have occurred during the last eighteen months. ... It cannot be accepted that France should again be exposed to the perils of a hazardous affair like the one that has just unfolded on the *Hauts-de-Meuse* heights, without anyone being brought to account except stooges or petty subordinates.

Here's a second extract:

> I shall not consider, therefore, ... whether sensible dispositions were adopted at the outset of operations so our armies could carry out their manœuvres; whether the methods of waging the war, once the fronts became static, have been thoroughly understood; whether every step has been taken in good time for conducting this siege warfare properly; whether the importance of heavy artillery and trench mortars has been grasped straightaway; whether the working methods and employment of staffs – especially the misuse of liaison officers – have really been appropriate to the actual situation.

The conclusion is short and blunt: 'Eliminate those commanders who are so burdened by the old and outdated doctrines that they are incapable of adapting to the circumstances of the current warfare.' This was unambiguous. Commanders burdened by the 'old doctrines' were the men at GQG, with Joffre first and foremost. They had to be 'eliminated', which is a most brutal word, one that stands in sharp contrast to the guarded style in which this sort of script is usually written.

It amounts to a real indictment and smacks of a settling of accounts. It would have been less of a surprise had it had been written by a civilian. But for the assembled Council of Ministers it was particularly astonishing since it came from a soldier who shared a collective responsibility for the matters he denounced. Besides, we can be sure that Galliéni's note simply repeated the basic points of what he had not hesitated to imply beforehand in private conversations. The Ministry of War was full of mobilized reservist officers, which made it an ideal tool for conveying to the media and the parliamentary chambers what the Minister said.

Joffre found Galliéni's note unacceptable, and it sounds over the top even to us today.[56] Just two years earlier, Galliéni had belonged to both the Supreme War Council and the Supreme National Defence Council, and he had been a party to all their decisions. During the brief period of around ten days when he had been in charge of the 6th Army, his command methods had been no different from those of Joffre and GQG. He had wanted to be given a mobile field army at the very moment when manœuvring had become impossible. So what military expertise did Galliéni have that permitted him to talk in such a way? On each of the points he raised, how had he suddenly gained an intuition about what must or must not be done? Where had this sudden intuition come from? What revelation had produced this flash of awareness? Did he possess a magic formula that enabled him to trot out so many certainties about the future and to discover the secret of how to win the war?

Of course not. The only reason why Galliéni produced his note at the council was that the tension between him and Joffre had reached breaking point. The result was immediate disquiet at the heart of the government. Galliéni had produced copies of his note for every member of the Cabinet, yet only Poincaré was willing to take one. It is unclear whether Galliéni threatened to resign if his demands were turned down. As it was, Briand and Poincaré pressed for him simply to be replaced on health grounds, with the Minister of the Navy, Lacaze, filling in for him until the situation was calmer.

*   *   *

The story ends here. Galliéni resigned soon afterwards and was admitted to a clinic at Versailles to undergo surgery. He died on 27 May 1916, as a result of complications following a second operation. His death was announced by GQG in a General Order on the 28th, signed by Joffre and ending with the words: 'Everybody should eternally remember him as one of the country's best servants.' Predictably, Galliéni's supporters instantly protested that the praise was inadequate. Nor did Joffre attend the funeral. Briand, whose relationship with his Minister of War had progressively deteriorated, paid no other tribute to the dead man than *Veni, vidi, vessie* ('I came, I saw, I died of a bladder affliction').[57] The remark does Briand credit, and may his words never be forgotten by any soldier who is tempted to interfere in politics!

According to Gheusi, a decision had been made sometime earlier to replace Joffre with Galliéni as generalissimo.[58] But he appears to have been taken in by what was just a rumour spread by those who hoped that propagating it would make their wish come true. Galliéni's name had repeatedly been mentioned whenever the tension rose between GQG and the government, but by 1916 it was too late, since his health was no longer up to it.

What conclusions should we draw? Galliéni was a great leader, as is proven by all he did overseas, even if colonization is regarded today in an altogether different light. Like every great leader, he had a well-developed ego. He regarded the impending war as his war, and the command of troops in action during a European conflict as the crowning of his career and the fulfilment of his destiny. Yet the war failed to break out in the final years before his retirement. When he had his chance to become the Commander-in-Chief designate in 1911, he lacked the know-how, ability and will to seize it. He alone really knew why he turned Messimy down. When war did finally come in 1914, he wanted to take control, and this seemed all the more feasible given that the holder of the post was his man (or so he thought) and given that his political ally, Messimy, was once again the Minister of War.

Galliéni tried everything, yet nothing went the way he wanted. He knew that his note of 7 March 1916 would be his last, and he had worked on it with Boucabeille for months.[59] It was one last attempt by a rather desperate man who sensed the end coming and preferred to try and drag down with him the rival whom he had failed to supplant. Galliéni's conduct did not prevent his name from being used by Joffre's enemies right up to the end of the war. During the closed parliamentary sessions, Galliéni was regularly quoted by politicians such as Maginot, whose efforts to make him speak from the dead are a measure of his own rabid hostility to Joffre.

Galliéni esteemed Joffre before the war, but in the way that a teacher might esteem a gifted pupil while nursing the hope that the pupil would never become his equal. As it turned out, the pupil tried to shake off his mentor's tutelage and live his own life – and what a life it was, at an exceptional moment in French history. The master promptly blamed it on ingratitude and simply could not stomach playing second fiddle. Beneath it all lies a familiar story: a grand old man is replaced by his heir and suddenly realizes that he has handed over power too soon. Joffre caused Galliéni to botch his exit.

One final point. Galliéni is the only one of all the general officers of the war not to be skewered by the self-righteousness of our era. No bloodbaths have been laid at his door, no criticisms directed against him that he sacrificed his soldiers in pointless offensives. This apparent innocence, associated with the title 'Saviour of Paris', has been enough to make him an untarnished hero, placed on a lofty pedestal, and naturally enough he was also perceived as being the victim of Joffre's greed for glory and of GQG's unscrupulous and predatory nature. This is one further reminder of how the public's gratitude is often linked to the way in which it perceives events, rather than to what a person has actually done.

Chapter 7

Gnawing Away

It seems to have been Joffre himself who came up with the expression *grignoter*, meaning 'to gnaw away'. He used it to answer members of parliament and ministers when they demanded to know why the results of the offensives launched throughout 1915 had been so disappointing. Hence the events of that year became known as the *grignotages*. They constitute a gloomy page in the history of the war – perhaps the gloomiest page of all, since it seemed such a bloody and demoralizing year after the hopes instilled by the victory of the Marne.

Before going into details, I need to explain why people at the time felt like this. As always in war, there was a mismatch between the purely intellectual way in which a commander might understand or justify an attack and the often distressing consequences of him putting it into effect. Joffre was reluctant to visit dressing-stations and hospitals, on the grounds, he said, that it would make him incapable of ordering further offensives.[1] He was not alone in this: many other commanders before and since have reacted similarly. Nor was he an insensitive man. The deeply personal letters published by his various biographers show that Joffre was a human being with feelings and knew what he was doing when he signed operational orders that were going to send tens of thousands of men to their deaths. Yet he signed them anyway and should not be accused for this reason alone of having deliberately ignored the consequences of his actions.

When an idea is translated into reality, what used to be mere words on a piece of paper turn into human suffering, grief and death. These are completely discordant states and it is humanly impossible to pass seamlessly from one to the other. We need to turn once more to the philosopher Pascal, as we did in Chapter 2, for only with his help can we understand the unbridgeable chasm that lies between the realm of the mind and the realm of the heart. We must accept that we can never fill this chasm, and yet it is vital that we do not adopt just one of the two approaches – the rational or the emotional – since the truth lies somewhere in both of them, and we must discard neither. Nor, in seeking this unattainable truth, should we condemn a man who sees only one approach, especially if he has endured physical or psychological suffering. We must listen to him, but only to the extent that his understanding of the truth does not make him rule out the possibility that truth can also lie in the other approach.

Static front

By the end of September 1914, in the wake of the Battle of the Frontiers, a new phase of the war was beginning as the front stabilized from the North Sea to Switzerland. The armies became static and faced each other in direct confrontation, and the line barely shifted until 1918. The Western Front at the end of 1914 was 720km long, of which the British occupied 50km and the Belgians 20km. The front consisted of two parts. The first (roughly two-thirds of the total length) ran from the North Sea to Verdun, and the second (the other one-third) from Verdun to Basle. Although this latter part was active after the start of 1915, it formed something of a secondary theatre of operations, for the Allies made their main attacks in the first part.[2]

The Battle of the Frontiers was immediately followed by what has been termed the Race to the Sea. This simply consisted of each side trying to turn the other's northern flank, and it ended in the Battle of the Yser. These costly actions came to an end in November 1914, when the fighting could no longer be sustained because both sides were exhausted and faced a crisis caused by the shortage of artillery ammunition. In the middle of December, Joffre launched his first offensive in Champagne and in Artois; it resumed in February 1915 and ended in mid-March. A new offensive in Artois was made in May and June, followed in September by a second offensive in Champagne and again in Artois. These ended in October. Next came the German offensive at Verdun, starting in February 1916, followed by the Battle of the Somme at the beginning of July.

To help you follow the events of 1915–16, the battles are listed in chronological order in Table 1. None of the actions brought about a permanent change in the military situation, nor did any of them sway the political mood

Table 1: Key battles of 1915–16.

Month	Major offensives	Local operations
1915, Jan		Soissons, Crouy, Hartmannswillerkopf
1915, Feb	Champagne	Les Eparges, Arras, Notre-Dame de Lorette
1915, Mar	Champagne	Les Eparges, Vauquois
1915, Apr		Les Eparges, Bois d'Ailly, Bois-le-Prêtre
1915, May	Artois	Hartmannswillerkopf
1915, Jun	Artois	Bois-le-Prêtre
1915, Jul		Le Linge
1915, Aug		Le Linge
1915, Sep	Champagne, Artois	
1915, Oct	Champagne, Artois	
1916, Feb – Dec	Verdun	
1916, July – Nov	Somme (with the British)	

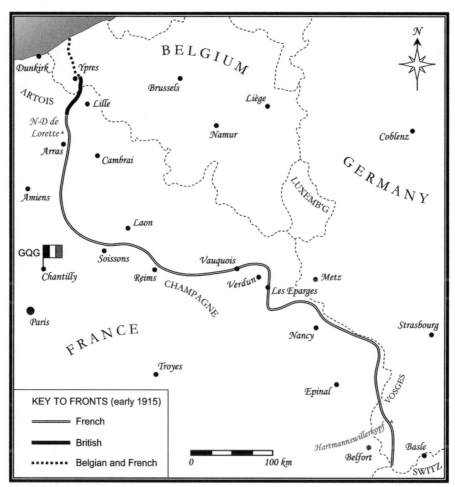

The Western Front in 1915.

within the coalition. Joffre therefore appeared to have failed completely with the strategy he had implemented, and that was a major reason why he lost his job as generalissimo. He was unable to come up with another spectacular achievement to equal that of the Marne. Once his stock of reputation had been spent, he became vulnerable, and the consequences were fatal as regards his continuation in command of the French armies.

What did Joffre intend? He pursued two simultaneous objectives: first and foremost to liberate the occupied part of France, and secondly to assist the Russians in a bid to 'relieve the pressure on our Eastern friends'.[3] Liberating the lost areas of French territory entailed throwing the occupier back beyond the frontier. The first requirement, therefore, was to break (or 'puncture') what was termed 'the crust' – in other words the enemy's trenches and the obstacles out in front that were swept by the enemy fire. If the attackers were successful, they would find themselves out in open countryside once more and free to manœuvre. Up until 1918, military commanders were obsessed with achieving a breakthrough. As for helping the Russians, offensives were often launched with the aim of drawing in the German reserves and preventing the *Großer Generalstab* from putting too much pressure on Russia. (Whereas the Germans were content to remain on the defensive in the West in 1915, they took the offensive on the Eastern Front.)[4]

These were fairly precise strategic goals, but Joffre also had the more general objective of trying to retain the initiative. Every commander-in-chief in history has sought to impose his will rather than be imposed upon. This was the same as what Foch and Grandmaison advocated. If Joffre wanted to attain these objectives as far as possible, he had no alternative to attacking all the time, and preferably in important sectors, as this was the only way to keep the enemy in suspense.

In addition to these main aims, there were secondary ones that have been poorly understood. It was neither desirable nor possible to leave troops at rest in the front line, lest their morale and energy declined rapidly and lest the enemy, drawing reassurance from the passivity of his opponents, gained a 'moral ascendancy' over them. This explains why so many actions were carried out, ranging from a mere raid by some tens of men to an operation mounted at regimental or even divisional level. Furthermore, many large-scale offensives ended in interminable confrontations, in which the violence built up to a climax before one or other of the two sides backed down.

Most of these attacks have been judged harshly and have been added to the list of operations condemned as devoid of any aim, sense or justification. Three of them (they are included in Table 1) became notorious: Les Eparges, Vauquois and the Hartmannswillerkopf. Yet in every case, there were objective military reasons for the attacks. The crest of Les Eparges, for example, commanded extensive views over the Woëvre, and similarly the Vauquois hill dominated the ground west of Verdun. 'Views' meant being able to observe the enemy's movements and above all to adjust artillery fire so it was accurate. The bitterness of the fighting clearly shows the importance that both sides placed on these locations. Les Eparges was just a minor hill, slightly more than 1,000 metres long and 700 metres wide, or less than 1 square km in extent. The struggle to control it began in mid-February 1915 and ceased for the time being at the end of April. The two sides sought to take or retake Point X in a series of attacks and counter-attacks, yet neither really managed to gain the upper hand.[5] Fighting continued there until 1918.

In almost every case, the aims pursued were derisory – or rather appeared derisory – compared with what was at stake in the war. Fighting might continue for weeks in order to gain an observation point or correct the course of a 50-metre stretch of trench system, leading to extremely heavy losses but no decisive result. This came to be seen as indicative of an absolute contempt for human life on the part of blood-thirsty commanders who cared nothing about the misfortunes of their men.

What was people's understanding of the war at the end of 1914 and early 1915? Above all, how did they intend to wage it? The main analogy was siege warfare, something that every soldier of the time had at least heard about. The enemy trenches were equivalent to a fortress that had to be captured, and it was only natural to think of using the same methods – based on sapping and specialized artillery – that had been prescribed by Vauban almost two centuries earlier and more recently had been set down as doctrine in the *Instructions on siege warfare* of 1909. In 1923, a Major Baills wrote:

> A typical conversation about this was overheard at the start of 1915 between two officers, one of whom was on the staff and the other in the engineers. The staff officer was moaning about the army becoming dead-locked in such a way, and said that this new form of warfare came as a complete surprise. But the engineer officer pulled a little blue book from his pocket (the *Instructions on siege warfare* of 30 July 1909) and handed it to him with the words: 'That's what the war will be like ...'[6]

The war was indeed unexpected and disconcerting, for field and siege warfare were poles apart. Nothing had been said about this novel form of field warfare in any of the regulations except that of 1913, which nobody had read or had the time to read (see Chapter 2). Besides, the analogy with siege warfare was only partly relevant, since in this case the 'fortress' could still communicate with the rear as it had not been invested. Since it was just a quasi-fortress, the enemy could feed in as many reinforcements as necessary. Even if the siege was successful, it did not result in the enemy surrendering, and so victory remained elusive. It was unclear what was then to be done, assuming of course that an attacker ever got to that stage.

All kinds of experiments were tried out. Attackers pushed their jumping-off parallels as close as they could to the enemy trench, so their troops were exposed in the open for the shortest possible time. They also identified the best combination of width and depth of attack. In other words, the frontage had to be wide enough so as not to expose the attackers to counter-attacks from a flank, and a decision had to be taken whether to make a series of attacks or to try and take all the lines of defence one after the other in a single stride.

Working out how artillery could be used effectively was just as difficult. For instance, howitzers were essential for hitting enemy trenches since the trajectories of their shells were almost vertical. But the question was where to site their firing positions. If they were too close to the lines, they would be subjected to the enemy's counter-battery fire. If, on the other hand, they were too far away, they would have to be moved forward as an attack progressed – and that would be practically impossible over the cratered terrain of a battlefield. How could the fire be adjusted for accuracy if the target was hidden on a reverse slope? Was zone fire better than fire delivered against specific targets? It was also necessary to lift the barrage just before the infantry attacked – or even better to try rolling the artillery fire forward at the same rate at which the infantry advanced.

How was an attacker to deal with the wire strung in front of the trenches? Not all of this wire was barbed wire, but it survived even the worst bombardments intact since it was too thin to be destroyed by the blast from shells. This was the complaint repeatedly heard from the infantrymen, who were caught and stopped by these types of snares while under artillery and machine-gun fire.

What protection could be found? Soldiers instinctively dug in. Initially, they made simple excavations, enough to cover a man who was lying down or kneeling, but largely lacking in artifice. The holes were then widened and linked to form a continuous line in which the infantrymen could stand up. The course of the line began to grow more sophisticated. Ideally, it zig-zagged as a precaution against enfilade fire, with loopholes being made through which men could fire. The number of defence lines was then increased to at least three. The first trench became the firing trench, while the others became what were called support trenches and were spaced out in depth at distances greater than the likely dispersion of the artillery fire.[7] The trenches were linked to those in front or behind by communication trenches, which followed a winding course and enabled the soldiers to go from one trench to another without leaving cover. The position had to be equipped with a basic level of the necessities of life for the men who were there. Latrines, cook-houses, first-aid posts, command posts and other such facilities had to be incorporated into the layout.

As the artillery bombardments increased in violence, it became necessary to create some protection from both the shells and the weather. Shelters began to be either buried underground or given the overhead protection of logs nailed together and covered with earth. Weapon emplacements (notably for machine-guns) were also established, while out in front of the positions were barriers – mostly belts of wire. But the artillery fire grew ever more intense and heavy calibre pieces were used. The ground was left completely cratered and it became necessary to dig deeper and stronger shelters. The best protected shelter was known as 'bomb-proof', but could withstand no more than a single hit by a 210mm shell. Concrete had to be used for greater protection.

All the staffs published instructions to guide and advise the infantrymen, but these were just 'provisional'. It was not until 21 December 1915 that GQG brought out its *Instructions on fieldworks for the use of troops of all arms* – a comprehensive document codifying what needed to be done on campaign. Its preamble made the point: 'The use of field fortifications ... actually strengthens the offensive spirit, rather than being incompatible with it.' Joffre signed over a dozen orders, starting on 5 October 1914, for the work of fortifying the front to be intensified and completed.[8]

Even so, the *Instructions* of December 1915 included a reminder at the end about a note that GQG had sent to the army group commanders that August. The following lines appeared in bold letters: 'First-line units are not permitted to get support troops to prepare their trenches for them.' This was a sign, if any were needed, that infantrymen and their officers were unenthusiastic about perfecting their defensive systems – in common with the attitude that has always prevailed in the French army. The pessimistic Fayolle even wrote during one of his moments of discouragement: 'As for the men, they prefer to get themselves killed rather than do any work.'

Establishing a trench system along the entire front had the big advantage of reducing the density of troops in the first line. As a result, the Commander-in-Chief was able to form reserves to guard against the danger of an enemy breakthrough and to give him the means for exploiting a success that he was still striving to achieve, even if it seemed unlikely to materialize. When Joffre wrote a note to the Minister of War on 17 March 1915, he added in an appendix concerning the operations in Champagne: 'The Commander-in-Chief was able to form a reserve of several army corps at the start of February, since improving the trench systems had made it possible to reduce the number of troops holding the front.'[9] He often wrote in similar vein.

It had become practically impossible to return to mobile warfare, yet that was not as obvious to Joffre and his army commanders as it is to us today. Fayolle revealed his confusion and disenchantment after the Battles of Artois and Champagne when he wrote in his diary:

> I am perplexed. I no longer believe it possible to break through, at least not in the present circumstances. So what are we going to do next spring? The failure in Champagne has cost us 60,000 men. Will we resume where we left off and lose even more men for gains equally limited and incomplete?[10]

This did not stop Fayolle from starting to feel hope again whenever a new attack was launched, only to revert to despair after a further setback. His outlook also changed as he rose through the hierarchy: initially in his diaries he often criticized Foch, but he ended up speaking in a way not all that different from him.

Joffre strove throughout both 1915 and 1916 to find the right formula that would enable him to exploit the slightest success by unleashing his cavalry divisions. He obsessively tried to find *the* solution, rather like an alchemist trying to discover the philosopher's stone. He was unable simply to refer to the regulations and find a ready-made solution, for the regulations were far too theoretical to be put into effect on the actual ground.

Joffre's approach to the problem did contain some consistent features. First, he gradually escalated the level of the offensives, progressing from army corps to army and then to army group. Next, he added attacks along the entire front so as to surprise the enemy and draw off his reserves. Finally, he increased the amount of artillery – both light and heavy guns – as the new weaponry arrived.[11] Above all, he built up an adequate stock of ammunition. (It was not until the end of 1915 that rather more generous allocations of ammunition could be made, especially for the 75mm guns.) In May 1915, Joffre summed up his ideas in another letter to the Minister of War: 'I respectfully point out that we need to seek a decisive outcome on our front by increasing the power of our attacks . . .'.[12]

But Joffre failed to find his philosopher's stone. His failure inevitably had an adverse effect on public opinion (to the extent that censorship allowed it to exist), on parliament and on the government. It did not help that Joffre was always claiming in his letters that it was possible to break through and that, if he failed to do so, there were various reasons why – and he made sure he listed them. All the notes he wrote were structured in much the same way. As an example, we'll consider a six-page letter from him to the Minister of War in August 1915, about the course of the offensive in Artois that May.[13] He mentioned a succession of points, starting with the quality of the artillery preparation:

> The 10th Army's attack had been prepared with meticulous attention to the smallest details. Every precaution had been taken to preserve the advantage of surprise.[14] Nor had moral preparation been neglected, for the men knew what was expected of them.

Joffre then set out the results: 'The enemy had suffered heavily. . . . The total figure for the [enemy's] losses during May is reckoned to be 80,000. . . . French losses reached 67,391 men.' Joffre had to admit: 'Nevertheless, as the offensive dragged on, it gradually lost its chances of success. . . . It was therefore impossible to exploit the breaking of the front, which was the initial objective of our offensive.' There followed some explanations, which contained 'lessons' – such as reserves intervening too late and from too far away, the excessively narrow front of attack, and the inadequate support provided by the British. Here's the final paragraph:

> The results of a manœuvre based on the lessons of the Arras operations can be awaited with confidence. Even if the Arras operations have fallen short of gaining a decisive success for the French armies, they nonetheless have helped prepare the way by teaching lessons that complete and supplement those that were learned in Champagne. This is why I am determined to . . . assemble the resources needed to prepare a general offensive consisting of several powerful and simultaneous attacks.[15]

The letter reads like a report written by someone conducting experiments. We can understand why the government, and politicians more generally, began to grow weary of a general whom they reckoned should be regarded with some justification as a sorcerer's apprentice. Poincaré was among those who were particularly forceful in giving vent to their impatience. Joffre imperturbably defended his actions in the same way. It never changed and can be summed up as: I intended to do such-and-such, with these resources. I did not succeed, but I know why and I am sure that adopting a different approach will prove successful.

Joffre wrote a subsequent letter to the Minister of War on 3 October 1915, at a time when he was preparing to relaunch the Second Champagne offensive. It contains the sentence: 'It can be said that the successes in Champagne give us the certainty of final victory.'[16] Yet the 'certainty' was really no more than a hope. We gain the impression once more that Joffre's approach was similar to that of an engineer who is proceeding by trial-and-error since he does not know the right balance of ingredients to use. Politicians found this completely intolerable, for their usual restiveness brooked no delay. Joffre might well invoke 'the chances of war' in his letters to the Minister of War, yet he repeated the phrase so often that it was ignored. It was in the year 1915 – and particularly in its closing stages – that a deep schism between the politicians and the military really began to become established. It now becomes easier to understand why France plunged into the risky venture of operations in the Eastern Mediterranean – anything seemed better than the costly stagnation and never-ending slog of the Western Front.

Losses mounted even though the front remained more or less static. In 1917, Abel Ferry asked GQG for the total number of losses (killed, missing, captured, or died while receiving medical treatment) since the start of the war.[17] Table 2 sets out the statistics for 1915, which amount to 1,428,000 men.

Table 2: French losses in 1915, Western Front.

Period	Killed, missing or captured	Evacuated to the interior of the country	Total
1914, Dec – Jan (1915)	67,000	18,000	85,000
1915, Feb – Mar	62,000	171,000	233,000
1915, Apr – Jun	134,000	306,000	440,000
1915, Jul – Aug	45,000	145,000	190,000
1915, Sep – Nov	125,000	279,000	404,000
1915, Dec – Jan (1916)	20,000	56,000	76,000
Total	453,000	975,000	1,428,000

Included in this figure are 453,000 men who were permanently lost – men who never returned to the armies – or the equivalent of slightly under three 'classes' (annual intakes) of conscripts.[18] Those soldiers evacuated to the interior of the country were basically wounded men, and many of them were too seriously injured to return to the front. In little more than a year, therefore, the war had 'consumed' about five years' worth of those Frenchmen liable to be mobilized – and they were the youngest years.

The quest for a decisive outcome

At the time of Joffre's removal at the end of 1916, he was preparing a new offensive following the check to the one on the Somme. His replacement, Nivelle, adopted this new offensive as his own, though in a much modified form. Yet Nivelle experienced the same lack of success, and Joffre claimed the war would have ended in 1917 if he himself had remained in post. 'My basic idea', he wrote in his memoirs, 'was that the 1916 battle had dislocated the enemy's defensive positions beyond repair, and that the German reserves had been so worn down that we could not fail to gain decisive results if we made a supreme effort.'[19]

Was this true or false? Obviously, the answer is not that clear-cut, especially since Joffre was writing with the benefit of hindsight. Had he really enjoyed a chance of success, or were his critics right to regard his perseverance as no more than stubbornness? We should start by recognizing that his plan of action for 1915 was designed effectively. He was successful in his obstinate efforts to ensure that the Allied armies acted in a unified manner, even if he proved unable to unify their command, something that still lay beyond the bounds of possibility at this stage. The two conferences at Chantilly in December 1915 and November 1916 were personal successes for Joffre. We should also note the determined way in which he formed new reserves.[20] Furthermore, he significantly increased the amount of heavy artillery by issuing his decree about the fortresses, while also producing a plan at the end of 1915 to improve its quality by bringing new artillery pieces into service.

As Joffre pointed out, he made each new offensive stronger than the one before. Just three French army corps took part in the First Champagne offensive, but six in Artois in May 1915, and then fourteen (ten plus four) in the Second Champagne. The Battle of the Somme in 1916 involved three British armies and two French, with artillery in proportion. As for the 1917 battle, Joffre intended to use four French armies (or roughly half the available French manpower) and two British armies, while also making permanent improvements to Allied coordination.

Occasional successes did occur, notably during the Battle of the Somme. They were very limited and for various reasons could not be exploited, but they did enough to create the belief that exploitation was not just a pipedream. The British had the same outlook. Since the Allies had apparently come so close to success, the notion spread – at least among the staffs[21] – that they were almost there and that with a bit more of something and a bit less of something else, it hopefully would become possible once more to break through into open country.

What Joffre said and wrote to the government was neither wrong nor deceitful. As a good engineer, he really did draw lessons from all his setbacks, including on the tactical level. This was shown by a note of 16 April 1915 that tried to set out the preconditions for a successful general offensive. It was shown again, slightly later, by the *Instructions on small-unit actions*.[22] In short, the war was considered and analysed step by step. It had a logic to it, and the objective of achieving a breakthrough. Joffre's determination to draw the German reserves to the Western Front played an important role in the East and probably saved the Russian army from collapse – in much the same way as the Russian offensive of Tannenberg in August 1914 had contributed to the recovery on the Marne. But French political circles were never likely to understand that argument, and – as Poincaré made clear to Joffre – that was what the government had to contend with.

Important innovations made their appearance in 1915 and early 1916, and almost all of them were instigated by GQG. The changes to the uniforms are well-known, involving the introduction of the 'horizon-blue' colour and the adoption of the Adrian helmet. Many other improvements were in progress, such as the development of wireless communications installed in airplanes,[23] and the perfection of procedures for adjusting the accuracy of artillery shoots (something that was done 743 times in Champagne-Artois between 1 September and 15 October 1915, to the benefit of the 4th Army). Nor should we forget the tanks: Estienne, the creator of the Assault Artillery (later known as the armoured corps) met Joffre himself at the end of December 1915 and secured his backing for the realization of his dream.[24] Many other achievements came to fruition at this time, proving that Joffre and GQG were making use of what we would now call feedback. Even before the war, Joffre had always been keen to exploit new technology, not least in the field of aviation. It was he who had insisted on the creation in 1913 of the Ministry of War's twelfth directorate, that of aviation and aerostation (flying in lighter-than-air craft, such as balloons and airships).

Officers' attitudes – mainly those of reservist officers – depended on their seniority: the more junior they were, the less they shared Joffre's outlook. They knew about the scale of the casualties but not about the gains, and in their eyes the series of apparently disjointed and unjustifiable attacks lacked any coherence. Why were so many men being killed? This is the question that can be found in the diaries written by the *poilus* and by those officers who served alongside them. For obvious reasons, they could not be told openly that no one knew exactly what should be done and that many different tactical combinations were going to be tried out in the hope of finding the right one. Nor did the shortage of artillery ammunition help, for it meant that the high command at this time was still trying to find a rough-and-ready compromise between its resources and requirements.

This period also marked the start of the grumbling about staff officers, who were unfairly accused of being out of touch with the war they were waging. Members of parliament were soon demanding that staff officers be sent to the front and replaced by officers from combat units. There was a degree of justification to this change in that almost none of the personnel in post in 1915 had seen action and that they failed to adapt their schemes to fit specific circumstances. Yet they had at least been trained for the job, and many of them were qualified staff officers. The change caused several weeks of disruption while the new staff officers learned their duties on the job and made up to some extent for their lack of training.

Roger Maurice, who appears to have been a reservist officer, wrote in 1918:

> At the start of 1915, most staff officers still had no experience of commanding troops in action. They had never seen the soldiers at close quarters: they had never lived with them, and had merely caught sight of them from time to time during a rapid visit to the trenches. They were therefore living in a world of delusions. ... Neither their Staff College training nor their service on the staff had taught them to attach enough importance to these numerous details. This touches on one of the reasons why the troops disliked and 'discounted' the staffs.[25]

Ideally, Maurice's whole article ought to be quoted, but you are free to look it up if you want to find out more. Maurice added that 'a general rarely had any more personal experience than his entourage', and he backed up this claim by recalling some events that he apparently witnessed himself.

Some mobilized members of the Chamber of Deputies made similar statements, including Abel Ferry and also Messimy, the former Minister of War. This is what Poincaré recorded being told when Messimy paid him a visit at the start of January 1915:

> They are living in an ivory tower at GQG and are largely unaware what is happening on the front. They order partial offensives so they have something to include in the communiqués, but these offensives are very bloody and are doomed to failure.[26]

Yet Messimy did not explain what he would call a 'partial offensive' if it succeeded – he did not define the criteria for success. In fact, he did not want any offensive at all. Messimy proved from his service as a general that he was a capable tactician, but he often had difficulty at higher levels and his ideas about the war show that he tended to be more of a politician than a strategist.[27]

*   *   *

In conclusion, Joffre was not wrong to try and break through. That was the way in which the war could be won, and how Foch did win it once he had the necessary resources and once the Allied armies had been placed under his sole command. As the German army demonstrated in 1918, it was possible to achieve a breakthrough, even without tanks, simply by adopting different tactics. Joffre would inevitably have been criticized had be opted for either total inactivity or a frenetic series of offensives. Instead, he tried to find a middle road that, after being gradually perfected, might have brought victory, perhaps in 1917. But this obliged him to wage war actively, whereas the Germans had chosen to wait on the Western Front and to focus most of their effort against Russia.

It is therefore doubtful whether Joffre could have acted differently. Yet neither was the government wrong to fear that a hypothetical victory – it was always promised, yet never actually materialized – would come at an intolerably high price for the French nation. The casualty figures, if extrapolated at the same rate through the coming months and years, would exhaust the available manpower and be the direct cause of permanently undermining the French army and country.[28] For this reason, it was not only inevitable but also desirable that politics should find its way back into the conduct of the war. From 1915, the continuation of the war meant that it affected every sector of the nation, and the direction of the war had to revert increasingly to civilian hands, unless a military dictatorship took over.

Furthermore, despite the harsh lessons of August and September 1914, the offensive spirit continued on occasion to be misapplied. Such mistakes cost fewer lives during the period of trench warfare. Even so, a state of mind can not be changed in just a few months, and some officers who carried out attacks lacked the tactical competence they should have displayed.

Chapter 8

Verdun

The Battle of Verdun was not the only reason for Joffre's dismissal, but certainly contributed to it, as did the failure of the Somme offensive. The Commander-in-Chief was bitterly criticized on three counts: the supposed inadequacy of Verdun's defences, the disarming of the forts, and the lack of interest shown by himself and GQG in indications that the battle was impending.

Some months after the start of the German attack, the first closed session of the parliamentary chambers was held. It was like unleashing a frenzied pack of hunting dogs, for the members of parliament had been obliged to remain silent for almost two years and had built up vast mountains of resentment. Joffre's departure initially came as a great, collective release – a purging of the frustrations of both individual politicians and parliament as a whole.

Highpoint of the war
Let's start by running through the facts of what happened. The Battle of Verdun was fought from 21 February to 15 December 1916, and during this period of almost ten months the French army was worn out in a defensive battle it was often on the verge of losing. The battle cost the French 380,000 men killed, wounded, missing or captured, including almost 9,000 officers. German losses were only slightly lower. For the French, Verdun was the highpoint of the war: although its monthly casualty rates fell far short of those of the Battle of the Frontiers, the sheer duration of Verdun made it unmatched.

Why Verdun? There is no obvious answer to this question. Falkenhayn revealed his intentions when he wrote his memoirs after the war: 'If [the enemy] declined to fight [for Verdun] and let the objective fall into our hands, the moral impact in France would be enormous. The zone in which the attack was to be made was closely restricted, and so Germany would not have to use troops in such large numbers that all the other fronts would be weakened to an alarming extent.' Falkenhayn added: 'In the French sector of the Western Front, objectives were lying well within our reach for whose retention the French high command would be bound to throw in every man they had available.'

Falkenhayn supposedly wished to 'bleed' the French army, in order to provoke a crisis of morale from which France could not emerge unscathed. This could actually have worked to some extent, but the German staff misjudged the French government's resolve, and overestimated its readiness to accept a compromise peace. For the Germans, it was a matter of pinning down as many French troops as they could and keeping open a sort of weeping sore, while relying as far as possible on artillery fire in order to spare their own infantry.

Yet the Germans probably had additional, more ambitious objectives. If they had managed to break through, nothing would have prevented them from attempting with their left wing what their right wing had failed to do in Belgium in 1914. Nevertheless, Falkenhayn restated his desire to limit the numbers of troops engaged to fifteen divisions, with plenty of artillery support. This was in keeping with his stated intention, and he resisted pressure to change his mind, including from the German Crown Prince who was entrusted with the command of the troops at Verdun. Hence the front of the attack was deliberately restricted at first to just 12km and it lay solely on the right (or east) bank of the Meuse. In theory, an attack launched on such a narrow frontage would be unable to break through into open country, but opinions about what was possible might change if the attack managed to make good progress.

Verdun was a symbolic place because of its history. The French had no option but to defend the city tenaciously, for its abandonment would have dealt a psychological blow to the country and its political circles. It had been a fortress for two centuries and had recently been transformed. It now lay at the centre of an entrenched camp built at great expense in the 1880s by Séré de Rivières. It was one of the few such camps to have been modernized. Concrete had been used to cover the forts' above-ground structures of earth and masonry, and metal turrets had been installed to protect machine-guns and 75mm and 155mm artillery pieces. So-called Bourges casemates had been built in the gaps between the forts, and were equipped with one or two 75mm guns (usually two) in order to protect the forts with enfilade fire. Concrete had also been used to make shelters and various defensive works, whose value became clear in due course. Not all the forts had been modernized, owing to a shortage of funds, but the most important work had been done during the pre-war period (at some locations, concrete was still being cast when the war was declared).

Verdun had been saved by Sarrail's 3rd Army in 1914, but the front curved round at an angle of roughly 160° and formed a pocket with the city in the centre. The south-eastern part of this pocket was then occupied by the Germans and remained in their hands until 1918, constituting what was known as the Saint-Mihiel salient.[1] Many of the French defences on the eastern side of Verdun were sandwiched between the German lines and the Meuse valley, in an area less than 10km deep. In the northern part of the pocket, the German lines crossed the Meuse to the side of the *Mort Homme* ridge, which became famous as one of the main focal points of French resistance.

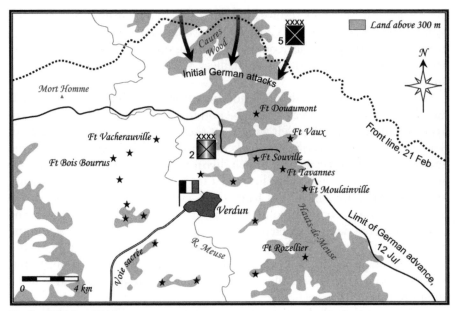

Battle of Verdun, 1916

At the start of 1916, the French had five divisions and two brigades along this circular arc, which was over 100km long. Opposite them were nine German divisions. This meant an average ratio of one French division for just over 15km of front. According to the ratios of the time, it was a quiet sector, and it had been so ever since the clashes of 1914 had ended. Units on both sides regarded themselves as being at rest, and this attitude had unfortunate consequences for the French.

The pocket was badly served by communication routes, which were partly in the hands of the Germans or under the fire of their artillery in the area of Aubréville.[2] The French had to be content with what usable links they had, not that these amounted to much. There was a light railway called the *Meusien* whose single track had a gauge of 1 metre. There also existed a secondary road that became the *Voie sacrée* or 'Sacred Way'. But in 1915 the French had begun to examine the possibility of supplementing the *Meusien* with another railway line – a standard gauge line built beyond the range of the German artillery. The *Meusien* itself had been improved in December 1914 with the construction of unloading platforms and the addition of a second track to some sections. These improvements had doubled its capacity in a year. In short, Verdun never suffered any shortages during the entire war, and the logistical arrangements continued functioning at an acceptable level.[3] I should mention that Verdun, in common with all the other entrenched camps, also had a network of 0.6-metre gauge railway lines. These lines were still in place and made it possible to bring supplies right up close to the units.

The battle went through several phases and produced many unexpected developments. The German attack began a week late, on 21 February 1916. Stunned by artillery bombardments of unprecedented violence, some French units disintegrated or were wiped out, and the local command reeled under the shock. By the 24th, the German army was within reach of the actual fortress city of Verdun – the very nucleus of the Fortified Region – but for various reasons failed to exploit its advantage. De Langle de Cary (the commander of the Central Army Group) ordered the evacuation of the Woëvre region, which lay east of the *Hauts-de-Meuse* heights on which the line of forts stood, and he was even on the verge of giving the order to abandon the right bank of the river.

On the 25th, Castelnau dashed over to see the situation at Verdun for himself, and Pétain, the commander of the 2nd Army, was placed in charge. At the same time, Joffre reiterated his order to hold on to the right bank of the Meuse. On the 26th, the Germans captured Fort Douaumont without a fight, for by this stage the fort was occupied by only a skeletal garrison. In just five days, the French army had lost 25,000 men and 125 artillery pieces.

Pétain shored up the defence and tried to form lines of resistance to block the most likely lines of attack. He sent more artillery to the left bank, where it was protected from the German infantry so long as the attack continued to be restricted to the right bank. Joffre was beginning to badger Pétain to switch to the offensive: 'The best way of checking the enemy's onslaught is to make an attack yourself.' Pétain was not ready for that, although he did have 666 heavy guns available by 1 March.

Divisions were beginning to melt away, but the two sides adopted completely different methods of reinforcement. The Germans left the same units in place and simply topped them up with replacements when necessary. The French, in contrast, used what was called the 'revolving door': they relieved each division every two days (in due course this became two divisions every three days). This was a more humane system, but considerable losses were incurred during the reliefs – losses that might amount to nearly a quarter of a unit's strength. Almost all the infantry divisions of the French army experienced Verdun, and some of them did so several times. During just the period from 21 February to 15 June, as many as sixty-six divisions were rotated through Verdun, out of the ninety-five that existed in the French army at that time. There were no quiet days at Verdun. The artillery was always firing, resulting in levels of ammunition consumption that would have been unthinkable some years before.

I do not intend to follow the battle's various swings of fortune. If you want to find out about the key episodes, you can obtain background information from the many written sources and from some internet sites of variable worth. In reading about Verdun, you will experience something of the battle, though without truly understanding it. Nor will you really grasp what happened, for unless you visit the battlefield you will be unable to visualize the terrain and comprehend the bitter actions that were fought to capture a 'hill', cross a valley or secure an outlet into open ground. The countryside of the Woëvre is cut by many valleys, and the only extensive views are to be found at certain points on the crests – points such as Douaumont, from where you can see equally well to both east and west.

The fighting continued into December 1916, with lulls whose length varied between different sectors. The Germans, after being checked on the right bank, resumed the offensive on the opposite side of the Meuse, preceded as always by massive artillery bombardments. They then attacked again on the right bank, or on both banks, gnawing away at the intervening distance as they drew ever closer to Verdun in the hope of driving the French back on to the left bank of the Meuse. By thrusting alternately on either bank, they penetrated to little more than 3km of Verdun and were now level with Fort Souville, although they were unable to capture the fort itself. The outcome hung by a thread.

At the start of May, Pétain was succeeded by Nivelle at the head of the 2nd Army, but kept an eye on Verdun in his new post as commander of the Central Army Group. Joffre and Pétain disagreed in a major way over how the battle should be fought. Joffre wanted to hold back troops for the forthcoming Somme offensive, which was to be launched jointly with the British, whereas Pétain wanted to devote the French army's resources to Verdun alone.[4] The question soon became politicized, since the first closed session of the Chamber of Deputies took place in June 1916.

The key episodes during the German attack were the capture of Fort Douaumont soon after the start of the battle – German propaganda made much of this success – followed several weeks later by the capture of Fort Vaux on 6 June. Conversely, the retaking of these two forts by the command team of Mangin and Nivelle marked the beginning of the end for the German thrust on the *Hauts-de-Meuse* heights. The unleashing of the Somme offensive at the start of July relieved the pressure on Verdun almost immediately.

Was Joffre surprised?

The first criticism that has been directed against Joffre is that he failed to see the attack on Verdun coming. In a way, he accepted this point, for he wrote in his memoirs fifteen years later: 'In strategic terms, Verdun was unjustifiable from the German perspective.'[5] It is clear that he had still not grasped what the Germans had been trying to do. The engineer in him could see no logic to the German plan, and his unimaginative mind had almost entirely discounted the possibility of an attack on Verdun. Yet at the same time, he added a rather contradictory statement: 'The truth is that the attack did not catch us unprepared.' It is this latter claim that I shall now examine.

The French and British armies were simply not large enough to be ready to oppose every potential threat along the 600km front. By using intelligence, it was possible to analyse the threats and identify the most probable ones. It was also possible to deploy reserves at suitable locations so they could intervene with a minimum of delay at the points that came under attack. In 1916, Joffre had about forty-five divisions in reserve. Twenty of them were held at the level of the three army groups, and the other twenty-five were at Joffre's own disposal. He had arranged motor-vehicle and railway transport so he could whisk these reserves to wherever they were needed. This was a normal pre-caution, since the policy was to occupy the line with no more troops than were absolutely necessary.

What did Joffre know about the danger of a German offensive against Verdun? The rather paradoxical answer might be: everything and nothing. Until 1 November 1915 (which marked the end of the Champagne offen-sives), he was not particularly worried since the Fortified Region of Verdun never had under thirty-two battalions of active troops and thirty-four of Territorials. At the end of 1915 and the start of 1916, the Operations Depart-ment of GQG was busy preparing the Somme offensive. During this time, it continued to watch out for dangers in other zones of the front, but Verdun remained of little, if any, concern for a long while.

GQG had no specific intelligence on Verdun until almost the end of 1915. The front there was quiet, but many rumours had circulated during the year about an impending German offensive. These rumours buzzed around the staff, yet it was only at the start of December that they grew more consistent and a significant increase in German railway traffic was detected in the region of Longuyon. Pierrefeu relates that the head of GQG's Intelligence Depart-ment, Colonel Dupont, was convinced that Verdun would be attacked, and did not hesitate to say so in the corridors of Chantilly.

The signs increased in January 1916. On the 4th, the Ministry of War received a piece of intelligence that was reckoned to be reliable, about an imminent attack on Verdun. On the 10th, GQG's intelligence summary was still undecided between Verdun and Flanders. Information began to pour in at the start of February, but not until the 10th did GQG know for certain that a German attack on Verdun was imminent, and even then was it unable to tell whether this would be the main attack or simply a diversion.

Yet the Germans had been busy in the Verdun sector since October 1915. They sought to strengthen their three existing defensive positions (the third of which had barely been begun). The initial priority was the first position, which was made continuous. Immediately behind it, villages were turned into what were known as *places d'armes*, which were simply cantonments sur-rounded by the various facilities needed for everyday life. From these *places d'armes*, 0.6-metre gauge railway lines fanned out to the front. The pace of work picked up at the start of January, and the Germans began building their famous *Stollen* or large, concrete shelters.[6] The work intensified even further in the middle of that month and continued day and night. The Germans were sufficiently well equipped to cope with the frozen ground and to work as if it was a more favourable season than mid-winter.

How much was known by the local French commander – General Herr, the commander of the Fortified Region of Verdun? A note from his Intelligence Department, dated 15 January 1916, concluded that even if an attack was to be expected on the Western Front, 'it was very doubtful that Verdun would be the German objective'. It justified this opinion by casting doubt on the statements of civilian refugees (there seem to have been many of them in the region), who all said that an offensive was going to be made against Verdun.

General Herr himself did not share his Intelligence Department's scepticism. On 16 January, he wrote to General Dubail, whose command included the Fortified Region of Verdun. In his letter, Herr took the statements of deserters and prisoners far more seriously. Above all, the appearance of the *Stollen* in the Verdun sector was a sure sign that something was afoot.

In contrast, other officers continued to express doubt about the likelihood of a German attack on Verdun. They based their arguments on the fact that the opposing lines were sometimes separated by more than 1,000 metres. It was believed at the time (wrongly, as it turned out) that an attack could be launched only from so-called 'jumping-off' parallels. These had to be positioned close enough to the objective for the attacking troops to be exposed in the open for as short a time as possible, and yet far enough away for them to have proper support from their own positions. An attack had never yet been launched from so far away from the defender's trenches. General Herr remained uneasy and knew that something was being prepared, even though he was unsure exactly what or where, and so he demanded reinforcements.

The German attack was meant to have been launched on 13 February. Yet the Intelligence Department of the Fortified Region of Verdun produced another note on that very day, entitled 'Development of the German defensive systems on the front of the Fortified Region of Verdun, from September 1915 to January 1916'. That's no misprint: the layout of the German positions really was described as defensive. The Intelligence Department was not exactly becoming more perceptive.

Yet the situation was about to be made clearer, especially by aerial photographic missions flown at the end of January and middle of February. An assessment of the 18 February missions concluded: 'Germans clearly intend to shelter considerable numbers of troops in their first positions opposite the Fortified Region of Verdun. Works have been continued very energetically since mid-January. These works are particularly visible in the following sectors [etc.] . . .'.[7] The sectors turned out to be those that were attacked some days later. The note added: 'The intelligence obtained shows clearly that the

Germans intend to make a serious attack north-east of Verdun.' All this information was picked up on 18 February, five days after the intended date of the German attack. Even so, it seems likely that General Herr had already received some previous indications. Indeed, we know that certain units were placed on alert several times. For example, an officer with the 164th Infantry Regiment in the Herbebois sector noted an initial alert on the morning of 16 January. A second alert followed on 11 February, two days before the planned date of the attack: 'Warning from a *chasseur* officer that the enemy would attack the French front at one o'clock ...'. On the 13th, the intended day of the attack, a general alert placed the troops in their combat positions. In short, the commander of the Fortified Region of Verdun knew what to expect long before the aerial photographic reconnaissances, for there is no way the information could have failed to reach his level or that anyone else could have ordered the alert.

Joffre personally visited the area on 19 February and met all the key generals of the coming battle. He left in confident mood, for he wrote in his memoirs: 'I gained the assurance that everyone was awaiting the gathering storm with calmness.'[8] By the time the attack was launched on the 21st, the overall situation of the Fortified Region of Verdun had been transformed since the end of 1915. Matters had progressively improved following an inspection by Castelnau on 23 January. The 54th and 67th Divisions were transported to Verdun, followed by the 14th and 37th. The 16th and 48th arrived on 20 February. Artillery reinforcements, in addition to those artillery units contained within the infantry divisions, were also sent to Verdun.

By 21 February, Herr had available 138 active or reserve battalions, or a total of 130,000 men, as well as around thirty battalions of Territorials. They were supported by 388 pieces of field artillery and 244 pieces of heavy artillery.[9] Against them the Germans used 208 battalions, or 250,000 men, and 882 field guns, of which 700 were heavy (with a calibre greater than 77mm).

At 7.15am on 21 February, the attack began with shells pouring down.[10] The 30th Corps (72nd, 51st and 14th Divisions), which was holding the northern and north-eastern sector, was practically wiped out in two days. Panic set in, as an eyewitness described:

> After the [reinforcements] had crossed the Etain road, all the tracks were found to be crammed with every type of vehicle and with dispersed soldiers of every arm who were flowing back to the rear. The march to the front was hindered by this tide of men fleeing the enemy, and the sight of them hardly encouraged the soldiers who were heading into action.[11]

Despite the recent warning signs, the attack came as a shock. The French troops were badly prepared for what befell them, though it is difficult to see how they could have been better prepared. They failed to stand their ground, and the fugitives probably included many men from the various support services. In contrast, some other units held out as long as they could under the bombardment and fell back only when ordered to do so. They included Driant's *chasseur* battalions, despite the fact that these *chasseurs* were reservists from Paris and northern France.

We can now answer the question whether Joffre and GQG were surprised by the German attack on Verdun. The answer is yes and no. They were surprised in the sense that something was happening at Verdun without anyone believing it. But they were not surprised in so far as the signs of the imminent offensive were detected early enough for reinforcements to be put in place as a precaution. This is how we should interpret Joffre's claim that 'the attack did not catch us unprepared'. The reinforcements were kept at a distance from the front, so they would not be 'consumed' too soon, and so they could be committed to a different zone should that become necessary.

Inadequate defences?

Let's turn to the second criticism that has been levelled at Joffre, namely the inadequacy of Verdun's defences. All the evidence points to the same conclusion: on the whole, Verdun's lines of defence were inadequate. It was more a problem of quality than quantity, but it's easy to see how the two could be confused, and how the poor quality of the defences could lead to claims that nothing had been done. Underground shelters covered with just earth and logs simply could not protect their occupants for hours on end under bombardment by artillery of greater calibre than 105mm. The first shells blasted away the overhead cover, allowing the subsequent ones to penetrate. The theory that two shells never fell in the same place was just an illusion. Experience had made attackers realize that if they wanted to break through they had to concentrate massive amounts of artillery and limitless stocks of ammunition.

Some of the defensive systems at Verdun dated from the fighting in 1914. The region had been much contested back then, and the sort of trenches that had been dug were those described in the *Instructions on fieldworks for the use of infantry units*. They were primitive, for the soldiers had not yet been taught by experience. The trenches did not form a continuous line, were not linked to each other by communication trenches, and their shelters and wire entanglements were either inadequate or non-existent. In short, not much work had gone into these defensive systems. When the men of the 85th Infantry Regiment went into the line near the plateau of Haudremont, 'they found no more than works that had only just been begun and rudimentary wire entanglements. No shelters or communications existed. ... The soldiers found that the only protection existing on the line of defence consisted of some sections of trench.'

But the defences were not this deficient everywhere. Up to four successive positions existed in the sector held by the 72nd Infantry Division, although not all of them had been completed.[12] (Caures Wood, held by Driant's *chasseurs*, lay within this sector.) These defensive positions included trenches, shelters (some made of concrete), wire entanglements and communication trenches. The first position was 12km in extent and consisted of a series of three lines: the first line was composed of various trenches, then came a support line known as the S Line, followed by a line of redoubts or R Line. The second position consisted of individual defensive works located on a reverse slope but not yet totally finished. The third was still in its early stages and a fourth had been begun after Castelnau's inspection but was likewise incomplete. Much remained to be done, therefore, but it is untrue to claim that Verdun lacked any defensive systems, especially in the zone that bore the brunt of the German bombardment and onslaught.

The existence of these defences was of limited help. A continuous German bombardment of about ten hours turned Caures Wood into what looked like a lunar landscape. No works on a line of defence could possibly withstand such an overwhelming pounding indefinitely. The best method the French knew of constructing trenches in 1915 was set out in a regulation.[13] The shelters it prescribed were merely the standard construction that could survive the impact of a single heavy artillery shell (with a calibre of at least 155mm). It also described concrete shelters, but even these could not be guaranteed to withstand prolonged shelling and they had a serious drawback – they could be built only by a specialized workforce that had to be provided by the engineers.

The tactical layout of the defence complied with the *Instructions on siege warfare*. The ground was organized with centres of resistance sited at certain locations. These centres of resistance consisted of strongpoints arranged in such a way that they covered each other's flanks. The strongpoints were known as *macarons*[14] or as 'beans' (because of their shape), and they lay at the heart of an argument that raged within the staffs and elsewhere over the question of continuous or discontinuous lines. Members of parliament criticized GQG, and hence Joffre, for a tendency to favour the *macaron* over the continuous trench (the latter required many more men to hold it).

Let's examine how the controversy arose about the state of Verdun's defences. We have seen that some members of parliament were serving as reservist soldiers or officers, which meant that they were both soldiers and politicians at the same time. Among them was Lieutenant-Colonel Driant, a graduate of the officer-training school at Saint-Cyr, the Deputy representing the Department of the Meurthe-et-Moselle and a member of the Army Commission.[15] At Verdun, he commanded two reserve battalions of light infantry in the northern sector – the 56th and 59th Battalions of *Chasseurs à pied* – and as a member of parliament serving in uniform he had one foot in Caures

Wood and the other in Paris. He was convinced that the Germans would attack in the Verdun–Nancy region and did not refrain from sharing this intuition with anyone who would listen. He was familiar with the Verdun sector and with the deficiencies of the defensive system in that zone.[16] In August 1915, he wrote to Deschanel (the President of the Chamber of Deputies) to inform him of his concerns and to ask for 'manpower, tools, barbed-wire'. His letter added: 'If the chain of command replies that I am wrong, that everything is ready and that all is going well, then it is mistaken and out-of-touch.' Deschanel replied that he was forwarding Driant's letter to the Minister of War, but we do not know the Minister's response.

Three months later, in November, Driant examined the defences covering Nancy and Lunéville, and noted that in some sectors they were pitiful. On 1 December, he raised the matter in a meeting with Briand, the President of the Council of Ministers, who referred him to Galliéni, the new Minister of War. (A friend who recorded Driant's visit added that 'if it had been a question of Verdun, where [Driant] was serving as an officer, he would have reported the deficiency to his superiors instead.' The fact that Driant had not done so is therefore significant: his concerns were not specifically about Verdun.) The upshot was that Galliéni sent a letter to Joffre on 16 December, pointing out the 'defective establishment of defences in the regions of the Meurthe, of Toul and of Verdun'. Inevitably, this was later seen as evidence of the Minister of War's foresight and was contrasted with GQG's failings and those of the Commander-in-Chief.[17] Yet Galliéni's letter to Joffre was not the result of concern specifically about Verdun. Nor did Driant imply that Verdun's defences were a special concern when he wrote other letters at this time while at Caures Wood. During the closed session of the Chamber of Deputies in June 1916, Briand stated that Driant had mentioned to him the village of Arracourt in particular – yet Arracourt was not at Verdun at all, for it lay 15km east of Nancy.

We have already seen in Chapter 6 how Joffre reacted to Galliéni's letter. His reply referred to all the orders he had given, especially the instructions of 22 October 1915 to his chief subordinates.[18] He added: 'In the regions specified in your despatch ... there exists a series of three or four defensive positions that are either finished or in the course of being completed.' It was a rash reply, and its contents are surprising even if the phrase 'in the course of being completed' could be interpreted in all sorts of ways. It was, of course, inaccurate, for there was a tendency at every level of command to confuse projects that were still no more than plans with projects that had actually been completed. Joffre would have been wiser to delay replying until he had sent officers to check the actual situation for him.

Yet if we look beyond Joffre's indignant response, we can detect a growing realization at GQG that something was happening in the Verdun region requiring its attention. The incident added strength to General Herr's subsequent letter of 16 January 1916. Along with other pieces of information, it confirmed the existence of the threat and prompted Joffre to send Castelnau to the spot. After a three-day mission of inspection beginning on 23 January, Castelnau returned to Chantilly to give his report. The impression he brought back, he said, was that 'in general, the defences wholly met the terms of the directives that had been issued, and ... the works that had been created were satisfactory'. Nevertheless, instructions were issued with a view to increasing the available resources. This was the start of a build-up in the numbers of troops and, more generally, in the resources of the Fortified Region of Verdun.

What did Castelnau see during his inspection? (He was accompanied by Driant.) He visited part of the northern front in particular – it was on this front that the defences were in their most advanced state – and also the front on the left bank of the Meuse where they were still very rudimentary. He declared that he was more pleased that he had expected. Some weeks later, on returning from an inspection on the front of Foch's army, he said: 'It's not half as good ... as what I saw at Verdun.'[19]

Even so, the reinforcements that were sent after Castelnau's inspection arrived with little time left for completing the defensive systems. Above all, time was needed to ensure the whole deployment was properly integrated. Setting up the artillery fireplans, for example, or burying the telephone networks sufficiently deeply, could not be done at the wave of a magic wand, and procedures between the infantry and artillery had to be perfected if these two arms were to be coordinated.[20]

Various reasons explain the deficiencies we have noted. There was a sense that Verdun was a quiet sector where nothing happened, and this has been confirmed by many veterans who were with units in the sector before the German attack. Once concern began to grow about Verdun's defensive system and the need to put it in a proper state (or restore it to a proper state), the number of men doing the work was clearly too small, and the continual demands for reinforcements are a persistent theme running through this story.

The productivity of the workforce was extremely poor. The infantryman was there primarily to fight rather than dig, and he also had to live in the position, which meant doing sentry duty, patrols and various fatigues. Some of the divisions sent to Verdun needed to rest and retrain, and so they were not permitted to share in the work. But the most important point was that the French infantryman (and his superiors) hated being a navvy and readily left the work to the engineers, who lacked the numbers to do it. What was actually achieved in practice, therefore, bore no relation to what ought to have been possible according to the theoretical manuals. Digging a 1-metre long section of trench involved excavating about 1 cubic metre of earth. As a rough estimate, it took a full hour for one man to clear out 1 cubic metre of soil (assuming no pick-axe work was needed). Since the enemy did not exactly refrain from trying to obstruct the work, what actually happened on the ground was light-years away from the theory.[21]

Men could not create a line of defence on their own. They needed tools and supplies, including plenty of wood in the form of logs or squared timbers. Also required were such items as tarred paper for waterproofing shelters, wire for stretching in belts in front of the positions, and nails and cramp-irons for fastening pieces of wood to each other. The infantryman had merely the tools that had been issued to him as part of his personal kit, and these quickly wore out, leaving him with nothing. He therefore had to be provided with at least spades and pick-axes from what was known as the park. But the French army remained short of tools and supplies for a long time. It was impossible to do everything simultaneously, so tasks had to be prioritized, and Verdun was not a priority.

The condition of the troops left much to be desired. For example, the 72nd Infantry Division, a reserve division, had been based at Verdun since mobilization. It had undergone several reorganizations and was composed of regiments from just about anywhere. Lieutenant-Colonel Grasset had this to say about the state of its soldiers:

> These men were kept without any respite in a wretched and very tough existence. They saw no end to this situation in the near future, and had something of a fatalistic outlook. Their appearance ... was a far cry from that of the soldiers of 1914. Their clothes were faded, full of holes or roughly patched up, and protruding from underneath could be seen the sleeves and collars of thick, woollen sweaters ... Instead of képis ... they generally wore polo caps, bérets or massive mufflers, and covering everything else they had such items as rugs or leather coverings.[22]

Elegant clothes do not necessarily make for efficiency, yet a unit in such a state certainly lacked the dynamism it soon needed.

The Fortified Region of Verdun could hardly be said to be in a perfect state to resist an attack on 21 February 1916. Yet even if work had begun earlier on building the defensive positions, it is doubtful whether they would have been in an adequate state to check the Germans. After the initial onslaughts of 21, 22, 23 and 24 February, GQG knew that it had a big battle on its hands. Verdun was now a priority whether GQG liked it or not – and it was most unwelcome to Joffre, who was focused on the impending Battle of the Somme on which he had staked so much. Yet despite the new priority accorded to Verdun, the situation there in June was worse than it had been in February. The attack was exceptional because of its sheer violence, and holding out at Verdun took more than previous situations had required. What happened on the right bank of the Meuse on 21 February was simply unprecedented. Not until the start of the Somme offensive did Verdun begin to subside as a constant source of concern and as the weeping sore that Falkenhayn had hoped to create – and the French army continued to struggle with difficulties almost until the end of 1916.

Disarming the forts

The final criticism that has been levelled at Joffre is that he disarmed the forts, and that the local commanders even tried to destroy them. As you would expect, this allegation has been made repeatedly by devotees of fortifications, but it has also been supported by many historians. Taking their lead from a Deputy called Engerand, these historians have assumed that Séré de Rivières' work was a permanent solution to the problem of how to protect both France in general and Verdun in particular.

We need to go back to 5 August 1915, when two decrees appeared. The first of them modified some of the articles in a previous decree (the decree of 7 October 1909, which set out regulations on fortress duties). The governors of those fortresses and fortified regions that lay within the Army Zone were now placed under the orders of the French Commander-in-Chief. (Paris was excluded from the scope of these changes.) This meant that all the resources of the fortresses were at Joffre's disposal. The second decree aligned the wording of the *Regulation on the handling of large units* (dated 28 October 1913) with these new arrangements. Instructions about fortresses were then issued, confirming that their role was no longer separate and distinct from that of the field armies, and specifying that they were subordinated in the same way to the high command.

On 9 August, Dubail issued instructions creating the fortified regions. He pointed out that 'defending such a vast fortified region [as that of Verdun] can be done only by manoeuvre'. He directed that those responsible were to:

> Decide on the course and configuration of the successive lines of defence that are to be created to ensure the field armies remain in touch with each other ... and consider the new role that Verdun's permanent defences should play within this new concept.

Dubail stated that the successive lines 'should make as much use as possible of the existing defences and the works of the entrenched camp'. For example:

> The part of the former main defence zone situated behind the currently-held front from Fort Bois Bourrus to Fort Douaumont and ... Fort Rozellier ... is to be kept ... in its present state with its means of defence:
> 1. The forts with the artillery installed in their turrets and their own means of defence;
> 2. The batteries that still have their guns.

In short, there was no longer any difference between the field armies and the fortified zones. All the fortresses' resources were now at GQG's disposal. The role of a fortress governor continued to exist for the time being, but was abolished at the end of August. (The post of garrison commander was created to take responsibility for the various depots and branches of service, including the engineers, artillery and logistics branches.)

The major innovation of the fortified region was to site the first defensive position far out in front of the fortress and to supplement it with at least two or three positions further back. Each successive position contained several lines of resistance. There was no intention of leaving the forts unused, for quite the opposite was true: they were incorporated seamlessly into the defensive system. The concrete outworks for the infantry (there were as many as twelve of them) proved at least as useful as the forts, and other outworks were also prominent. Thiaumont, for example, was taken and retaken six or seven times in all, and was wiped out by the shelling.

What averted a complete catastrophe was the defensive organization of the ground, with strongpoints and centres of resistance arranged in depth on successive lines. This meant that the defensive works became important only when the course of the battle happened to make them useful. In most cases, they had precious little value as active elements. Although the forts did play an important role, it was a passive role far removed from that originally intended for them. They served as shelters,[23] and did so to such an extent that it sometimes proved necessary to restrict access to them, and to evict the command posts and various organizations that tended to establish themselves inside without good reason. The Germans turned Douaumont into a sort of haven during the several months that they retained the fort. It became a stopping-place in the journey between the rear and the front, as well as a depot and field hospital. Several thousands of men used it, either in going forwards into the line or in returning from it. The Germans restored the fort, but installed no weapons in it other than those required for its self-defence. We should also note that when the French troops had fallen back earlier in the battle, they had simply bypassed Douaumont instead of occupying it, for it was questionable whether the fort had any usefulness as an active defensive work, except as an observation post for artillery. That was just about its only real military value by 1916.

We have seen in Chapter 3 that Joffre, a former Director of Engineers, had clearly been perplexed before the war about the relevance of permanent fortifications. In 1915, he simply put into effect what he had already advocated during those pre-war years. He was very up-to-date in his outlook and regarded war as a dynamic process. He believed that the only valid reason for making war static was to fight at a time and place of his own choosing. In order to respond to changing circumstances, he had to be able to move and adapt all the scarce resources available to him. But General Coutanceau, the commander of the Entrenched Camp of Verdun and the governor of the fortress, saw matters differently and remained attached to siege warfare. Coutanceau's vigorous protests to a parliamentary delegation came to nothing, yet he caused GQG much trouble by getting Dubail to intercede – even though Dubail was the man who had created the Fortified Region of Verdun in the first place.

Whenever we deplore the French army's mania for the offensive in 1914, we must be careful to add a qualifying note, for the defensive remained very attractive in the minds of many generals of the time. Yet the very nature of warfare had changed and the limitations of permanent fortifications had been revealed by the destruction of forts in both Belgium and France. Joffre's pre-war predictions had turned out to be correct, and everything suggests that he then simply implemented measures that he had envisaged some years earlier.

From now on, GQG could use the resources of the Entrenched Camp of Verdun as it thought best. It certainly needed them. Three pressing needs explain the decisions that were taken during the summer of 1915. The first was the desire to replace the resources that the French army had expended during the previous year, namely the hundreds of thousands of men who had been killed, wounded or captured. The second and similar need was to re-equip the field artillery (the 75mm guns), as it had been badly depleted by battle damage and by accidents when shells exploded prematurely inside the gun barrels. Verdun had about forty 75mm guns in the Bourges casemates, along with ammunition for them, and these guns could be used almost immediately by being mounted on a field gun carriage. Another thirty-odd 75mm guns had been installed in turrets to enable the forts to defend themselves, but they all had shortened barrels, which meant they could not be used in the field and so they were left in place.

The third pressing need was the creation of a heavy artillery arm. The only available pieces belonged to the de Bange system, and were basically long-barrelled 120mm guns and long- and short-barrelled 155mm pieces. Fortunately, most of these pieces had already been removed from the forts and were no longer in their traverses. The equivalent of forty-three batteries was withdrawn in October 1915.[24] (The number of actual pieces is uncertain, as is their type, for the totals might include 95mm, 90mm or even 80mm pieces, which were already obsolete.) The Galopin or Bussière retractable turrets were each armed with one long- or short-barrelled 155mm, or occasionally two for the Bussière turret. These pieces had to be left in their turrets as they were impossible to remove.

How much artillery, therefore, had been taken away from Verdun by February 1916? The 75mm guns were no longer in the same locations as before, but at least some of the guns had been reassigned to divisions as a result of the Fortified Region of Verdun being reinforced since September 1915. The artillery of the 132nd Division, for example, had been increased to nine batteries, or thirty-six pieces, by the creation of a *groupe* ('brigade') of

75mm batteries. It was much the same story with the de Bange pieces, except that the turret guns were still in place, and those guns that were not in turrets had been assembled to form the nucleus of a heavy artillery that would otherwise have been practically non-existent. It is true that only about forty heavy pieces remained at Verdun at the end of 1915, yet it was possible to bring more pieces back to the Fortified Region quickly, and indeed that is exactly what happened. It is usually forgotten that the artillery pieces had been immobile and vulnerable until their removal, since they had been mounted on their firing-platforms in the open. When the pieces returned, on the other hand, they could be transported either by road, with caterpillar tracks on their wheels to reduce the pressure on the ground, or by railway.

It is interesting to list the artillery that was in the forts of Verdun on the first day of the German offensive, and compare it with the amount that had been there in 1914. It amounted to seven 155mm turret guns (compared to seven in 1914), twenty-eight 75mm turret guns (compared to twenty-eight) and thirty machine-gun turrets (compared to thirty). There were no longer any 75mm pieces in the Bourges casemates, whereas about forty-six had been there in 1914, but we have seen what happened to them. It is nonsense, therefore, to say that Verdun was disarmed, and in due course we shall consider the way in which these artillery pieces were used.

During the closed parliamentary session of 17 June 1916, the Minister of War, General Roques, listed what GQG had withdrawn from fortresses throughout France.[25] The total amounted to 165 infantry battalions, forty companies of engineers, forty-one field batteries, 134 batteries of foot artillery, 1,144 machine-guns, 1,814 pieces of field artillery and 2,313 heavy artillery pieces, along with millions of shells, cartridges and other such items. This was a lot, and all this weaponry had been standing idle while the war raged. Nor should it be forgotten that 25 per cent of the number of troops mobilized in 1914 were mobilized in the fortresses.[26]

*   *   *

It is worth considering Verdun's fortifications from another perspective. The Germans brought up some 420mm howitzers, which had already demolished the forts of Liège and Namur, and used them to bombard not just Fort Douaumont but also Fort Moulainville. Major Harispe, who commanded the garrison of Moulainville, personally experienced these bombardments. Several years later, he wrote:

> A fort similar to those built for the last war is not strong enough to withstand 420mm shells. If you have to abandon a fort when it comes under bombardment, is it still a fort? If a fort is unable to protect its garrison by stopping heavy shells from smashing their way through, is it fulfilling its role as a fort? Most of the forts were not bombarded with 420mm shells,

which explains why misleading notions have taken hold and why claims
have been made that Verdun's forts played a role.[27]

Both Douaumont and Moulainville were evacuated by their garrisons when
under bombardment by 420mm shells.[28] The occupants actually had to take
refuge in trenches outside the forts.[29] The Germans did this as well when they
were holding Douaumont, and Pétain also issued orders to the same effect.
Trenches were no more proof against 155mm shells than the forts were
against 420mm ones, yet on the whole soldiers were more likely to survive
outside the forts than inside them.

The forts played little role in the actual fighting. Only Forts Douaumont,
Vaux, Souville and to a limited extent Tavannes are ever mentioned in this
respect. Yet Verdun had a total of about fifty defensive works, ranging from
forts to small infantry outworks. Well over half of them were never involved
in the battle, unless they came under long-range artillery fire. Regardless of
whether or not they had been disarmed, they were of no use at all – in most
cases they could not even fire at German units since they were too far away.
The battle unfolded in an area no more than 6 or 7km deep. The only forts
involved were those mentioned above, to which can be added the fire from
the six guns of Moulainville, Vacherauville and Rozellier. This amounted to a
total of nine 155mm and eight 75mm guns – and the latter were reduced to
just four once Forts Douaumont and Vaux had fallen.

Besides, all except one of the artillery pieces of the forts had shortened
barrels. Their range was only around two-thirds that of the ordinary pieces:
4km instead of more than 7km for the 75mm; and 6.7km instead of 9km for
the 155mm. These pieces did little firing, and the reason was not shortage
of ammunition. The Bussière turret of Fort Souville fired just 600 shells
of 155mm calibre from 24 February to 12 April 1916. The 155mm turret of
Moulainville is said to have fired 6,000 shells during the entire Battle of
Verdun. Yet a normal battery of four or six guns could fire up to 1,000 shells
in twenty-four hours. The intensity of the fire from the forts compared to that
of the batteries outside was practically negligible. It had little effect on the
battle, except to the extent that scoring a lucky hit was possible. As far as can
be ascertained, the German artillery fired an average of 150,000 shots of all
calibres every day. The French artillery sometimes managed to fire over
140,000 shots in twenty-four hours, and much more than that during the
attempts to retake the forts. How could Joffre's critics be justified in claiming
that the handful of 75mm guns removed from the Bourges casemates would
have been more effective in their original locations than the numerous 75mm
batteries located behind the front line? The guns in the casemates would, of
course, have been well-sited, with fields of fire that had been perfectly regis-
tered, but they would soon have run out of ammunition.

* * *

Now let's turn to the issue of the destruction of the defensive works. General Herr did indeed issue orders on 24 February 1916 for the demolition of the forts to be prepared. This meant that a start was made on placing explosives in mine-chambers. When blown up, these were meant to destroy the concrete, masonry and other materials of the forts – yet it was not inevitable that an order would come for the actual destruction to be carried out. Precise rules had to be followed when demolishing a permanent structure such as a fort or a bridge. The order to trigger the explosion was just the final act in a long procedure that we do not need to go into here. At Fort Vaux, it seems that a mine-chamber was triggered by either a German shell or by an order given by an unknown French officer.

Was it better to lose Douaumont and Vaux, or to blow them up? It's a difficult question, but on balance it would probably have been better to blow them up. At least that would have avoided the obsession with recapturing them, for as it was the Gallic cock felt obliged to use all its energy to prove it was still alive and it paid a high price as a result. Nevertheless, Pétain decided to cancel the order for preparing the demolitions. On 1 March, he issued instructions to disarm the mine-chambers that had been created in the forts and casemates, but the explosives and equipment were to be stored on the spot, so 'the re-arming of the mines could be carried out with the minimum of delay'. Pétain was perfectly within his authority to give this order, and the consequences showed that his decision was justified in that it did at least provide the troops with shelters. But it was also risky: if Pétain had failed to check the German attack, the order would probably have been given to set off the demolitions – and this would only have been possible if enough time had been available to place the explosives back in the mine-chambers.

Let's consider the situation that had arisen meanwhile at Fort Moulainville. On 24 February, its battery storekeeper received the order from Verdun's directorate of engineers to complete the preparation of mine-chambers for destroying the fort. But the arrival of this order did not mean that the fort had been abandoned – far from it. An officer called Lieutenant Ménager had been sent to take command of its artillery, and he actually had to order his soldiers to prevent the storekeeper's men from entering the gun turrets intent on preparing them for demolition. We can only conclude that both parties were doing their duty in carrying out their apparently contradictory orders. It was only natural for Lieutenant Ménager to fear that he would be prevented from opening fire on the Germans and even that he might be blown up by his own side. Yet we can hardly blame the command chain for trying to speed up the placing of explosives in the mine-chambers, given that it did not know when the Germans would reach the fort. The dilemma was a common one, seen throughout military history, and it has always been difficult to resolve. A crucial bridge, for example, can not be blown up too soon, but if the moment is left too late it will never be blown up at all. At Verdun in 1916, there was no inconsistency in making preparations to demolish a defensive work in order to prevent it from falling into enemy hands.

In purely military terms, Douaumont, Vaux and Souville were not particularly useful, except as shelters. Psychologically, however, they played a role out of all proportion to their actual significance. The Germans naturally played on this psychological card. The news that Douaumont had been taken or lost immediately went around the world. This was how the myth originated. The French were hoist with their own petard because they (the politicians in particular) had laid such emphasis – well before the start of the war – on fortifications and on the role of the fortresses, especially on the eastern frontier.

Verdun was one of the few fortified systems to have been modernized on a regular basis. It simply could not be allowed to fall. If the French lost one of the forts, they had to blame it on an accident, or even better on treason (one of their favourite concepts, since it absolved them of all responsibility). Above all, they had to retake the fort, in order to save the honour of the nation and avert a collapse in the soldiers' morale. In this respect at least, the response of the members of parliament was edifying.

* * *

So who, or what, was to blame for Verdun? Parliament was quick to condemn 'mistakes' and reckoned that big setbacks had to be attributed to suitably prominent scapegoats. Joffre and GQG were therefore blamed, in a classic case of *Vae victis* ('tough luck for the losers'). But the stark reality was that the war was still being waged on a shoestring even at the end of 1915 and the start of 1916. Everything was in short supply. Manpower itself was beginning to run out, but the worst deficiency was undoubtedly the heavy artillery, which was inadequate in both quantity and especially quality.[30] As is too often the case in a tight corner, audacity and morale were the only way – or at least were reckoned to be the only way – to compensate for inferior equipment and technology. Of course Joffre was responsible, but only because his position as Commander-in-Chief meant he was responsible for everything.

I shall close by quoting two different opinions about Verdun. One is Jean-Pierre Guéno's comment about the 'senior generals of the 1914–18 war, some of whom now deserve to be charged posthumously with crimes against humanity, given that their incompetence and inhumanity were so flagrant'.[31]

Philippe Grasset, on the other hand, began by quoting these lines by the poet Péguy:

Mother, behold your sons who have fought so hard,
Let them not be judged on their wretchedness alone.
May God grant them a little bit of this earth
That cost them so much and for which they felt such love.

Grasset then wrote:

> Each time I feel the same emotion. Each time, I weep once more. I do not have these tears when I recall any other event of our recent past. I also believe strongly that the Great War occupies a central and unique place in our history – in the history not just of France but of the world. ... Such a catastrophe, such a scale of suffering beyond the ability of any human mind to grasp, has to have some justification, something beyond earthly matters – and the soul with its ability to broaden and enlargen the mind must surely know this something intuitively.[32]

Even if the 1914–18 war should eventually slip from popular consciousness, Verdun will never be forgotten.

Chapter 9

Joffre and Politics

I'll start by adding some information to what we learned in Chapter 1. Joffre's surprise appointment as Commander-in-Chief designate caused neither outcry nor celebration.[1] Instead, the press seemed confused, for it had expected Pau to be picked. It published just a brief biographical sketch of Joffre, whose achievements in Madagascar had long since been forgotten and those in the Sudan even more so. No fuss or public relations campaign accompanied Joffre's appointment, and he remained practically unknown to the public at large almost until the very start of the war. His name was all but meaningless. Not until the debates about the Three-Year Law did he appear again in the newspapers, and even then it was the General Staff rather than the future Commander-in-Chief who attracted both the applause and the vilification.

Joffre did belong to the Freemasons, but he no longer attended their meetings or conventions. He was known to be friendly with *Monsieur* Huc, the editor of *La Dépêche de Toulouse*, a newspaper so influential in South-Western France that it could swing the outcome of elections. It was the South-West, too, that produced Joffre's strongest supporters and fiercest opponents. He managed to navigate the troubled times of the Dreyfus Affair and the controversy over the officers' personal files without giving anyone grounds to accuse him of being politically-committed – and that was quite some achievement in itself. The fact that it was André who bestowed his general's stars on him caused Joffre to be labelled a man of the Left, and he surely was so at heart, but he never advertised it.

Joffre had been appointed to his post by Caillaux's government, in which Messimy served as Minister of War. Power then passed to a new President of the Council of Ministers, Poincaré. His Minister of War, Millerand, was the first in a series of men in that post who carefully avoided clashing with the General Staff and its Chief in the period up to 1914. Etienne and Noulens continued to trust Joffre completely, as did Messimy on his return to the Ministry of War in 1914. Such constancy was rare in France at that time and it sustained Joffre's authority as Chief of the General Staff. By the time war broke out, he had attracted barely any criticism in either parliament or the press.

However, the Three-Year Law had begun to make both friends and enemies for Joffre in politics. In the eyes of Socialists and some Radicals, he was hardly an ideal Republican, and strong hostility to him began to appear. He came under incessant political attacks from Doumer, Accambray and

Chautemps, as well as from some more obscure members of parliament who had won seats in 1914 in the last of the pre-war elections.[2]

Millerand, a Socialist who had moved towards the centre ground, remained Joffre's best protector until the end of the summer of 1915. The Commander-in-Chief was able to conduct the war sheltered from parliament and its members, and in particular from the presidents of the Army Commissions in the Chamber of Deputies (General Pédoya) and in the Senate (initially Senator Freycinet, then Clemenceau). Allegations were later made that Joffre had become the real Minister of War and some truth lay in these charges, as can be seen from the tone of some of his correspondence with the Minister.

Wartime problems
The first significant problems emerged following the start of the war. What status should be accorded to those members of parliament and ministers who had been mobilized? No clear-cut position was adopted on this question because parliament was so quick to adjourn – it did so on 4 August 1914, with an assurance from the President of the Council of Ministers, Viviani, that the campaign would last just six weeks. But in December the government returned to Paris in the wake of the Battle of the Marne and the parliamentary chambers reconvened. Joffre then asked the Minister of War to clarify the position of those members of parliament who had been mobilized. He wrote in a letter of 18 January 1915: 'If they prefer to carry out their military duty, they will be subject to all the duties and obligations of mobilized soldiers. If, on the other hand, they are to sit in parliament, they will be detached and a replacement will take over their command or military post.'[3] This stated the matter plainly enough, and Joffre gave some specific examples to back up his request for clarification. For instance: 'When a mobilized Deputy returns to Paris, is he free to discuss the actions of his past and future superiors when he speaks in the Chamber?'

It was a good question, but was never answered. Parliament preferred to declare itself in permanent session, and this ploy allowed the mobilized Deputies – there were slightly more than 200 of them – to continue shuttling between Paris and the front. This supposedly enabled backbench Deputies to carry out both their military and parliamentary duties at the same time. Yet Léopold Marcellin took a different view and bluntly wrote that it 'provided those who had been mobilized with an excuse to avoid returning to the trenches' – an allegation that I shall neither confirm nor refute.[4]

Joffre's troubles came largely from these mobilized Deputies. The war as they described it to their fellow members of parliament was limited to their personal experiences – and the vast majority of them witnessed it from a very low level because of the rank they held. They were no more than captains, meaning that they were just company commanders. The few exceptions tended to be Deputies who were former officers, as they already held a rank in the army reserve. Nor were all of them to be found in the trenches. Some simply served as officers in the supporting services, or fell into the category of those labelled 'shirkers'.

Among the biggest 'trouble-makers' were such men as Accambray (a captain), Ybarnegaray (a second-lieutenant), Abel Ferry (a corporal, then a second-lieutenant, while at the same time remaining within the government until 1915), Maginot (a private, then a sergeant, though he was wounded early on and did not return to the front thereafter) and Messimy (a former government minister who was quickly promoted major).[5] The result was just as Joffre had predicted. The war amounted to what these men saw of it, at the particular locations where they happened to be.[6]

Obviously, they were not to blame for what they experienced. Yet the accounts they gave on their return about what they had seen of the war could not fail to disturb the vast majority of their colleagues, who at the same time were being overwhelmed by letters from constituents serving in the army. How were these politicians to take a broader perspective and ponder the best way of winning the war, rather than focusing on haphazard incidents? When confronted with the dark side of the conflict – the scale of the casualties and the massive population displacements from the war zone – it took great moral strength if not to forget these aspects then at least to take a balanced view of them. The Deputies lacked the mental toughness to do that, and the nature of their role in parliament had made them more accustomed to knocking things down than building them up. The Third Republic had a strong legislature, but weak executive – not because it had been designed that way constitutionally, but because in practice members of parliament had grown thoroughly used to treating governments like a game of skittles.

The *Union sacrée* ('Sacred Union') of August 1914 could not long withstand the swings in fortune of the opening phase of the war. The combined effect of the Battle of the Frontiers, the danger to Paris, the government's transfer to Bordeaux, the fruitless offensives and the heavy casualties served to inflame the Deputies. They soon stepped up their efforts, first in demanding answers to their questions and then in undermining the men in charge. Nor did the political divisions help smooth matters over. The 1914 elections had given a majority to the Left, which was composed of Socialists and Radicals determined to scrap the Three-Year Law. The Left was hardly fond of the military and, since it could no longer take up its usual stance on national defence, it resorted instead to bitter, relentless criticism of those who were responsible for it.

For the first time since the proclamation of the Republic, France was discovering the problems involved in maintaining a parliamentary democracy while waging a war in Europe. No precedents existed to provide guidance. Vital issues could not be addressed in plenary sessions, lest the enemy gained useful information. More open debate was possible in the commissions, but just forty-four (later sixty) Deputies belonged to them. This did not satisfy the backbenchers, who were desperate to have their views heard. A compromise was found by assembling the parliamentary chambers in closed sessions, and I shall return to this in due course.

Everyone remembered the great moments of the French Revolution. Some of the Deputies saw themselves as political commissars sent to the armies by a new National Convention, adorned with a tricolour sash and empowered to decide whether or not to impose the death penalty on generals who were trying to fight the war. Messimy often urged Joffre to have no hesitation in executing commanders who proved unreliable. All this helped to inflame parliament, and when it assembled the atmosphere of the session soon became highly-charged.

*   *   *

The second difficulty that Joffre encountered was the parliamentary commissions' insistence on sticking their noses into his 'business'. The Army Commissions of both the Chamber of Deputies and the Senate included representatives of every political group of the two assemblies. It was within these commissions that discontent first emerged. They had not assembled when war was declared and had left for Bordeaux along with both the chambers. It was on returning to Paris that they held their first meetings, and they immediately made clear that they intended to see matters for themselves and supervise them. They initially did so in a minor way and refrained from extending their activities into the Army Zone, but they soon grew more ambitious and tried to expand the area of their supervision.

Joffre, who was consulted by the Minister of War, was flatly opposed to such attempts. General Pédoya, the President of the Army Commission in the Chamber of Deputies, stated: 'Considering that the commission has an important duty to fulfil and a responsibility to the country, [I] ask for a pass to be given to this commission's members, enabling them to travel at any time by motorcar, railway or even on foot, inside the Army Zone.' But Joffre replied on 20 February 1915: 'I respectfully inform you that it is impossible to comply with your request.' He added: 'I take the view that while operations are on-going, there can be no parliamentary supervision of the high command's actions, nor of the functioning of the army's support branches.'[7]

The Commander-in-Chief never wavered in refusing to allow parliamentary supervision inside the Army Zone. Yet the dispute was clearly far from over. Pédoya managed to get to Dunkirk, despite the risk of being imprisoned. When Millerand visited the Army Commission on 7 May 1915, Pédoya bluntly declared: 'The commission has decided that its members will go wherever I, the president, think it is worth sending them.' On 20 June, the commission won the argument, but with restrictions that prevented it from acting as it pleased. In particular, it was obliged to give forewarning of what it intended to do, despite its earlier opposition on this point. Joffre eventually gave way after Galliéni was appointed Minister of War – Galliéni was keen to exercise his ministerial authority. Even so, it was the end of 1916 before the commission could do more or less what it wanted.

Nor did the Senate find it any easier. The President of its Army Commission was refused permission when he wanted to visit Verdun. Some days later, a mission to the entrenched camps of Eastern France was blocked as well, and many other incidents could be described. For example, when the Budget Commision tried in August 1915 to find out how many men were on the staffs, it was asked why it wanted to know.

By the time Joffre left his post, the commissions had regained all their prerogatives, and never relinquished them again. The Commander-in-Chief may in fact have taken the wrong approach. As he knew full well, his position was legally untenable. Since no precedent existed for the parliamentary commissions' working method, nothing prevented one from being created from scratch. This would have been quite easy at the start of the war when everyone was trying things out and the contentious issues had not yet surfaced. But Joffre's stubborn refusal irritated the members of parliament, and in any case they were kept informed of events – or at least had the impression that they were – by many letters reaching them from the front. (The writers of the letters included officers at all levels, and not all of them were reservists.) Joffre might have defused the pressure had he taken a pre-emptive approach. Instead, he simply stonewalled, and that did nothing to prevent the most damaging stories from spreading by word-of-mouth.

During the first half of 1915, two secret reports, three months apart, were sent to certain Deputies, most of whom were on the Left or Left-of-Centre. The authors were clearly military men, who were probably serving in General Sarrail's 3rd Army and were perhaps writing under the guidance of civilians. The first report was entitled *Situation before the declaration of war, and operations from August 1914 to January 1915*. It was a real denunciation of the Commander-in-Chief and heavily criticized everything he had done since Plan XVII: 'It is not possible for just one man, even if he is General Joffre ... to appoint the army and army group commanders on his own and without supervision. It is not possible ... for France to leave its fate in the hands of just one man, who lacks ... the necessary depth for this task.' The Commander-in-Chief was criticized for bestowing all the rewards on generals 'who lacked any ties to the Republic'.

The second report was entitled *Note on the military situation on 20 April 1915*. It set out Joffre's assets and liabilities, and predictably the liabilities far outweighed the assets. Strangely, the author (or perhaps authors) argued in favour of establishing a sort of council where operational decisions would be taken collectively – a proposal that certainly raises my eyebrows.

It was probably no coincidence that these reports were followed by a letter from Accambray. Dated 18 November 1915, it was sent to Briand, the new President of the Council of Ministers. Accambray clearly knew about the two reports and he intensified the criticism of the Commander-in-Chief. His conclusion was clear-cut: Joffre had to be removed from his command, on the grounds that he was not up to the task. Those army group commanders who were reckoned to be lukewarm Republicans – Dubail, Foch and above all Castelnau – also had to be sacked. What Accambray proposed was simply to appoint Sarrail as Commander-in-Chief. Sarrail had been Ruffey's replacement in command of the 3rd Army, but had been jettisoned by Joffre in July 1915 after failing to achieve much in the Argonne. Joffre then wanted to give him command of just an army corps, but Sarrail furiously turned it down, the Deputies on the Left had an adrenaline rush and the Minister of War found himself in a predicament. Eventually, Sarrail was prevailed upon to take command of the forces sent to Salonika. At the time, these forces were directly under the Minister of War's authority. But a decree was issued that December raising Joffre to the command of all the French armies, and so Sarrail once again found himself under his orders. Joffre distrusted Sarrail's sudden whims and in May 1916 rebuked him by telegraph over a minor matter: 'In future, as a commander you need to show a level-headedness and sense of discipline that you have totally lacked.'[8] But Sarrail's interests were vigilantly defended by the entire Left wing of the Chamber of Deputies, for he alone of France's generals was believed to be whole-heartedly Republican.

* * *

The campaign against Joffre was then ratcheted up several notches when both the Chamber of Deputies and the Senate met in closed sessions. The government had been reluctant to countenance these sessions, but the first were held on 16–22 June and 4–9 July 1916. Briand, the President of the Council of Ministers, and Roques, his Minister of War, were present so they could answer questions from the members of parliament.[9] It was no different from an ordinary meeting of the Chamber of Deputies, except that the press was absent and the public galleries were empty, which in theory made it possible to discuss any topic without the risk of valuable information being given away. But the reality was somewhat different. Even if the shorthand record of the debates remained confidential for a long time, there was nothing to stop certain Deputies from informing journalists and political friends what had been said. Indeed, this seems to have been exactly what happened. Another closed session was held in the Chamber of Deputies on 28 and 29 November, and then in the Senate on 19–23 December 1916.

By now, almost two years had passed without parliament having been able to assemble for an *unrestricted* discussion of the war. The pressure of the pent-up resentments that had accumulated in that time can be imagined. Such matters as the artillery issues, the war in the Balkans, the Dardanelles, Verdun, and the government's relations with the high command were all discussed, either because the questions that were raised were included in the Orders of the Day, or because the Deputies were unable to contain themselves and instinctively broadened the debate. Among the most critical of them were Maginot, Accambray, Margaine, Abel Ferry, Renaudel and Bénazet.[10]

Here's a flavour of what was said.[11] A Deputy called Delahaye stated: 'When governments are weak or powerless, as is the case with the [defensive] organization of the Army Zone, then the people have the power, through their representatives, to ensure that their wishes are heard.'[12] Next Renaudel denounced the 'chess-players of Chantilly' – this was a lousy play on the French word *échecs*, which can mean either 'chess' or 'setbacks' – and he added that 'a purge needed to be carried out'. Another Deputy, Hennessy, declared: 'So we'll not stop dragging [the government] back to the Battle of Verdun, because that is where the proof lies of the incompetence of our high command.'[13] The June closed session ended on an Order of the Day that decided 'to create and set up a direct delegation that, with the government's help, would provide effective and on-the-spot supervision of all the branches responsible for supplying the army's needs'.

It had not been a good start. The November closed session centred more on questions relating to the operations in the Balkans and on the commander of the forces in that region, General Sarrail. To a man, the whole of the Left harried Joffre and the government for always 'bullying' Sarrail. Chaumet declared: 'There is an element in the way he has sometimes been treated that has not merely been distressing for himself and his pride …'.[14]

Joffre's fall

Joffre sensed that people and power alike were slipping away from him. First and foremost among them was his old friend, General Roques. Roques was a graduate of the *Ecole polytechnique* and a veteran of Tonkin and Madagascar, and thanks to Joffre had succeeded him as Director of Engineers. When Roques became Minister of War, Joffre might have thought that Galliéni's period as Minister would prove to have been just an interlude and that Roques would support him as solidly as Millerand had always done. Yet it turned out that Roques wanted to exercise real power as Minister and thought he could manipulate the great beasts of parliament by feeding them concessions, the most important of which was parliamentary supervision.[15] As a result, Joffre's prerogatives disappeared bit by bit. The names of officers whom he proposed for promotion were crossed out and replaced by others. He was obliged to part from his closest assistants: General Pellé, Colonel Buat (formerly Millerand's principal private secretary, he had become a hate-figure for members of parliament) and Major Bel (the head of GQG's Personnel

Department, a formidable man who was feared for the hold he supposedly had over the Commander-in-Chief). Several of Joffre's old comrades – loyal men from the black days of August and September 1914 – left their posts when they reached the age limit, to the government's relief. De Langle de Cary, Dubail, Villaret and d'Urbal were thus put aside, and there would have been delight in some quarters had Foch and Castelnau followed.

For Joffre, it was the end. At first, there was a pretence of leaving him with a share of the responsibility for conducting the war. But he was then removed altogether, although the blow was softened by his elevation to the dignity of Marshal of France. Bugnet wrote:

> In their haste to see the endless nightmare draw finally to a close, people were prepared to take a gamble rather than stick with him: anything was better, just so long as it was something different! People cling to hope, even illusory hope, and the problem with [Joffre] was that he had caused too many disappointments, even if those disappointments were exaggerated.[16]

Joffre had spent two-and-a-half years in command, and that was a long time indeed during so great a war. The men who brought him down had their come-uppance. In 1917, the Nivelle offensive failed bloodily and France was in danger of collapse. The army mutinies were the result not of political agitation – that played only a minor role – but rather of a general weariness. Catastrophe might have ensued had the Germans known more about what was happening. The French officers may not have joined the mutinies, but their morale had slumped and that slump seems to gone hand-in-hand with a loss of respect for the generalissimo. This became clear shortly afterwards, when it proved difficult to find officers who were willing to be Joffre's companions in his semi-retirement.

The members of parliament had acted as clumsily as the fabled sorcerer's apprentice. Tangled up in their fixed ideological beliefs, they proved incapable of implementing change and of establishing new methods of working, even though change had become unavoidable. Events showed that Joffre had definitely been correct to try and prevent members of parliament from eagerly pursuing a mix of roles – a mix that might see them firing a rifle and leading a section of troops on one day, and on the next proclaiming in a speech in the Chamber of Deputies that the orders from above were just a load of nonsense.

Appointing a soldier rather than a civilian as Minister of War was bound to cause further difficulties, yet it happened three times in succession (Galliéni, Roques and then Lyautey). The whole point of a general was to wage war, and so things were bound to go wrong if he was put in a position where waging war was the one thing he was unable to do because it was being waged by someone else (though theoretically in his name). The fact that the government always had a political hue aggravated the problem, for it was immediately assumed, rightly or wrongly, that the soldier in charge of the Ministry of War accepted the government's ideas, even if only because of the principle of collective responsibility. Weygand wrote: 'In France soldiers have always made execrable Ministers of War. Being closely involved in politics, they defend the government's interests better than those of the army. But at the same time, their lack of previous political experience exposes them to being led astray by the beguiling ease of compromise solutions ...'.[17]

It is difficult to see how the members of parliament made any worthwhile improvements to the conduct of the war. The government's relations with the high command should have been formalized before the war, at the same time as a war plan was drawn up. But more pressing concerns had required attention back then, and so it was left too late. After Joffre's fall, the process of appointing commanders-in-chief was left to the gossip and hazards of politics. The soldiers did not always play an honorable role in this, and in fact they just inflamed an already overwrought system. Mermeix recorded Briand as saying: 'Whenever a general comes to Paris to have lunch with a member of parliament, the number of candidates for the post of Commander-in-Chief increases by one. I was unaware that soldiers had so much influence over the civil power.'[18] Similarly, Poincaré declared: 'Whenever I meet someone in uniform, I'm given his opinion.' All too often, generals unburdened themselves in the midst of politicians who were eager to listen – and eager in particular to use the information they were told as ammunition against GQG and its chief, regardless of whether or not it was accurate. Painlevé was another person who complained about this.

In August 1916, Joffre learned that Franchet d'Esperey had used political connections to offer his services as Commander-in-Chief, and that Maginot had gone to sound out Foch in order to offer him the post. Later, Castelnau took steps to try and secure the command.[19] Before the Nivelle offensive in 1917, something unique in politico-military history was seen: a sort of informal council-of-war where those entrusted with carrying out their Commander-in-Chief's planned operations were asked in turn and in his presence to say what they thought about them.

Matters changed after Clemenceau came to power, for this eminent 'democrat' muzzled the parliamentary chambers. Ironically, he did so by applying the same methods for which he had previously criticized those governments he had declined to join. Parliament's heyday had lasted from mid-1916 to November 1917, but it was during precisely this same period that the French war effort lacked a clear-cut direction. Even if that was possibly just a co-incidence, it is clear that democracies invariably struggle to cope in extraordinary circumstances. As for Joffre, he had served France well for five years and was able to leave the stage with his pride intact.

Chapter 10

The Dismissals

This is a brief discussion of the *limogeages* or 'dismissals'. It is not the easiest chapter to write, firstly because the sources have gaps and secondly because the real reasons for the dismissals are often unclear from the records. Even when reports are available they have to be interpreted, since the style in which they were written tends to obscure what actually happened. It is not always understandable why points raised in the reports were deemed to be faults or mistakes. I shall identify the generals concerned solely by the first letter of their surname, purely out of respect for their descendants. Only in exceptional circumstances shall I use the full name.[1]

Sent to Limoges

The phrase *généraux limogés* usually means generals who lost their command, did not immediately obtain another one, and were compulsorily transferred to the 12th Military Region (whose administrative centre was Limoges) or else to some other city such as Besançon or Dijon. Not all the dismissed generals actually went to Limoges, but most were transferred to posts outside the Army Zone. We must remember that it was not Joffre alone who was responsible for the dismissals. Some generals (in many cases they were fortress commanders) were dismissed by the successive Ministers of War, Messimy and then Millerand. Decisions about the removal of less senior officers – colonels, majors and ordinary captains – were made below the Commander-in-Chief's level.

What we need is a systematic analysis of the dismissals, identifying why the officers concerned lost their commands. There were all sorts of reasons. Some men were removed for perfectly respectable medical reasons. Others had been wounded or had become so stressed that they were temporarily unable to remain in post. Many were simply labelled 'exhausted' and sent on leave to recover their health, but were assigned a different command when they returned some weeks later.

Stress, or combat strain, became an aspect of the war that could not be ignored. Fear, setbacks and heavy casualties were obvious causes, but even more important were physical and nervous exhaustion and the impossibility of letting go and relaxing. Most of the dismissed generals had 'cracked' before they were removed. The only fault that can be attached to most of them is that they failed to foresee the situation in which they found themselves and did not prepare for it. It was the state of their nerves, more than any inherent incompetence, that prevented them from continuing to direct their units in action. Any general who failed to organize his command post for the long-haul ceased to be of much use after 48 hours spent without sleep while receiving an avalanche of bad news. Claims that the generals were insensitive to casualties are much exaggerated.

Some commanders committed suicide, either at the front or following their dismissal.[2] In 1914, generals received no training in how to withstand the pressure for a long period. They were not even aware what lay in store for them, since they had no previous experience of modern warfare. Battles were not expected to last longer than a few hours, yet at the start of the war nearly every unit fought for over two months with few breaks. 'Guts' and 'moral strength' could not suffice for everything.

Numerous accounts exist of generals who clearly lost all control of themselves, collapsed in tears, and were unable to calm down and think. Their incapacity to direct the battle was obvious to their assistants, many of whom were in no better state. Some commanders completely failed to hide their demoralization, and General Legrand-Girarde, whom we have already met, frankly admitted to having broken down in front of a subordinate.[3] Much scorn has been poured on the care that Joffre took to preserve his health – including his copious meals and his eight hours of sleep – yet it does much to explain his remarkable mental stability. In contrast, Joffre described Lanrezac's state when they met on 28 August 1914: 'I was struck by his physical condition: his face was etched with exhaustion; yellowish skin, bloodshot eyes ... with gestures that revealed the state of his nerves.' Nor was Ruffey in any better shape after several days of battle, and I'll return to both these generals in due course. Stress was by far the foremost cause of incapacity. If a general no longer commanded his unit, or if he commanded it badly, it was usually because he lacked, or had lost, the necessary physical and mental state.

In August 1914, the French army required about 160 *généraux de division* and 260 *généraux de brigade*. The first were to lead the armies, army corps and divisions, and the second just the brigades. Included in these statistics are the generals needed for cavalry, artillery or engineer commands, and for the staffs. Yet the numbers of those available were just 120 *généraux de division* and 220 *généraux de brigade*.[4] The shortfall had to be filled by using reservists, yet these were inevitably elderly since the age limits for active service were 60 years for colonels (some of whom commanded brigades), 62 for *généraux de brigade* and 65 for *généraux de division*.

Many of these older officers were physically unfit and had long since give up horse-riding. Yet horses were essential for moving about during operations, and any general had at least two of them at his disposal. In that era, regular horse-riding was not simply a means of staying healthy, it also demonstrated the rider's fitness for operational duties. A commander who could ride was able to move about on the ground, and this ensured he was close to his troops – something that was essential if he wanted to know what was happening. Any commander who was unable to move around had no chance of keeping track of the battle and could not impose himself on the operations, as he would no longer be directing them. More than one officer defended himself against allegations of exhaustion by referring, if not to his prowess at horse-riding, then at least to the fact that he made a habit of it.

*   *   *

In theory, Joffre lacked any power over the appointment and dismissal of generals or colonels. All these officers, commanding regiments, brigades, divisions, army corps or armies, were appointed by the Council of Ministers and held what was known as a 'letter of service', in other words an official letter of appointment. The officers owned their rank and could not be demoted. Compulsory retirement was possible only after the Supreme War Council had deliberated and given its opinion, and then a decision would be made by the President of the Republic. That was how the Faurié Affair was dealt with after the Grand Manœuvres of 1913 in South-Western France. Transferring an officer to another post was easier and required just a straightforward transfer order, even though there might be an underlying implication that the officer was being relieved from his command.

On 15 August 1914, Messimy notified Joffre that he was having the 1912 Law changed to allow a general officer to be compulsorily retired without the need for the Supreme War Council to deliver an opinion.[5] Instead, the Commander-in-Chief would simply send a report to the Minister of War. On 24 August, Messimy informed Joffre: 'I again urge you to be merciless. I want some cowardly or incompetent commanders to be executed *in the real sense of the word*.[6] Messimy specified the procedure to be followed for those who were spared 'execution': they were to be placed under strict arrest at the residence that they gave as their place of retirement, and a report was to be sent to the Minister of War. He concluded: 'These people must not be allowed to stroll idly about.' I have already emphasized Messimy's state of intense exaltation: he believed he was living through a repetition of 1792 and borrowed his ways of doing things from the great classics of literature. In the event, no general was executed, for Joffre wisely let the Minister of War know that he had neither the time nor the means to have the necessary indepth enquiries made. Messimy left office some days later, after sending Joffre numerous letters in the same vein. His replacement, Millerand, was just as concerned about the issue, but did not advocate such extreme steps and used more moderate words.

Joffre had already written on 13 August to inform his army commanders: 'If you have noted the least shortcoming among the generals or unit commanders under your orders – or should you do so – you are to report the officers to me as a matter of urgency and they will immediately be replaced. This will not rule out the possibility of more serious measures being taken against them.' Joffre now had the assurance of the Minister of War's backing and he was setting his sights not only at the generals, but also at the colonels in command of regiments. But his same letter of 13 August also asked that officers and generals who particularly distinguished themselves should be reported to him, so he could appoint them to posts that became 'vacant'. The result was a vast and irregular succession of personnel movements to and fro, and some units were commanded by several generals in succession – which is not exactly ideal in terms of promoting efficiency!

Using the relevant archive records, I have compiled a list of no fewer than ninety-six officers whose transfers were ordained by GQG between 12 August and 30 September 1914.[7] Most of the officers in question were generals. They include fifteen who were put at the Minister of War's disposal between 12 and 31 August. (It is, however, an incomplete list, for some men – such as Lanrezac and d'Amade – seem to be missing from the register.)

When a decision was taken to dismiss someone, it was rare for the initiative to come from Joffre, although it was occasionally known to happen. Normally, he waited until he received reports about officers who merited removal. He did not intervene if his chief subordinates were satisfied with their officers, although he might sometimes ask for information about a specific individual.

Joffre's liaison officers have often been accused of having taken the 'scalp' of certain generals such as Lanrezac. But their actions have to be seen in their proper perspective. Joffre never relieved officers solely on the advice of his liaison officers, and if necessary he went personally to assess what he had been told. Consider, for example, the messages exchanged on 20 August between Joffre and General Ruffey, the 3rd Army's commander. It all began when Major Bel returned to GQG and reported that the commander of the 14th Hussars, Colonel R——, ought to be forcibly retired on the grounds of 'physical and moral unfitness for active operations'.[8] Joffre at once requested Ruffey by telephone: 'Confirm this assessment for me as a matter of urgency by a personal telephone message.' In almost every case, three people – sometimes four – either took the decision or were party to it. They were the immediate superior or superiors of the officer in question, the general commanding the army in which he was serving, and Joffre, who had the final say. The Commander-in-Chief lacked the time to assess a case and ponder its ins and outs in the calm of his office, yet no decision was taken blindly and on the basis of mere denunciations as his enemies liked to claim. His liaison officers did play a role, but were more likely to have done so by bringing back their overall impressions and an idea of the general atmosphere. This can be seen by reading between the lines of the reports from Alexandre, the liaison officer with the 5th Army.[9]

The army commanders often acted as a restraining influence, and appeared cautious and extremely scupulous when it came to putting their complaints in writing. This has helped create an impression that Joffre acted arbitrarily, yet in reality he was willing to reconsider his decisions. On 23 August, for example, he took care to inform General Ruffey that he was granting his request to remove General L—— and General G de La M—— from their posts. But he added: 'If events ... should cause you to change your mind about these general officers, I would be very amenable myself to reconsidering the steps that have been taken.' Indeed, on 25 August he cancelled his decision regarding the commander of the 8th Division, 'given the audacity that General de L—— has shown during the action of 22 August and the subsequent days.'

On the other hand, when Joffre thought the information he had requested was either insufficient or totally biased, he sent a reprimand to wayward subordinates so they would state matters objectively. In August 1916 he had a letter sent to Foch about the replacement of Colonel H du T——, the commander of the 264th Infantry Brigade:

> But he can not pass over General R——'s report, which is so vague and tediously confused. The misgivings expressed by the commander of the 132nd Infantry Division are utterly superfluous – they can not fail to complicate the high command's decision-making, and they betray General R——'s hesitant and indecisive character.

Hence this business in itself caused General R—— to be seen as 'indecisive', which was hardly a good sign 'on the eve of the action'. General R—— accepted the rebuke he received some days later, but he had had a narrow escape.

Some men were given a dose of their own medicine. Lanrezac and Ruffey, who commanded the 5th and 3rd Armies respectively, were assiduous in condemning subordinates – this was especially true of Ruffey. They both demanded the removal of numerous officers, until their own turn came to be relieved of their commands. I have felt free to identify these two generals, since Joffre himself has much to say about them in his memoirs. They disappeared from the order of battle and never returned.

Ruffey was fairly blunt in his assessments. He reckoned that 'Colonel C—— [was] completely panic-stricken and is said to have destroyed his flag'. He also complained that 'the state of mind of some general, field and company officers of the 5th Corps is atrocious'.[10] He added: 'The *généraux de division* are completely demoralized and fail to hide their shortcomings properly from the soldiers they command.' His assessment of a third man, General B——, was: 'Did not understand the situation.' Ruffey was removed from his command on 30 August 1914 by Joffre in person.[11] Twice he wrote to the Minister of War and to the Commander-in-Chief, seeking another command even if it was at a lower level. He was practically begging, as is clear from this letter of 13 December: 'More than three months have passed since I was last at the front. What a torment! I respectfully ask you for any command at all, even a division.' Ruffey tried again some months later, on 22 May 1915. This time he sent a letter directly to Joffre, once more offering his services. He emphasized: 'I respectfully ask you to make use of me in the operations that are likely to unfold in the near future against the German fortresses in Eastern France and especially against Metz–Thionville and Strasbourg.' Joffre did not reply and Ruffey was never given another command at the front. The fact that he was put permanently on the shelf was probably connected with a memorandum he wrote expressing doubts about Joffre and Maunoury.[12]

I have already said much about Lanrezac in previous chapters. He seems to have been less set than Ruffey on trying to have some of his army's generals replaced. However, I can mention the case of Sauret, the commander of the 3rd Corps, who was nowhere to be found during much of the Battle of the Sambre. On 25 August 1914, Lanrezac sent GQG a five-point report by telephone, condemning Sauret's command failings. For an entire day, Sauret had been completely ignorant of the locations of his troops. He was sacked on the grounds of 'professional inadequacy' and replaced by General Hache.

Lanrezac himself was relieved on 3 September, though Joffre had hesitated right up until the end to give him the chop. It is difficult to tell whether Lanrezac deserved his removal, since the controversy surrounding the decision grew enormously inflated after the war and has obscured the objective reasons – some did exist – that lay behind it. Joffre devoted several pages of his memoirs to this incident – proof, were any needed, that it left him scarred.[13] Admittedly, Lanrezac had endured ten stressful days of defeat and relentless retreat. But he really does seem to have fallen out of step with his Commander-in-Chief, and his ongoing friction with Sir John French risked undermining whatever remained of the cooperation between the Allies. Lanrezac's indecision is confirmed by many witnesses, along with his stubbornly cautious and uncertain attitude.[14] His replacement was Franchet d'Esperey, the commander of his army's 1st Corps.

Other examples can be mentioned, such as General Pouradier-Duteil of the 14th Corps, which was engaged at the Sainte-Marie Pass in 1914. On 15 August, he asked for two colonels to be removed, but he himself was relieved on the 23rd.[15] His army commander, Dubail, then relented and gave him another chance, only for Joffre to uphold the dismissal. According to Pouradier-Duteil's grandson, Paul, the reason was that Joffre wanted to give command of the 14th Corps to one of his protégés, General Baret, which may or may not be true.

* * *

The reasons given to justify the removals fall into three categories: physical, moral and professional unfitness. As a general rule, physical and moral unfitness went hand-in-hand if the physical problems stemmed from the stress of battle rather than from illness. But some officers really were sick, or else were wounded, while others had undergone a physical shock and survived only by a miracle. One example was General D——, who had to be evacuated after a heavy calibre shell exploded nearby and killed two of the runners he had available for carrying his messages.

Exhaustion and the need for rest were often mentioned and used to justify someone's removal. Spells of leave were granted fairly readily, but sometimes the officers concerned did not return to their units afterwards, being relieved for good. De Langle de Cary requested the removal of General B——, the commander of the 70th Reserve Division, who was suffering from a 'symptomatic trembling and [was] hesitant in the way he spoke, slow on the uptake'. A worrying state of nerves was detected in one major, and 'precautions [had] to be taken to prevent Major de L—— from blowing out his brains'. Another man, a cavalry colonel, was stated to have 'emphysema'.

Joffre refused to tolerate officers who lost their composure, or those whose words or actions seemed to betray weakness, indecision or lack of confidence. In his memoirs, he often mentioned his pleasure at seeing calmness and resolve in his chief subordinates and in their staffs. The words 'calm' and 'confidence' appear frequently in his writings, and it is true that any general who loses control of his nerves is liable to find that he automatically loses the ability to command. Similarly, defeatism, or a failure to believe in victory, led directly to an officer's removal, especially if he expressed it in the presence of subordinates.

The third category of reasons for relieving generals was professional incompetence, and it was frequently cited. It is difficult today, with insufficient evidence, to list the lapses that were recorded and assess how much truth lay behind them, but they varied widely. They ranged from the muddle-headed general who did his subordinates' work for them, to his counterpart at the opposite end of the scale who failed to issue any orders and was nowhere to be found. Many sacked generals were accused of multiple, and sometimes contradictory, mistakes, such as either misusing advanced-guards or forgetting to use them altogether. More frequently, generals were simply accused of professional inadequacy, and if details were given at all, then it might be in such vague terms that it is difficult to work out what lay at the bottom of it. For instance, Dubail reckoned that General P——, the commander of the 55th Infantry Brigade, was 'incapable in respect of tactics and knowing how to handle a brigade'. What exactly is that supposed to mean? To take another example, Joffre asked for a report about two of the 5th Army's *généraux de division* who were apparently not 'up to their task'. D'Urbal thought that another *général de division*, General T——, the commander of the 16th Corps, 'commanded feebly'. One of General T——'s subordinates, General Xardel (whom we have already discussed in Chapter 5) was himself 'dismissed despite all the efforts he made to exercise his command'. I could give many similar examples.

Some of these professional inadequacies caused considerable casualties. For instance, a failure to take proper security measures was liable to result in units being surprised by German artillery and machine-gun fire while still formed in marching columns. Yet heavy losses never led automatically to removal, unless they had been caused by a commander's mistakes. I have found just one exception to this in the dossiers that I consulted, and that was the case of General L——, the commander of the 67th Infantry Division. He was rebuked for having made statements that were deemed to be damaging: 'It is unheard-of for a general officer to repeat the most damaging allegations made by the army's enemies, and write that a military operation should aim to get our men wounded.'

Occasionally, the reasons for dismissal were unconnected with purely military considerations. For instance, Joffre asked Foch in August 1915 to look into the case of General B——, 'who is said to have had a woman of loose morals brought to the town where his headquarters were located, and he supposedly lived with her for several weeks'. The general in question had already been spared dismissal some months previously, on the grounds that Foch's request for his relief – which was based on other reasons – lacked sufficient justification.

The impact

How did officers react to being relieved? It is rare to find any immediate reaction. Once decisions were taken, they appear to have been put into effect at once, which did not leave the officers in question much time to say what they thought. They were either transferred to other posts in the interior of the country or were left at home without employment. After some weeks or months of patiently awaiting events, many wrote to the Minister of War or the Commander-in-Chief – often to both – to ask for another posting and usually for another command.

To support their request, they often wrote a justification of what they had done at the time of their relief. General P——, removed from command of the 53rd Reserve Division, sent the Minister of War a typed, twelve-page vindication of himself. Sauret, the commander of the 3rd Corps at the Battle of the Sambre, who has already been mentioned, used eight pages to shift the blame for setbacks on to his chief-of-staff: 'My assistant always seemed to be trying to dump his duties on me, and I was obliged to be patient and forbearing with him because of the gravity of the situation.'

After a removed officer had taken up a post in the interior of the country, he would forward his request through the hierarchical channels. His superior would give an opinion, and would invariably conclude that the officer was fully fit physically and mentally and that the request was justified. Also attached in many cases was a certificate of a medical examination and follow-up examination.

One such request came from General B——, who had been an outstanding cavalryman before the war and had subsequently spent a period in command of the 103rd Territorial Infantry Division.[16] His request was annotated at GQG with a remark signed by Pellé: 'General B—— has been far from out-standing in command of the cavalry of General Brugère's Territorial divisions; recommend leaving him where he is.' Joffre added his decision in blue pencil: 'Recommendation accepted'. Despite this verdict, General B—— was given another active command a year later.

Some requests were made for more emotional reasons than others. General Exelmans – a descendant of Marshal Exelmans – reckoned that his name would be 'dishonoured' unless he was given another command. He was sub-sequently recalled to duty. General D——, the former artillery commander of the 10th Corps, asked Joffre to recall him to duty and added that he had already lost one son as a second-lieutenant, that another was currently serving with the army and that he found it 'the cruellest of penalties to be unable to do my duty – my full duty – like my sons'. In contrast, General K——, who had likewise lost a son, withdrew his request after a further son was killed in action.

Many generals who had been removed were in fact recalled to the front after the end of 1915 and given another command. But I'll now turn to a couple of rather unusual generals, Percin and Regnault. I've already said much about Percin, so I'll start with him. On 21 August 1914, General d'Amade sent a message to Joffre, in which he stated: 'The defensive organization of Lille, and the role that this fortress might have to play at any moment now, make it essential for General Percin to be replaced in command at once, owing to his age and exhaustion.' This helps explains the virulence of Percin's criticisms of Joffre and GQG: his role in defending Lille in 1914 had hardly been glorious and he needed to justify himself after the war.[17]

The second case is that of General Regnault. He was relieved from com-mand of the 3rd Infantry Division on the request of de Langle de Cary, officially on the grounds that he was physically exhausted and overworked, in common with many others. Transferred to the 9th Military Region – he became one of the deputies of the general in command there – he wrote a six-page letter to the Minister of War on 18 January 1916,[18] describing his mis-fortunes at length and making clear that he was not exhausted at all, since 'the following day he rode more than 65km on horseback' and the day after had to 'endure 75 hours of being transported in the same railway waggon as his horses'. He asked the Minister to have him given a new command at the front, and he was recalled to duty in December 1916. Yet he did not forget, and was one of Joffre's most virulent critics after the war, especially when giving evidence to the Briey Commission.[19]

* * *

Joffre paid a heavy price for the dismissals and removals. More than 80 per cent of the general officers who were in post when the war broke out suffered this fate during the first two years of the conflict, and the dismissals did not end with Joffre's fall. Those on the receiving end felt deeply humiliated and nursed a resentment of the Commander-in-Chief. This was especially true if they did not receive command of another unit, even a unit below the level of the one they had previously led. Failure to gain another unit command was a common outcome in the case of the oldest generals, who had been recalled to active duty in 1914, were tired and had practically no operational competence in this unfamiliar type of warfare. The poison of politics did not help matters. In 1914, a general was a figure of some standing and invariably knew at least a Deputy or a senator to whom he could unburden himself, and the results can easily be guessed.

It is clear that decisions to remove men from their post were made hurriedly, but this was 'tough luck'. The first months of a major conflict invariably result in a turnover within the high command. No exceptions to this rule exist: the Revolutionary wars, those of the Empire, the war of 1870 (to a lesser extent, owing to its short duration), the 1914 war and more recently the Second World War all ended with a new set of officers responsible for conducting operations.

If those officers who were simply transferred to another command are counted as being dismissed, then it is doubtful whether any general at all could claim to have been spared, even among those who commanded an army. Practically all the great names of the war, such as Castelnau, de Langle, Sarrail and Foch, experienced either dismissal or at least a loss of favour at one time or another. Even someone who exchanged command of a crack division for that of a less esteemed division could think of himself as dismissed, especially if his replacement was either a politician or regarded as one of GQG's favourites.

The ever-present threat of removal hardly fostered harmonious relations within an already deeply divided officer corps. Pre-war friendships and enmities became reinvigorated, and continued to wreak damage. Almost every general, when he was free to say what he thought, seemed to be intent only on bad-mouthing the comrade who had replaced him, and of course he claimed that his supercession was the result of influence.

The atmosphere on the eve of war in 1914 was not good. General Legrand-Girarde, who himself was one of those dismissed, wrote:

Did not an unfortunate spirit exist within the army's staff – the deadly result of a peace that had dragged on for too long, and of the frustrated ambitions of all these officers cluttering up the departments? Was not the old spirit of discipline lost through quibbling about plans, dreaming up regulations and being desk warriors? Since officers were unable to boost their chances of promotion on a battlefield, they instead tried to do so in public life and in the press.[20]

When Joffre gave this anthill a mighty kick in mid-August 1914, he was simply doing what his predecessors had done during the Revolution, though without the excesses that Messimy was apparently ready to accept. The alternative, which Joffre was neither willing nor able to tolerate, was a bunch of second-raters. It is fitting to close by pointing out that the most prominent of all the dismissed officers was none other than Joffre himself.

List of French Governments, 1911–20

President of the Republic:	**Armand Fallières** **from 18 Feb 1906**
Caillaux Ministry	from 27 Jun 1911
President of the Council of Ministers:	Joseph Caillaux
Minister of War:	Adolphe Messimy
1st Poincaré Ministry	from 14 Jan 1912
President of the Council of Ministers:	Raymond Poincaré
Minister of War:	Alexandre Millerand
	Albert Lebrun (from 12 Jan 1913)
3rd Briand Ministry	from 21 Jan 1913
President of the Council of Ministers:	Aristide Briand
Minister of War:	Eugène Etienne
President of the Republic:	**Raymond Poincaré** **from 18 Feb 1913 (to Feb 1920)**
4th Briand Ministry	from 18 Feb 1913
President of the Council of Ministers:	Aristide Briand
Minister of War:	Eugène Etienne
Barthou Ministry	from 22 Mar 1913
President of the Council of Ministers:	Louis Barthou
Minister of War:	Eugène Etienne
1st Doumergue Ministry	from 9 Dec 1913
President of the Council of Ministers:	Gaston Doumergue
Minister of War:	Joseph Noulens
4th Ribot Ministry	from 9 Jun 1914
President of the Council of Ministers:	Alexandre Ribot
Minister of War:	Théophile Delcassé
1st Viviani Ministry	from 13 Jun 1914
President of the Council of Ministers:	René Viviani
Minister of War:	Adolphe Messimy
2nd Viviani Ministry	from 26 Aug 1914
President of the Council of Ministers:	René Viviani
Minister of War:	Alexandre Millerand

5th Briand Ministry   from 29 Oct 1915
President of the Council of Ministers: Aristide Briand
Minister of War: General Joseph Galliéni
                                                       General Pierre Roques
                                                       (from 16 Mar 1916)

6th Briand Ministry   from 12 Dec 1916
President of the Council of Ministers: Aristide Briand
Minister of War: General Hubert Lyautey
                                                       Rear-Admiral Lucien Lacaze
                                                       (acting, from 15 Mar 1917)

5th Ribot Ministry   from 20 Mar 1917
President of the Council of Ministers: Alexandre Ribot
Minister of War: Paul Painlevé

1st Painlevé Ministry   from 12 Sep 1917
President of the Council of Ministers: Paul Painlevé
Minister of War: Paul Painlevé

2nd Clemenceau Ministry   from 16 Nov 1917 (to Jan 1920)
President of the Council of Ministers: Georges Clemenceau
                                                       (and Minister of War)

Notes

Note: SHD refers to the *Service historique de la défence* (the Historical Branch of the French armed forces, at Vincennes).

Chapter 1: An Unconventional Choice (pp. 1–16)

1. Mayer, Emile (Lieutenant-colonel). *Trois maréchaux: Joffre, Galliéni, Foch*. Gallimard, 1928. Joffre supposedly told the author: 'I would undoubtedly have hesitated had I thought that a war was bound to break out.' Emile Mayer had shared his schooldays with Joffre, had entered the *Ecole polytechnique* in the same class as Foch, and had met Gilbert (and Joffre again) at Fontainebleau. He was one of the few people who really knew these personalities through having studied alongside them in his youth, and he was able to relate several anecdotes that sound more plausible than others. In the 1920s–1930s, Mayer had long discussions with de Gaulle at the Dumesnil Bar, during which he shared some novel ideas about the next war.

2. Jaurès had much difficulty explaining to his party comrades why he had given in to his wife's wish for their daughter to make her Solemn Communion. Joffre, after the death of his first wife, remarried on 26 April 1905 in a civil ceremony, but the religious ceremony did not occur until 10 July 1924. (The reason for the delay was that the previous marriage of Joffre's second wife had ended in divorce in 1904, and so the religious ceremony appears to have waited until after her former husband had died.) Another anecdote underlines how different Joffre was from those around him. The Joffres, possibly on *Madame* Joffre's urging, owned a barge called *The Cygne*, which was moored at Bougival. He sold it some years following the war, after having frequently expressed a desire to cruise along rivers and canals (*The War illustrated*, 25 Jun 1916). I suspect that this was rather a bohemian lifestyle and one that was hardly common among the general officers of the era. There was a whole side to Joffre's personality that has a tendency to surprise.

3. In 1908, Joffre had commanded the 2nd Corps, which contained the 7th Infantry Brigade commanded by Castelnau. This was when Castelnau came to Joffre's notice.

4. 'The Jesuits on the General Staff', in *Le Courrier européen* (23 May 1913). This was a pacifist newspaper.

5. André had begun, with the help of the Freemasons, to record officers' religious beliefs on their personal files. Joffre had been put on the list of suitable general officers by André. To understand subsequent events, you constantly have to bear in mind that men such as Michel, Percin, Regnault and Sarrail had belonged to André's circle in one way or another.

6. The Xs tended to be somewhat on the Left politically, and men from Saint-Cyr on the Right. The encounter was also one between two aristocracies: on the one hand the old, long-established nobility, often Christian in belief, and on the other hand the more recent aristocracy, men who had risen by using their brains, and many of whom were atheistic.

7. Joffre was subsequently a professor of permanent fortification at the Joint School of Artillery and Military Engineering at Fontainebleau for a year-and-a-half. His precise and conscientious approach profoundly bored his pupils. How on earth could someone so deficient as an oral communicator have ended up as a professor?

8. Joffre, Joseph (Maréchal). *Mémoires, 1910–1917*, 2 vols. Plon, 1932, vol. 1, p. 15. Joffre did not write his two-volume memoirs by himself. Orderly officers did the work, but he carefully read through the passages that were suggested to him and often had changes made. He signed each page, and the finished book was held in safe-keeping by the publishing house Plon. It was published in 1932, a year after his death.

9. Joffre, Joseph. *Opérations de la colonne Joffre avant et après l'occupation de Tombouctou.* Berger-Levrault, 1895. This is the only publication known definitely to have been written by Joffre in person. It was also translated into English as *My March to Timbuctoo by General Joffre.* Chatto and Windus, 1915.

10. See Fraenkel, Roger. *Joffre: l'âne qui commandait des lions.* Italiques, 2004.

11. In his report on operations in the Sudan, Joffre described at least one action in which he may have been in charge: the action of Niafounke.

12. See, for example, the extracts from Castelnau's letters quoted in: Gras, Yves. *Castelnau, ou l'art de commander, 1851–1944.* Denoël, 1990, p. 30ff.

13. There is even an anecdote that Joffre could have become one of the officers of the *Commune* – the failed insurrection in Paris in 1871 – in common with another sapper, Rossel. An attempt was made to persuade him, but Joffre refused.

14. Joffre entered the *Ecole polytechnique* at his first attempt, at the age of 17, and was ranked fourteenth. This fact ought to have quashed completely any insinuations that he was slow on the uptake or not particularly bright, yet the same old clichés are repeated even today.

15. Kahn, Alexandre. *Life of General Joffre, cooper's son who became commander-in-chief.* New York, Frederick A. Stokes Company, [1915], p. 16.

16. The general in command of the army corps to which Joffre's 6th Division belonged noted in October 1906: 'Has made a particular study of tactics since assuming command of the 6th Division; will succeed in this as in any other military task he may undertake.' This was a perceptive observation.

17. Mayer, *op. cit.*, p. 85.

18. de Pierrefeu, Jean. *GQG secteur 1: trois ans au Grand Quartier Général, par le rédacteur du communiqué*, 2 vols. L'Edition française illustrée, 1920, vol. 1, p. 96. Pierrefeu, a literary chronicler before the war, drafted the communiqué at GQG after having been wounded at the start of the war. He was initially well-disposed towards GQG and Joffre, but his attitude gradually turned into one of systematic denigration. Pétain soon became his idol.

19. Legrand-Girarde, Emile (Général). *Un quart de siècle au service de la France: carnets 1894–1918, Madagascar, Elysée, Chine, loi de trois ans, guerre de 1914–1918.* Les Presses littéraires de France, 1954, p. 638. This is a remarkable but little-known book, written in a very outspoken style.

20. 'He was equally terse in speech and in writing', stated Legrand-Girarde. Joffre was really handicapped by his difficulty in expressing himself and in taking part in discussions during meetings where voices soon became raised and where it was common practice to interrupt the speaker. He remained silent when he should have been defending his position energetically.

21. d'Esme, Jean. *Le père Joffre.* France-Empire, 1962, p. 21.

22. In 1876, the following comment was made about him: 'Would mount fairly well if he had his heart in it.' He subsequently improved, but by 1911 had put on weight and lacked an imposing bearing. He was seen going at a trot more often than at a gallop.

23. Even officers as respectable as Gambiez and Suire called him 'big Joffre' in their book *Histoire de la première guerre mondiale*, 2 vols. Fayard, 1968, vol. 1, p. 212. Joffre effortlessly attracted jibes and ridicule.

24. Sarrail, Maurice (Général). 'Souvenirs 1914–1915', in *Revue politique et parlementaire* (May, Jun, Jul, and Aug 1921).

25. Liddell Hart, Basil Henry (Captain). *Réputations.* Payot, 1931, p. 47.

26. Bonnal, Henri (Général). *Questions de critique militaire et d'actualité.* Chapelot, 1913.

27. We should add another point about Castelnau. The Left viewed him with a jaundiced eye not only because of the familiar reason of his militant Catholicism, but also because of something that is less well known, namely that he had served in the Army of Versailles and had helped suppress the Commune of 1871 at the *Gare du Nord* and the *Buttes-Chaumont.*

28. Percin, Alexandre. *1914: les erreurs du haut commandement.* Albin Michel, 1920, p. 121. The whole of Chapter 7 is devoted to systematically demolishing Joffre: not much of him is left by the time you reach the end.

29. Fabry, Jean (Lieutenant-colonel). *Joffre et son destin: la Marne, Verdun, la Somme, l'Amérique.* Charles Lavauzelle, 1931.

30. Poincaré, Raymond. *Au service de la France: neuf ans de souvenirs*, 11 vols. Plon, 1926–74. Vol. 5 (*L'invasion, 1914*), p. 226.

31. Messimy, Adolphe. *Mes souvenirs.* Plon, 1937.

32. 'Joffre et Lanrezac', in *Revue de Paris* (15 Jan 1933). Lardemelle had been dismissed by Sarrail in the Balkans.

33. Alexandre, René (Général). *Avec Joffre d'Agadir à Verdun: souvenirs, 1911–1916.* Berger-Levrault, 1932, p. 104.

34. Messimy was said to have promised Joffre's place to Sarrail.

35. We might also pause to wonder what Lyautey did to deserve his elevation to the marshalate.

36. It is clear from reading the writings of the 'Ancients' that there had indeed been a quarrel between the Ancients and the Moderns, dating from before the war, and that Joffre had consciously sustained the grumbling of the military bigwigs by

systematically giving preference to young officers rather than to the prominent soldiers who were already in post.

37. For example, we read in the *Documents politiques, diplomatiques et financiers* (Mar 1933), p. 127: 'Everything that has been published since 1919 has shown not only the former generalissimo's total ignorance, but also his equally limitless incapability.'

38. Margueritte, Victor. *Au bord du gouffre, août – septembre 1914*. Flammarion, 1919, p. 114. A former soldier and a well-known novelist and portrayer of the new moral standards. He was expelled from the Order of the Legion of Honour some years later, following the publication of his novel *La Garçonne*.

39. Napoleon's posturing on Saint Helena soon resulted in parallels being drawn between him and Christ's life and Passion. Some officers who accompanied the Emperor became his 'evangelists'.

40. *Napoléon à Sainte-Hélène*. Robert Laffont, Collection 'Bouquins', 1981, pp. 106, 107, 108.

41. Any alternative commander to Joffre would have had to have been a member of the Supreme War Council, or a political general such as Sarrail.

42. A popular description of a military leader is someone whose activity can be summed up as: 'Do nothing, get everything done by others and allow nothing to be done of its own accord.' That fits Joffre perfectly.

43. Bugnet, Charles (Commandant). *En écoutant le maréchal Foch*. Grasset, 1929, pp. 139, 140.

Chapter 2: The Offensive (pp. 17–42)

1. The expression 'Young Turks' became widely used and seems to have originated with Pétain. It referred to young officers, all of them qualified staff officers, who were serving on the staff and who were accused of waging *their* own war. The allusion is to the Young Turks movement, which helped create modern Turkey.

2. Joffre. *Mémoires, op. cit.*, vol. 1, p. 34.

3. Ténot, Eugène. *Les nouvelles défenses de la France: Paris et ses fortifications, 1870–1880*. G. Ballière et Cie, 1887. (1st ed, 1880), p.V.

4. Italy had not forgotten that it had lost Nice and Savoy, which had been annexed by France during the Second Empire.

5. 'Les règlements de manœuvre d'infanterie d'avant guerre', in *Revue militaire française* (Nov 1922).

6. 'La défense de la France', in *Nouvelle revue* (1890–1), vols 67, 68.

7. From an article in *Le Temps* (13 Dec 1905).

8. Foch, Ferdinand. *De la conduite de la guerre: la manœuvre pour la bataille*, 2nd ed. Berger-Levrault, 1909.

9. Foch, Ferdinand. *Des principes de la guerre*. Berger-Levrault, 1903.

10. See, for example, the articles in *Le Matin* from 11 Sep 1912 onwards, about the Grand Manœuvres of 1912. It is also interesting to examine *Le Temps* of the same period.

11. Percin, Alexandre. *Le combat*. Alcan, 1914.

12. 'La volonté de vaincre', in *Revue de Paris* (15 Jun 1912).

13. The Left and Far Left of the time, as distinct from today.

14. See the theory of the three 'orders', or realms, in Pascal's *Les pensées*.

15. Mayer, *op. cit.*, p. 22.

16. Joffre. *Mémoires*, *op. cit.*, vol. 1, p. 14.

17. de Grandmaison, Louis (Colonel). *Deux conférences faites aux officiers de l'Etat-major de l'armée: la notion de sûreté et l'engagement des grandes unités.* Berger-Levrault, 1911. It is not widely known that Grandmaison had served at Tonkin with Galliéni and Lyautey for two-and-a-half years. He had also served in Tunisia and Algeria. He was therefore a colonial, and it would be interesting to know what effect this experience might have had in the development of his thinking.

18. Ever since entering Saint-Cyr, he had earned an unbroken series of exceptional reports. One of those who reported on him during his time at the Staff College was Lanrezac, who nonetheless joined many others in 'crying wolf' some years later.

19. Debeney, Marie-Eugène (Général). *La guerre et les hommes: réflexions d'après guerre.* Plon, 1937.

20. Grandmaison gave many lectures during his career, starting when he was a captain, and had a gift for it.

21. de Grandmaison, Louis (Commandant). *Dressage de l'infanterie en vue du combat offensif,* 3rd ed. Berger-Levrault, 1908 (published in 1905, and reissued in 1908 with a preface by General Langlois).

22. *Ibid*, p. 19.

23. *Ibid*, p. 8.

24. Regnault, the chief of Grandmaison at the General Staff, was staunchly hostile to Joffre and fiercely scornful of the offensive, yet in 1911 he noted Grandmaison as someone who had the ability to 'rise to the most senior ranks'.

25. It was supposedly Lanrezac who came up with the sarcastic comment: 'Let's attack, let's attack ... anything and anywhere!' He also complained of the indiscipline of his troops, and I will return to him in due course.

26. Lanrezac, Charles (Général). *Le plan de campagne français et le premier mois de la guerre, 2 août – 3 septembre 1914.* Payot, 1920, p. 147.

27. 'Joffre et Lanrezac', in *Revue de Paris* (1 and 15 Jan 1933).

28. Laure, Emile (Général). *Pétain.* Berger-Levrault, 1941.

29. To be more precise, I should state that after 1886 so-called fortress and siege batteries began to be dispersed in positions on the exterior defence lines all around fortresses.

30. Yet no one accuses Millerand of being responsible for the mania for the offensive.

31. Joffre. *Mémoires*, *op. cit.*, vol. 1, pp. 39–40.

32. Z—— (Capitaine). *Vertus guerrières.* Payot, 1918. Every line rings true in this small and little-known book, which has nothing in common with either unbearable hagiography on the one hand and equally dreadful abuse on the other.

33. 'Doctrine *a priori* ou doctrine des circonstances', in *Revue militaire française* (1 Mar 1921).

34. *Le Correspondant* (10 May 1914).

35. My italics.

36. This trend started with Engerand, to whom I shall return in due course.

37. Section VIII.

38. 'Notre théorie de 1914 sur la conduite des opérations et les leçons de la guerre', in *Revue militaire française* (1 Nov 1923).
39. My italics.
40. SHD Carton 1 N 16.
41. Joffre. *Mémoires, op. cit.*, vol. 1, p. 36.
42. 'Les manœuvres du Languedoc', in *Revue des deux mondes* (15 Oct 1913).
43. 'Considérations du Grand Etat-major allemand sur les manœuvres françaises de l'année 1912'. Archives du 2e bureau. SHD Carton 7 N 673.
44. Something that will be familiar to those involved in setting up the Camp of Larzac in 1975–80.
45. 'Opinions allemandes, la guerre actuelle', in *Revue militaire générale* (Apr 1909). The article caused a big stir both in Germany, where it was commended by Wilhelm II, and also in France.
46. Except possibly for Russia.
47. Joffre. *Mémoires, op. cit.*, vol. 1, p. 40. Ideally, I would like to quote the page in full.
48. *Ibid*, vol. 1, p. 32.
49. *Ibid*, vol. 1, p. 35.

Chapter 3: Plans (pp. 43–66)

1. Ténot, Eugène. *Les nouvelles défenses de la France: la frontière, 1870–1882.* G. Ballière et Cie, 1887 (1st ed 1882).
2. See for example: SHD Carton 7 N 1168.
3. SHD Carton 1 N 10.
4. SHD Carton 2 N 1.
5. Underlined in the original.
6. SHD Carton 2 N 1.
7. Joffre. *Mémoires, op. cit.*, vol. 1, pp. 117–18.
8. The Germans themselves reckoned that 'the transitory use' of the routes through Belgium did not amount to a violation of the country's neutrality – as was seen at the start of the war.
9. 'Caractère et durée d'une guerre franco-allemande', in *Revue militaire générale* (Aug 1907). It was around the time of this article that the Schlieffen Plan took its final form.
10. *La guerre d'aujourd'hui.* Reissued in 2009 by Editions du Trident.
11. Read two articles by Maitrot (Général): 'L'invasion par la Belgique' and 'L'invasion par la Suisse et l'Italie', in *Le Correspondant* (10 Sep and 25 Nov 1911).
12. One of the conditions of this commitment was the improvement of the Russian railways, and this resulted in the famous loans from France.
13. SHD Carton 2 N 1.
14. French, Viscount of Ypres (Field Marshal). *1914.* Constable and Company Ltd, 1919, pp. 9, 10–11.
15. In 1919, parliament decided to create a commission that could study the state of metallurgy in France, following a question in the Chamber of Deputies about the problem of Briey. France had in fact been deprived of the bulk of its iron-ore resources when Briey was abandoned at the start of the war. This commission, whose *rapporteur* was Fernand Engerand, the Deputy for the Calvados, heard from the principal generals who had been in command during the war, including

Joffre. One thing led to another, and the commission ended up being transformed into a commission of inquiry, notably about the events that had occurred at the start of the war. The depositions did not always reflect well on those who gave them, and the soldiers were often roughly handled. In particular Joffre, was called on to give evidence on 4 July 1919, was harried by questions from the president and appeared hesitant and uncertain in his replies.

16. Joffre. *Mémoires, op. cit.*, vol. 1, pp. 143–4.
17. See, for example, Fraenkel, *op. cit.*
18. To find out more, you can read the articles published under the title 'La doctrine de défense nationale', in *Revue militaire générale* (Oct, Nov, Dec 1910).
19. Joffre. *Mémoires, op. cit.*, vol. 1, p. 145.
20. *Ibid*, vol. 1, pp. 143, 145.
21. 'Reserves' in this sense should not be confused with the word 'reserve' used in the opposite sense of 'active'. This is something I shall address in due course.
22. The classification of the German army's personnel differed somewhat from that of the French. The so-called *Ersatz* units included the surplus men in the various depots who had not been incorporated into the active or reserve units. The *Landwehr* and *Landsturm* grouped together those troops whose French counterparts belonged to the Territorial army or to the Territorial army reserve.
23. 'La guerre actuelle', in *Revue militaire générale* (Apr 1909). Article translated from the *Deutsche Revue* (Jan 1909).
24. SHD Carton 1 N 16.
25. Herbillon, Emile (Colonel). *De la Meuse à Reims: le Général Alfred Micheler*. Plon, 1934.
26. SHD Carton 7 N 1771. Colonel Demange was a member of the Military Staff Committee, and as such was earmarked to serve in wartime in one of the army headquarters.
27. Extracted from a report entitled *Mémoire pour servir à l'établissement d'un plan de guerre*. SHD Carton 9 Y D 489. This document, which is fifty-seven typed pages long, is remarkable in every respect. It was never finished, but was probably drawn up with a view to developing a Plan XVIII. Its author lacked enough time to address the problem of Belgium, but devoted ample attention to the issues in Alsace and Lorraine.
28. SHD Carton 1 N 11. By 'the basis of the plan', I mean that what the council had to approve or reject was not the plan itself, but simply the basis on which the plan was to be established.
29. A march on foot, of course.
30. The 'W' in Army W stood for Wilson, the British general who worked with the French General Staff in developing the British disembarkation plan.
31. Fortunately, not all the planned forts were actually built.
32. Engerand, Fernand. *Le secret de la frontière, 1815–1871–1914. Charleroi*. Bossard, 1918, pp. 141–2.
33. Nor must we forget that the Germans lost their gamble on the British not intervening.

Chapter 4: Preparing for War (pp. 67–88)

1. The peacetime army was not the same as the wartime army, and had a smaller establishment. This has always been the case, in every conscripted army.
2. This was the period when the Republican opposition was delighted to see 'the priests carrying backpacks' – the priests having hitherto been exempt from military service.
3. de Gaulle, Charles. *La France et son armée*. Plon, 1938.
4. Jaurès, Jean. *L'armée nouvelle*. Editions de l'Humanité, 1919.
5. The Niel Law of 1868 continued to envisage a rather hybrid system.
6. Jaurès, *op. cit.*, p. 487.
7. Legrand-Girarde, *op. cit.*, p. 490.
8. SHD Carton 1 N 10.
9. This option was discussed again in due course when General Mangin advocated using *la force noire*, or 'the black troops'.
10. Mahon, Patrice. 'Le service de trois ans et les armemen[t]s allemands', in *Revue des deux mondes* (15 Apr 1913). Mahon's article was a good argument in favour of the Three-Year Law.
11. His speech was printed and published in several editions. I have used the following edition: *Jean Jaurès et la défense nationale: discours sur la loi de trois ans prononcé à la Chambre des députés les 17 et 18 juin 1913*. Editions de l'Humanité, 1917.
12. Joffre had previously addressed the Army Commission in an equally unimpressive way, which hardly comes as a surprise.
13. Three cadres laws were passed in succession in 1911, 1912 and 1913: they applied to the artillery, the infantry and the cavalry.
14. Instructions of 21 November 1913.
15. All the figures in this section have been rounded up or down.
16. I'll briefly give some details of composition so readers can visualize the scale of the strengths of the established structures. The French and German armies were organized into companies (250 men), battalions (four companies constituted a battalion), regiments (three battalions constituted a regiment), brigades (two regiments constituted a brigade), divisions (two brigades constituted a division), and army corps (two divisions constituted an army corps). These are not hard and fast figures, for many exceptions existed, and this was especially true at the start of the war. The subsequent manpower crisis brought many changes.
17. The modified Schlieffen Plan that emerged from the original version of 1905. I have no intention of going into this topic here, as it would be too long and complicated. The essential point is that in 1914 Joffre did not know how the Germans planned to defeat him.
18. Joffre. *Mémoires, op. cit.*, vol. 1, p. 308.
19. Also overlooked was the increase in the number of artillery batteries from 177 to 203.
20. Provided they had adequate cadres. The cadres were not sufficient for forming reserve corps.
21. Many reservist officers had resigned following the Dreyfus Affair and the Two-Year Law. The problems of providing cadres became insolvable.

22. The Directorate of Financial Control still exists and is more indispensable and heeded than ever. It is practically the only directorate that has survived. In theory, it was entrusted with checking that the Ministry of War's expenditure was in order. But, with the tacit agreement of successive Ministers, it soon ended up supervising the appropriateness of that expenditure.

23. Alexandre, *op. cit.*, p. 31.

24. The regular resources became insufficient and the State had to raise a large loan of 815 million *francs*, at an interest rate of 3.5 per cent. Providing security for the loan proved difficult.

25. The approximate number of 75mm guns in 1914 was 4,500.

26. The mortars were intended more specifically to be included in the siege trains and used for besieging fortresses.

27. Purists will be interested in the following figures, given in a document of July 1913 from the Intelligence Department: 2,395 long-barrelled 120mm guns, and 1,389 long-barrelled 155mm guns. The total almost equals that of the 75mm guns. SHD Carton 7 N 1785.

28. In an article in the *Grande revue* (25 Jan 1913).

29. The remark exemplifies the mindset of Clemenceau, who was hostile to soldiers. To call one of the designers of the 75mm gun a criminal is going a bit over the top.

30. When Major Malandrin invented the disk named after him, it was thought that the problem was solved at a stroke. His famous disk was fixed to a shell and gave it a curved trajectory, thus making it possible to turn a 75mm gun into a howitzer. But this substitute device was abandoned during the war, since its performance turned out to be unsatisfactory.

31. The type of cannon was defined by the barrel length, which was given in calibres. A howitzer was a cannon with a barrel length between 12 and 14 calibres. The barrel length of a long-barrelled cannon might range from 18 to 45. (It was 27 for the long-barrelled 155mm de Bange.)

32. Rimailho was a gunner from the *Ecole polytechnique*. He designed and organized the production of the 155mm quick-firing cannon. The 120mm Baquet (named after its designer) was a short-lived piece that proved unsatisfactory. General Baquet was the Director of Artillery in 1914, but resigned from his post the following year, having been the target of particular abuse from Humbert and Clemenceau.

33. SHD Carton 7 N 2. This was exactly the sort of demand an engineer would make.

34. Messimy was one of those who made the allegation. This amounted to effrontery on his part, for in 1903 (he was already the Deputy for the Seine by this stage) he had a little booklet published, in which he advocated reducing the military budget by 150 million *francs* by making cuts in units and staffs. (Messimy, Adolphe. *La paix armée: la France peut en alléger le poids.* Paris, Giard et Brière.) In 1907, Messimy again advocated cuts, this time in the 'high command'.

35. The Germans themselves took artillery and ammunition from the forts they had systematically demolished. Maubeuge, for example, provided several dozen long-barrelled 120mm pieces, and some tens of thousands of shells.

36. If we were to examine the problem of the funding granted to the Minister of War, it would require a whole chapter to itself. A bill tabled on 16 January 1914 set a spending figure of 487 million *francs*, including more than 200 million for barracks and the acquisition of land intended for the construction of what the bill called 'training grounds'. The main points of this bill were contained in a law passed in the middle of July. Priorities changed, of course, after the war broke out.
37. Except for the problem posed by the shortage of heavy artillery.

Chapter 5: Battle of the Frontiers (pp. 89–112)

1. Joffre. *Mémoires, op. cit.*, vol. 1, p. 120.
2. Note that in 1940 it was through the Ardennes that the Germans directed their offensive, though admittedly in different circumstances.
3. Recouly, Raymond. *Joffre*. Editions des Portiques, 1931, p. 78.
4. Brécard (Général). 'Mes missions en Belgique', in *Revue de Paris* (1 Feb 1934).
5. The daily account sent by the Army General Staff (Paris) about the deciphering of intercepted German messages can be consulted at the SHD (Cartons 5 N 9 and 5 N 19). It is hard to find any useful information in it.
6. Viollette did his best to exert pressure where it hurt.
7. When the French attack, they really get stuck in!
8. This was contrary to the Grandmaison 'doctrine' – proof were it needed that his lectures were more theoretical ideas than a doctrine that was actually followed.
9. Castelnau later denied tenaciously that he had wanted to abandon Nancy.
10. Many reasons have been put forward to explain why the two armies were not transferred. The question of the transfer seems to have sparked a discussion at the heart of the *Großer Generalstab*.
11. Messimy, wildly carried away by excitement, urged Joffre to carry out executions, as in 1793. You should read the letters he sent to several generals at this time, and note their tone. As Bugnet says: 'He makes up in volume for what he lacks in weight.'
12. A more nimble version of this existed for the cavalry.
13. Lanrezac's point of view deserves respect. He set it out in detail in his book *Le plan de campagne français et le premier mois de la guerre*. Payot, 1920. An opposing point of view, equally deserving of respect, is that of Lieutenant Spears, whom we have already mentioned. Spears, Sir Edward. *En liaison, 1914*. Presses de la Cité, 1967. See also Engerand. *Le secret, op. cit.*, chapter 3. Bear in mind that Engerand later wrote another book, which glorified Lanrezac.
14. At the Rethel meeting, Sir John French was worried about why the Germans had come to the Meuse, and Lanrezac supposedly replied: 'To go fishing.' It is unclear whether or not the anecdote is true, but it is credible enough given Lanrezac's character.
15. In the same interview he added: 'The audacity, ardour and training of a unit: these are what constitute the true cutting-edge of war.' It will be noted that training is ranked only third.
16. de Gaulle, *op. cit.*
17. Lintier, Paul. *Avec une batterie de 75: ma pièce, souvenirs d'un canonnier, 1914*. Plon, 1916.

18. General Xardel commanded the 62nd Brigade of the 16th Corps, belonging to the 2nd Army. The recollections he wrote have never been published and were not intended for publication.
19. de Gaulle, *op. cit.*, pp. 239–43.
20. This was true as regards the French left wing.
21. de Gaulle, *op. cit.*, p. 219.
22. *Les armées françaises dans la Grande Guerre*, tome 1, vol. 2. Annexe no. 158.
23. Italicized in the original.
24. *Les armées françaises dans la Grande Guerre*, tome 1, vol. 2. Annexe no. 821.
25. Joffre. *Mémoires, op. cit.*, vol. 1, p. 303.
26. Percin, Alexandre (Général). *Le massacre de notre infanterie, 1914–1918*. Albin Michel, 1921. Percin was a most competent artilleryman, but his vision was limited to the 75mm gun, whose use he had long studied.
27. 'Données statistiques sur les forces françaises 1914–1918', in *Revue militaire française* (1 Jun 1934).
28. Admittedly these percentages were for the whole duration of the war.
29. The army's training was hardly helped by the Right brandishing the threat of a *coup d'état*, or by the Left having the Sisters of religious communities expelled from the country.
30. Incidents between officers – such as duels, refusals to salute, or refusals to shake the hand of a comrade – were never so numerous as in the period 1895–1910.
31. You should read the first lesson in Foch's book, *Des principes, op. cit.* The lesson is entitled 'On the teaching of war', and states that 'the outcome in war is a function of f (a, b, c … , k, l, m) = 0', and he dwells at length on the variables of this function f! Foch has been accused of drowning his discourse in mathematics.

Chapter 6: Joffre and Galliéni (pp. 113–136)

1. Galliéni, Joseph-Simon (Maréchal). *Les carnets de Galliéni*. Albin Michel, 1932. These diaries bear testimony to Galléni's attitude on this point on almost every page from the end of 1914. I should add a brief explanation about *Les carnets*. They were published, probably in an expurgated form, by Galliéni's son in 1932, with notes by Gheusi for the greater glory of Galliéni. Anything with the potential to undermine the 'good cause' was probably omitted. Even so, *Les carnets* are interesting, for they vividly show the gossip, tittle-tattle, true indiscretions and false rumours that were prevalent in this little civilian and military world. On practically every page, you find Galliéni pulling Joffre to pieces.
2. One-and-a-half columns of congratulations by Galliéni appeared on the front page of the *Journal officiel de Madagascar et dépendances* (28 Mar 1903), year 19, no. 790.
3. SHD Carton 9 Y D 408.
4. An important reason for Galliéni may have been the fact that Joffre was a colonial and had not attended the Staff College in the same way as other officers. Galliéni used to ask qualified staff officers – such as Lyautey on his arrival at Tonkin – to forget everything they had learned.
5. Messimy. *Mes souvenirs, op. cit.*, pp. 77ff. Confirmation of this is nowhere to be found in Galliéni's writings. Long after the war, doubt was cast on whether Galliéni had actually been called on to serve, and he was no longer around to

confirm whether it was true. He does seems to have been consulted at least. Joffre did not expand on the conditions under which he had been appointed, and he made no mention of Galliéni. It is worth remembering that Messimy was the Minister of the Colonies before his appointment as Minister of War.

6. In the French army of the time, there existed two 'mafias': the *colo* and the *métro*. (For the sake of this discussion, we'll leave aside the question of officers' political affiliations.) These 'mafias' were subdivided into the Xs and the Cyrards, into officers who were qualified to serve on the staff and those who were not, and above all into Catholics and non-Catholics. In the midst of such a mesh of networks, it can be difficult to identify an officer's connections.

7. Poincaré, *op. cit.*, vol. 5, p. 363.

8. SHD Carton 1 N 10.

9. When Galliéni did contribute to the discussion, his views tended to be in line with Joffre's.

10. Galliéni. *Les carnets, op. cit.*, p. 25. Joffre's hope was fulfilled when Galliéni returned to active duty some years later.

11. *Ad latus* means someone who is at a person's side, as a potential successor.

12. Galliéni asked for these three active army corps through Messimy even before he was appointed. Messimy relayed the demand in the form of an order issued to Joffre. But instead of obeying, Joffre took advantage of the way the order was worded ('to be carried out in the event of the manœuvre that is currently in progress being checked'). Joffre. *Mémoires, op. cit.*, vol. 1, pp. 313ff. The demand for the three active army corps resurfaced as a *leitmotiv* throughout the duration of Galliéni's command.

13. *Ibid*, vol. 1, p. 368.

14. *Ibid*, vol. 1, p. 330.

15. Galliéni, Joseph-Simon (Maréchal). *Mémoires du maréchal Galliéni*. Payot, 1928, p. 188. Galliéni's memoirs were written in 1915, but published much later.

16. Gheusi, Pierre-Barthélemy. *La gloire de Galliéni: comment Paris fut sauvé, le testament d'un soldat*. Albin Michel, 1928, p. 164.

17. There are several versions of this statement, and it was surely said in one form or another. Jean d'Esme has Joffre saying: 'I am well aware that it would have been me, and me alone, who lost it.' d'Esme, *op. cit.*, p. 174.

18. Except for the railways, since the layout of the rail network was a star-pattern centred on Paris.

19. For once, Joffre personally took Galliéni's call, despite his reluctance to use the telephone.

20. Lyet, Pierre (Capitaine). *Joffre et Galliéni à la Marne*. Berger-Levrault, 1938. Colonel Lyet was later the editor-in-chief of the *Revue historique des armées*.

21. Bugnet, Charles (Lieutenant-colonel). *Rue Saint-Dominique et GQG, ou les Trois dictatures de la guerre*. Plon, 1937, p. 88. The chapter entitled 'Galliéni: l'énigmatique' is one of the most insightful analyses of the relationship between Joffre and Galliéni.

22. Joffre. *Mémoires, op. cit.*, vol. 1, pp. 389–90.

23. The first clashes began around 11.00am on 5 September.

24. A fact that readily explains why some failures occurred, which we shall come across in due course.
25. Though by the time the battle ended, von Kluck was on the verge of turning the 6th Army's northern flank.
26. The reason for the uncertainty on this point is that Joffre received information from the British, whose Royal Flying Corps apparently detected the start of the change of direction from 31 August.
27. Read in particular pages 159–61.
28. Galliéni remained under Joffre's orders for as long as Paris remained in the Army Zone. The only occasion when he recognized his subordination to Joffre can be found in a private letter of 3 September to his 'dear Joffre', in which he wrote: 'I have just received from the Minister the letter placing me under your orders ....'
29. Messimy. *Mes souvenirs, op. cit.*, p. 226.
30. Galliéni. *Les carnets, op. cit.*, notes of pp. 52–3.
31. SHD Carton 6 N 52.
32. SHD Carton 5 N 131.
33. Galliéni. *Mémoires, op. cit.*, pp. 240, 246. (Letters of 8 and 11 Sep 1914.)
34. Poincaré, *op. cit.*, vol. 5, p. 500.
35. Bugnet, Charles (Commandant). *En écoutant le maréchal Foch.* Grasset, 1929, pp. 139–40.
36. A few more details about Spears' book, *Liaison 1914* (Spears, *En liaison, op. cit.*). The British have the gift of talking in a light-hearted manner about serious matters, and this was particularly the case with Spears. He reveals a sense of humour that is impossible to translate into French, and it makes his prose a delight to read even today. But we must never forget that he was writing for British readers. For his opinion on Galliéni, see p. 434ff.
37. SHD Carton 23 N 72.
38. Note the phrase 'investing army'. Even though the Battle of the Marne had been fought by field armies, the Military Governor of Paris stuck to the regulations and continued to think as the governor of a fortress.
39. You may also wish to consult Leblond, Marius-Ary (pseud). *Galliéni parle: entretiens du 'Sauveur de Paris', ministre de la Guerre, avec ses secrétaires*, 2 vols. Albin Michel, 1920, vol. 1, p. 68.
40. Gheusi, Pierre-Barthélemy. *Guerre et théâtre, 1914–1918: mémoires d'un officier du général Galliéni et journal parisien du directeur du théâtre national de l'Opéra-Comique pendant la guerre.* Berger-Levrault, 1919, p. 115.
41. Poincaré, *op. cit.*, vol. 5, p. 364.
42. SHD Carton 5 N 271. A bit later, Dubail was agreed on for this post – the important thing was to exclude Galliéni.
43. SHD Carton 23 N 17. In the same letters, Galliéni gives vent to his usual grievances.
44. SHD Carton 5 N 132.
45. This is a reminder of the problems of allocating sparse labour resources. Men were required everywhere at this time to construct lines of defence on the front, including at Verdun.
46. Poincaré, *op. cit.*, vol. 7 (*Guerre de siège, 1915*), p. 193.

47. 'Bayle' was Major Bel. Galliéni, too, had his 'gang', including the head of his military cabinet, Colonel Boucabeille.
48. Poincaré, *op. cit.*, vol. 7, p. 297.
49. It was at this time that Galliéni and Castelnau drew closer to each other.
50. Ever since the start of the war, politicians were inundated with letters from civilians and above all from soldiers.
51. Driant was the son-in-law of General de Galliffet. Driant was less critical than is popularly believed, and his letters were not so much allegations of negligence as straightforward observations.
52. Joffre. *Mémoires, op. cit.*, vol. 2, p. 200.
53. This was not totally illogical. Two reasons explain the decision: political pressure from the 'ground-roots' and Galliéni's aggressive attitude towards qualified staff officers.
54. Those Deputies who had been mobilized preserved the alarming privilege of going from the front to parliament, or even to the government if they were ministers such as Abel Ferry. I shall say more on this in due course.
55. Gheusi. *La gloire, op. cit.*, pp. 178–203.
56. Not a word about this is contained in Joffre's memoirs.
57. *'Nous avons pris une vessie pour une lanterne'* is another expression that has been quoted. Translated literally, it means 'we have taken a bladder for a lamp'. In other words, 'we have been labouring under a stupid illusion'.
58. Gheusi. *La gloire, op. cit.*, pp. 159–60.
59. Boucabeille's role in this matter ought to be better known.

Chapter 7: Gnawing Away (pp. 137–149)
1. Fabry, *op. cit.*, p. 90.
2. In the Vosges, 1915 was one of the most active and bloody years of the war.
3. Joffre. *Mémoires, op. cit.*, vol. 2, p. 97. Joffre added: 'It has to be realized that this fundamental reason lay behind all the offensives I conducted from May 1915 onwards.'
4. The Germans had not been able to withdraw enough forces from the Western Front to strengthen the Eastern Front.
5. Point X was what the point was called on the detailed military maps. Les Eparges saw the start of mine warfare.
6. Baills (Commandant). 'L'instruction de 1909 sur la guerre de siège', in *Revue militaire française* (1923).
7. The trenches formed what were known as *points d'appui* or strongpoints. These strongpoints were grouped into centres of resistance dotted across the terrain. The intervals between the centres of resistance were swept by enfilade fire – at least, that was the theory.
8. He even appended a copy of a German regulation to the order of 5 October 1914.
9. SHD Carton 7 N 4.
10. Fayolle, Emile (Maréchal). *Cahiers secrets de la grande guerre.* Plon, 1964, p. 133. Fayolle, a gunner who had studied at the *Ecole polytechnique*, was brought out of retirement in 1914 and placed in charge of merely a brigade, but then rose through every level of command and was later appointed a Marshal of France. He was a devout Christian and a perfect soldier. His doubts can be seen in every line

of his diaries, which were definitely not written for publication. His is a book that plays a different tune.

11. GQG issued a note on 20 November 1915 to reorganize the heavy artillery.
12. SHD Carton 5 N 132.
13. SHD Carton 7 N 4.
14. Securing surprise seems very uncertain. This was not for lack of trying, but the problem was how to put tens of thousands of men and hundreds of guns in place without the enemy finding out. That did not stop Abel Ferry from coming up with some solutions!
15. The 'general offensive' is is a reference to the Second Champagne offensive. Joffre congratulated himself in this same note for the additional heavy artillery he had obtained as a result of downgrading the importance of the fortresses.
16. SHD Carton 5 N 132.
17. SHD Carton 6 N 152.
18. An annual intake contained between 180,000 and 190,000 men who were theoretically liable to be mobilized. In reality, the number of men called up was larger (up to 280,000): this was the result of scraping the bottom of the barrel and assigning some men to posts somewhere other than in the front line.
19. Joffre. *Mémoires, op. cit.*, vol. 2, p. 367.
20. The French army increased in size in 1915, taking many of the remaining men in the depots.
21. Fayolle was an exception.
22. A remarkable, nineteen-page document exists, which is even more explicit. Intended for the British staff, it was written in English and entitled *Lessons of the September battles (especially the battle in Champagne) from the point of view of a combined offensive*. It was signed by Joffre, and dated 27 December 1915. SHD Carton 6 N 52.
23. See the periodical *Avions*, issues 171 and 174.
24. Ortholan, Henri. *La guerre des chars*. Bernard Giovanangeli, 2007, pp. 28ff.
25. 'Les états-majors et la troupe', in *Mercure de France* (16 May 1918), 203.
26. Poincaré, *op. cit.*, vol. 6 (*Les tranchées, 1915*), p. 22.
27. Messimy commanded a division by the war's end. He corresponded much with Galliéni until the latter's death, and even sent Galliéni the broad principles that he thought should govern future operations. He was also involved in the controversies surrounding the Nivelle offensive.
28. The French army's numbers began to fall from the end of 1916, and this downward trend became more marked in 1917.

Chapter 8: Verdun (pp. 150–170)

1. The salient was ultimately conquered in a major offensive by the fledgling US army.
2. Bernède, Allain. 'Verdun 1916: un choix stratégique, une équation logistique', in *Revue historique des armées* (2006), no. 242.
3. This does not mean that everything needed by the frontline soldiers reached them in a timely manner, for that was another matter altogether.
4. Joffre. *Mémoires, op. cit.*, vol. 2, pp. 197ff.
5. *Ibid*, vol. 2, p. 206.

6. These *Stollen* were between 8 and 10 metres underground, and contained latrines, kitchens, water and electricity supplies, and various stores. French combat soldiers never enjoyed such luxurious living arrangements. Although the French built deep dug-outs or bunkers, these had nothing like the same conveniences. The German word *Stollen* has several meanings, but the most appropriate one appears to be equivalent to the English word 'gallery'.

7. See a series of three articles by Paquet (Lieutenant-colonel). 'Avant l'offensive allemande sur Verdun (1916)', in *Revue militaire française*, vols. 23 and 24.

8. Joffre. *Mémoires, op. cit.*, vol. 2, p. 205.

9. From April, the numbers of French guns at Verdun were 744 pieces of 75mm calibre, and 576 pieces of heavy artillery.

10. If you wish to follow the opening events, you can refer to the *Journal des marches et opérations* (war diary) of the Fortified Region of Verdun. SHD Carton 26 N 71/1.

11. Rouquerol, J. (Général). 'La première crise de la bataille de Verdun', in *Archives de la grande guerre* (1923), vol. 16.

12. Keeping track of the numbering of the positions at Verdun is especially difficult.

13. GQG, 1er et 3e bureaux. *Instruction sur les travaux de campagne à l'usage des troupes de toutes armes.* 1915.

14. A *macaron* was a round item of confectionery, and was also a leather patch under the button of a belt loop.

15. Driant fought a duel with Percin, who received two wounds. Driant was also a fan of Déroulède and Barras. After leaving the army, he spent some of his time writing futuristic novels with more or less military overtones. He was a staunch opponent of Dreyfus, a fierce advocate of the offensive, and the founder of a Military League. He often went astray when he spoke in parliament before the war.

16. Jollivet, Gaston. *Le Colonel Driant.* Delagrave, 1918.

17. Of course, when the Minister of War was Galliéni, it was the oracle speaking!

18. Joffre. *Mémoires, op. cit.*, vol. 2, p. 200.

19. Castelnau was constantly clashing with Foch, for both military and personal reasons.

20. The archives of the Entrenched Camp of Verdun appear have been lost.

21. As a general rule, about 10 metres of trench had to be dug in order to create 1 metre of a defensive system.

22. Grasset (Lieutenant-colonel). 'Verdun, le premier choc à la 72e division', in *Revue militaire française* (Dec 1925).

23. Something that was recognized only very belatedly, when plans were being made for what developed into the Maginot Line.

24. The removals ordered by GQG can be followed in the war diary of the fortress of Verdun. SHD Carton 26 N 67/10.

25. The numbers given for artillery pieces ignored those in the park. The true numbers were therefore higher.

26. *Les armées françaises dans la grande guerre*, tome 1, vol. 1. Appendix II, p. 526.

27. Ménager, René (Lieutenant). *Les Forts de Moulainville et de Douaumont sous les 420.* Payot, 1936.

28. The vaults of Douaumont withstood the bombardment, but one of Moulainville's collapsed.
29. The impact of the 420mm shells on the concrete structures made the defensive work shake as deep as 15–16 metres, making it impossible for men to remain inside without running the risk of being driven mad.
30. The rate of fire was inadequate.
31. *Carnets de Verdun.* Librio, 2006.
32. On the website www.dedefensa.org.

Chapter 9: Joffre and Politics (pp. 171–179)

1. There was a notable exception. General Cherfils wrote with his usual acidity in *Le Gaulois* of 1 August 1911: 'The Republic would do better to draw the names of its army commanders from a hat …'.
2. Accambray was the Deputy of the Aisne in 1914. A graduate of the *Ecole polytechnique*, he had resigned from the army with the rank of captain. A member of the Radical-Socialist party, he became one of the most scornful critics of GQG and Joffre. After the war, it was discovered that he had apparently been in the pay of the German intelligence service, to which he had sent fairly insignificant reports through Switzerland. He never had to answer for it.
3. SHD Carton 5 N 132.
4. Marcellin, Léopold. *Politique et politiciens pendant la guerre*, 2 vols. La Renaissance du livre, c.1921, vol. 1, p. 63.
5. Abel Ferry was a complex character: although young and dynamic, he sometimes allowed his judgement to be clouded by a pugnacious anti-clericalism. He was able to describe personally at meetings of the Council of Ministers his experiences as a second-lieutenant. In 1917–18, he produced some often very discerning reports for the Army Commission. He was mortally wounded just weeks before the armistice.
6. Seventeen Deputies were killed during the war, or slightly under 3 per cent of the Chamber of Deputies (not all of whose members were liable to be mobilized).
7. SHD Carton 5 N 132.
8. SHD Carton 7 N 4.
9. Bugnet, Charles (Lieutenant-colonel). *Rue Saint-Dominique et GQG, ou les Trois dictatures de la guerre*. Plon, 1937. One of the book's chapter titles is 'Roques the nonentity', which says is all.
10. Margaine and Ferry were in the Radical Left party. Renaudel was a Socialist Deputy. Bénazet, who belonged to the Radical Left, had passed out of Saint-Cyr, had subsequently resigned from the army and was mobilized as a captain on the outbreak of the war.
11. All these quotations are from the report of the closed session of 16 June 1916, which can be consulted on the National Assembly's website.
12. Delahaye was one of the few Right-wing Deputies to state his opinion.
13. Hennessy belonged to the Democratic Left party.
14. Chaumet belonged to the Left-wing Republicans party.
15. Joffre told Roques: 'When you no longer have any little things to give them, you'll have to sacrifice some of the big ones. Then, once those have all gone,

they'll chuck you out.' Joffre. *Mémoires, op. cit.*, vol. 2, p. 392. This is precisely what happened.

16. Bugnet (Lieutenant-colonel). 'Lyautey, Joffre et Nivelle', in *La Revue hebdom-adaire* (29 Aug 1936).
17. In his preface to d'Esme's book. d'Esme, *op. cit.*, 1962.
18. Mermeix. *Joffre: la première crise du commandement, novembre 1915–décembre 1916.* Ollendorff, 1919, p. 179.
19. *Journal de marche de Joffre, 1916–1919.* SHAT/FEDN, 1990, pp. 81, 186.

Chapter 10: The Dismissals (pp. 180–190)
1. I will also refrain from giving references, so as not to overburden the chapter with notes. Most of the quotations are from the archives of the SHD (Cartons 16 N 487, 16 N 490, and 16 N 508).
2. For example, General B——, who was found hanging in the bathroom of his apartment on 1 December 1914, left a brief note: 'I have decided by my own free will to kill myself, as I am unable to live with being forcibly retired during the war.' SHD Carton 5 N 131.
3. Legrande-Girarde, *op. cit.*, p. 529.
4. The ranks of *général de corps d'armée* and *général d'armée* did not exist. The commanders of army corps and of armies were drawn from the body of *généraux de division* and could be recognized by their special insignia ('white feathers'). Nowadays, these ranks are 'appointments', and are distinguished by the wearing of four and five stars respectively on the sleeves.
5. SHD Carton 16 N 490. André Cousine and Pierre Rocolle give a figure of 162 of them by the end of December 1914.
6. My italics.
7. SHD Carton 16 N 508.
8. Bel was dubbed Fouquier-Tinville. He was promoted colonel, but was forced to leave GQG in 1916 and was killed in Italy at the head of his troops. Castelnau called him Robespierre, because he reckoned he was incorruptible. The main reason for the hatred directed at Bel was that he adamantly refused to oblige those who importuned him, especially those in parliament.
9. Alexandre, *op. cit.*, pp. 120ff. See also pp. 131, 132.
10. One of the divisional commanders of the 5th Corps, General P——, committed suicide on 10 August before his division had even been engaged. Unit moral is hardly likely to have remained unharmed by this.
11. It appears that Ruffey's immediate reaction was to accept his removal, for he dined with Joffre that same evening.
12. Ruffey was placed in charge of various inspectorates in the interior of the country, before being placed in retirement in 1917. The exact contents of his memoran-dum seem, however, to have remained confidential.
13. Joffre. *Mémoires, op. cit.*, vol. 1, pp. 370ff.
14. You may want to read what Spears has written about this. Spears, *op. cit.*, pp. 422ff. Read also Isaac, Jules. 'Le témoignage du général Lanrezac sur le rôle de la Ve armée', in *Archives de la grande guerre*, no. 29.
15. This general's grandson has written an apologia for him. Pouradier-Duteil, Paul. *Août 1914: enquête sur une relève.* Theopress Ltd, 1997. See also SHD Carton

16 N 487. Since this book defending him exists, I have revealed the general's name.
16. He was a former head of the President of the Republic's military household.
17. For more information on this matter, you can read the book by Lebas, Alfred Isidore (Général). *Places fortes et fortification pendant la guerre de 1914–1918: défense du Nord, camp retranché de Lille*. Payot, 1923.
18. This was after he had failed to receive a reply to two previous letters.
19. It was a typical story, for Regnault was relieved on the request of de Langle de Cary. Joffre merely confirmed the relief.
20. Legrand-Girarde, *op. cit.*, p. 124.

Select Bibliography

What follows is just a brief selection from the immense number of books published on the Great War. Details of English translations are given in square brackets at the end of the relevant entries.

Alexandre, René (Général). *Avec Joffre d'Agadir à Verdun: souvenirs 1911–1916*. Berger-Levrault, 1932.

Bonnal, Henri (Général). *Questions de critique militaire et d'actualité*. Chapelot, 1913.

Bugnet, Charles (Commandant). *En écoutant le maréchal Foch*. Grasset, 1929. [*Foch talks*. Trans by Russell Green. Victor Gollancz, 1929.]

— (Lieutenant-colonel). *Le Maréchal Joffre*. Alfred Marne et fils, 1932.

— (Lieutenant-colonel). *Rue Saint-Dominique et GQG, ou les Trois dictatures de la guerre*. Plon, 1937.

Conte, Arthur. *Joffre*. Olivier Orban, 1991.

Cousine, André (Général). Three articles on the *limogeages* (dismissals), in *Bulletin de la réunion des officiers de réserve*, nos 549, 550, 552.

Debeney, Marie-Eugène (Général). *La guerre et les hommes: réflexions d'après guerre*. Plon, 1937.

Engerand, Fernand. *Le secret de la frontière, 1815–18711914. Charleroi*. Bossard, 1918.

d'Esme, Jean. *Le père Joffre*. France-Empire, 1962.

Fabry, Jean (Lieutenant-colonel). *Joffre et son destin: la Marne, Verdun, la Somme, l'Amérique*. Charles Lavauzelle, 1931.

Foch, Ferdinand (Lieutenant-colonel d'artillerie). *Des principes de la guerre*. Berger-Levrault, 1903. [*The principles of war*. Trans by Hilaire Belloc. Chapman and Hall, 1918.]

— (Colonel). *De la conduite de la guerre: la manœuvre pour la bataille*, 2nd ed. Berger-Levrault, 1909.

Fraenkel, Roger. *Joffre: l'âne qui commandait des lions*. Italiques, 2004.

French, John Denton Pinkstone, Viscount of Ypres (Field Marshal). *1914*. Constable and Company Ltd, 1919.

Galliéni, Joseph-Simon (Maréchal). *Mémoires du maréchal Galliéni*. Payot, 1928.

— *Les carnets de Galliéni*. Albin Michel, 1932.

Gascouin, Firmin-Emile (Général). *L'évolution de l'artillerie pendant la guerre*. Ernest Flammarion, 1920.

de Gaulle, Charles. *La France et son armée*. Plon, 1938.

Gheusi, Pierre-Barthélemy. *Guerre et théâtre, 1914–1918: mémoires d'un officier du général Galliéni et journal parisien du directeur du théâtre national de l'Opéra-Comique pendant la guerre*. Berger-Levrault, 1919.

— *La gloire de Galliéni: comment Paris fut sauvé, le testament d'un soldat*. Albin Michel, 1928.

de Grandmaison, Louis (Commandant). *Dressage de l'infanterie en vue du combat offensif*, 3rd ed. Berger-Levrault, 1908.

— (Colonel). *Deux conférences faites aux officiers de l'Etat-major de l'armée: la notion de sûreté et l'engagement des grandes unités*. Berger-Levrault, 1911.

Gras, Yves (Général). *Castelnau, ou l'art de commander, 1851–1944*. Denoël, 1990.

Herbillon, Emile (Colonel). *De la Meuse à Reims: le général Alfred Micheler*. Plon, 1934.

— *Souvenirs d'un officier de liaison pendant la guerre mondiale: du général en chef au gouvernement*. Editions Jules Tallandier, 1930.

Jaurès, Jean. *L'armée nouvelle*. Editions de l'Humanité, 1919.

Joffre, Joseph. *Opérations de la colonne Joffre avant et après l'occupation de Tombouctou*. Berger-Levrault, 1895.

— (Maréchal). *Mémoires, 1910–1917*, 2 vols. Plon, 1932. [*The memoirs of Marshal Joffre*, 2 vols. Trans by Thomas Bentley Mott. Geoffrey Bles, 1932.]

— *Journal de marche de Joffre (1916–1919)*. SHAT/FEDN, 1990.

Jollivet, Gaston. *Le Colonel Driant*. Delagrave, 1918.

Kahn, Alexander. *Life of General Joffre, cooper's son who became commander-in-chief*. Frederick A. Stokes Company, [1915].

de Langle de Cary, Fernand (Général). *Souvenirs de commandement, 1914–1916*. Payot, 1935.

Lanrezac, Charles (Général). *Le plan de campagne français et le premier mois de la guerre, 2 août – 3 septembre 1914*. Payot, 1920.

Laure, Emile (Général). *Pétain*. Berger-Levrault, 1941.

Leblond, Marius-Ary (pseud). *Galliéni parle: entretiens du 'Sauveur de Paris', ministre de la Guerre, avec ses secrétaires*, 2 vols. Albin Michel, 1920.

Legrand-Girarde, Emile (Général). *Un quart de siècle au service de la France: carnets 1894–1918, Madagascar, Elysée, Chine, loi de trois ans, guerre de 1914–1918*. Les Presses littéraires de France, 1954.

Liddell Hart, Basil Henry (Captain). *Réputations*. Payot, 1931. [*Reputations*. John Murray, 1928.]

Lintier, Paul. *Avec une batterie de 75: ma pièce, souvenirs d'un canonnier, 1914*. Plon, 1916. [*My Seventy-five: journal of a French gunner*. Tandem Books, 1967.]

Lyet, Pierre (Capitaine). *Joffre et Galliéni à la Marne*. Berger-Levrault, 1938.

Marcellin, Léopold. *Politique et politiciens pendant la guerre*, 2 vols. La Renaissance du livre, c.1921.

Margueritte, Victor. *Au bord du gouffre, août – septembre 1914*. Flammarion, 1919.

Mayer, Emile (Lieutenant-colonel). *Trois maréchaux: Joffre, Galliéni, Foch*. Gallimard, 1928.

Ménager, René (Lieutenant). *Les Forts de Moulainville et de Douaumont sous les 420*. Payot, 1936.

Mermeix. *Joffre: la première crise du commandement, novembre 1915 – décembre 1916*. Ollendorff, 1919.

Messimy, Adolphe. *Mes souvenirs*. Plon, 1937.

Muller (Commandant). *Joffre et la Marne*. Editions G. Crès et Cie, 1931.

Painlevé, Paul. *Comment j'ai nommé Foch et Pétain: la politique de guerre de 1917, le commandement unique interallié*. Félix Alcan, 1923.

Percin, Alexandre (Général). *Le combat*. Félix Alcan, 1914.

— *1914: les erreurs du haut commandement*. Albin Michel, 1920.

— *Le massacre de notre infanterie, 1914–1918*. Albin Michel, 1921.

Pétain, Philippe (Maréchal). *La bataille de Verdun*. Payot, 1929.

de Pierrefeu, Jean. *GQG Secteur 1: trois ans au Grand Quartier Général, par le rédacteur du communiqué*, 2 vols. L'Edition française illustrée, 1920. [*French headquarters, 1915–1918*. Trans by Cecil John Charles Street. Geoffrey Bles, 1924.]

— *Plutarque a menti*. Bernard Grasset, 1923. [*Plutarch lied*. Trans by Jeffery E. Jeffery (pseud). Grant Richards, 1924.]

Poincaré, Raymond. *Au service de la France: neuf années de souvenirs*, 11 vols., Plon, 1926–74. [*The memoirs of Raymond Poincaré*, 4 vols. Trans and adapted by Sir George Arthur. William Heinemann, 1926–30.]

Raynal, Sylvain-Eugène (Colonel). *Le drame du fort de Vaux: journal du commandant Raynal*. Editions Lorraines Frémont, [1919].

Recouly, Raymond. *Joffre*. Editions des Portiques, 1931. [*Joffre*. Trans into English. D. Appleton & Co., 1931.]

Rocolle, Pierre. *L'hécatombe des généraux*. Lavauzelle, 1980.

Spears, Sir Edward (Major General). *En liaison, 1914*. Presses de la Cité, 1967. [*Liaison 1914: a narrative of the great retreat*, 2nd ed. Eyre and Spottiswoode, 1968.]

Ténot, Eugène. *Les nouvelles défenses de la France: Paris et ses fortifications, 1870–1880*. G. Baillière et Cie, 1887. (1st edition 1880.)

— *Les nouvelles défenses de la France. La frontière, 1870–1882*. G. Baillière et Cie, 1887. (1st edition 1882.)

Varillon, Pierre. *Joffre*. Frayard, 1956.

XXX (Général). *Plutarque n'a pas menti*. La Renaissance du livre, [1923]

Z—— (Capitaine). *Vertus guerrières*. Payot, 1918.

I have also consulted the unpublished diaries of General Xardel for the period from August to October 1914.

It is impossible to cite all the journal or review articles that I have used while writing this book. Most of them were found in such titles as: *Revue de Paris, Revue des deux mondes, Revue politique et parlementaire, Nouvelle revue, La Grande revue, Revue militaire générale, Revue militaire française, Le Courrier européen, Documents politiques, diplomatiques et financiers, Archives de la grande guerre, Le Correspondant, Armée et démocratie*. Almost all can be consulted and downloaded on 'Gallica', the website of the *Bibliothèque Nationale de France*, and I pay tribute to the BNF's efforts to digitize its collections.

I have also used several illustrated magazines, including of course *L'Illustration*, but also *Le Pays de France* and *Le Miroir*. British publications (*The War illustrated*) and their American counterparts provided some interesting information.

The *Service historique de la défense* (SHD) at Vincennes remains indispensable. Those archive boxes that I have consulted are cited in the references. Available at the SHD, on open-shelf access, is the French Official History, *Les armées françaises dans la grande guerre*. Numerous published documents from the archives can be found in its volumes of appendices.